Civil Society and Media in Global Crises

CIVIL SOCIETY
AND MEDIA
IN GLOBAL CRISES
Representing Distant Violence

Martin Shaw

PINTER

PINTER

A Cassell imprint
Wellington House, 125 Strand, London WC2R 0BB
215 Park Avenue South, New York, New York 10003

First published in 1996

British Library Cataloguing-in-Publication Data

A CIP catalogue record for this book is available from the British Library

ISBN   1 85567 387 8 HB

        1 85567 224 3 PB

Library of Congress Cataloging-in-Publication Data

Shaw, Martin

     Civil society and media in global crises : representing distant violence / Martin Shaw.

       p. cm.

     Includes index.

     ISBN 1-85567-224-3 (pbk.)

     1. War in the press. 2. Violence in the press. 3. Television broadcasting of news. 4. Broadcast journalism–Social aspects. 5. International relations–Social aspects. I. Title.

PN4784.W37S53 1996

070.4′4935502–dc20

                                                  95-43516

                                                      CIP

Designed and Typeset by Ben Cracknell
Printed and bound in Great Britain by Biddles Ltd, Guildford and King's Lynn

Contents

Preface

In *Global Society and International Relations* (1994), I wrote—as others have—about the emergence of a 'global civil society'. Few, however, have given empirical accounts of this contradictory and problematic development. I decided therefore to examine this issue in the context of the most serious tests to global society and the state-system, the wars of the post-Cold War years. In particular, I wanted to see how far institutions of civil society in the West, the centre of the global system, were able to *represent* society in the crisis zones, which were mainly peripheral.

Like many others, I started with the Gulf War. No one can ignore this, the most serious interstate conflict of the new era to date. Yet virtually all researchers—including people I respected—ended their accounts where President Bush tried (but in reality failed) to end the war, with the ceasefire of 28 February 1991. I thought it essential to examine responses to the revolts in Iraq in the aftermath of the Gulf War—the *other*, neglected Iraqi wars of 1991—and to compare them with other recent conflicts in former Yugoslavia and elsewhere.

These wars seem to me to set precedents quite as important as the Gulf conflict. The Kurdish refugee crisis has been recognized of course, as the first example of so-called 'humanitarian intervention'. While many had made assumptions about the role of the media in that crisis, no one had actually studied it (as I do in this book) or looked at the contrast with the media's role in the Gulf War itself (which everyone was writing about). Moreover, while so many had written about television in the Gulf, no one had systematically discussed the newspapers' role, which was also very important, albeit in a different way.

Discussion of the media, moreover, had failed to put it in the wider context of Western civil-society institutions. Studies of the Gulf War and other post-Cold War conflicts failed to examine how far institutions within Western civil societies actually represented globally responsible thinking and action. Despite the fashion for talking about social movements, no one had noticed how unimportant social movements were in the Gulf War and the other post-Cold War conflicts or asked why this was so.

This book, then, takes up themes which are central to current debates in sociology, political theory and international relations and examines them in the light of some realities of current global events. At the same time, I hope it helps us to think about the difficult question: how *do* we represent distant violence and those who are fighting and suffering in it?

This book is a theoretical argument centred in empirical social research. Given that my themes are large, the foci of my research have had to be highly selective. Although I would like to have written a comprehensive social history of Western responses to the conflict, I have actually selected certain aspects for closer examination and ignored many other related phenomena. I have focused my research on Britain, partly for pragmatic reasons but also because it was an important state in Western responses to the Iraqi crises. In Kurdistan it was the British media and public opinion which forced governments' hands.

I have discussed some kinds of civil-society institution rather than others and researched some media rather than others, partly because these seemed intrinsically important or raised particular issues which I wanted to discuss but also because I wanted to examine a number of cases in some detail rather than to cover everything superficially. Because my concern was institutions' representation of distant violence, in some areas I have concentrated on published data rather than carrying out 'behind the scenes' social research, which would in any case have required resources much larger than those at my disposal. I hope readers will understand the nature of these research dilemmas and forgive me where I have ignored an angle which they think ought to have been represented.

This book could not have been completed without the assistance of many others.

Above all, Roy Carr-Hill collaborated on the survey research which is described at a number of points, and co-wrote several articles on which I have drawn. He produced the tables in Chapter 14. Others who helped in the execution of the surveys were acknowledged in our earlier Hull University collaboration, *Public Opinion, Media and Violence: Attitudes to the Gulf War in a Local Population* (1991), and I wish to repeat my thanks here. This work would not have been possible without the financial support of the Joseph Rowntree Charitable Trust, the University of Hull, the *Hull Daily Mail* and the B & G Cadbury Trust.

I received invaluable help from Dorothy Sheridan and Joy Eldridge of the Mass-Observation Archive at the University of Sussex; Philip Taylor, Andrew Thorpe and Justin Charlesworth of the Institute for Communication Studies, University of Leeds; and the staff of the Brynmor Jones Library, University of Hull, Hull Central Library and the British Library at Colindale. Help, advice and references were also supplied by many colleagues, particularly Andy Alaszewski, Colin Creighton, Andrew Dawson and Greg McLaughlin.

Versions of parts of the argument in this book have appeared in a number of places, and I should like to thank the following editors and their publishers: Peter G. Forster, *Contemporary Mainstream Religion* (Aldershot: Gower, 1994); Ken Lunn and Martin Evans, *War and Memory* (Leamington Spa: Berg, 1996); Michael Morgan for the *Electronic Journal of Communications/Revue Electronique de Communications* special issue on the Gulf

War (1991); and Paul Thompson for *Renewal: Journal of Labour Politics* (1994). Colleagues at national and international conferences gave useful feedback on parts of the argument. More specific debts are acknowledged, I hope, in the text.

Last but not least I should like to thank my parents, Roy and Gwen Shaw, for their help and Joanna, Thomas, Isabel and Robin for variously encouraging me in and distracting me from various stages of this work over the last four years.

— Part I —

Concepts and Contexts

CHAPTER ONE

Distance, representation
and global civil society

People today are increasingly aware of living in a global society. The world is more unified, but simultaneously it appears more divided. A more integrated world is one with new conflicts, which reverberate rapidly around the globe. Individuals and communities are affected by distant disputes and especially violence. In the past people responded to local or national events and to epochal world conflicts which—once or twice in a lifetime—engulfed national societies. Today people are faced with a constant stream of wars, each of which is represented to us and demands, in a sense, our response.

How these crises affect not just government leaders but ordinary members of society, how we see them and how we respond are the main subjects of this book. Responses are shaped by many factors, chief among which are the nature of the crises, the ways they are communicated to us, the institutions and values in society to which we relate and our own experiences as individuals and communities. This study aims to examine the ways in which these elements combine to affect the representations of global crises today. Although the book focuses on one set of crises and one segment of world society, it raises issues which involve people everywhere, in situations which appear to arise every year in the present period. In this chapter, I shall discuss the concepts and contexts necessary to understand the processes of representation and response.

Global political crises

As the world has been unified over the last few centuries, connections between events in different parts have increased in density and intensity. For as long as European states have operated world-wide, states have seen their rivalries as involving global sets of connections: events in one region have impacted on the general pattern of rivalries and hence on interactions in other regions. Western political ideas have become increasingly universal.

The major crises of the state-system have therefore had global impact. The French Revolution of 1789 initiated a convulsion of the European state-system which led to wars across Europe and the areas in which the system had extended, most notably North America. Revolutionary ideas also spread far across the world. The Great War of 1914–18, after a further century of European expansion, was a European war with much stronger global reach. The ideas of the Russian Revolution had even more profound global ramifications than those of the French. The Second World War of 1939–45 was fully a world war, with an Asian-Pacific war equal to the war in Europe; only South America was not directly incorporated into the conflict. The victorious ideologies of Western democracy and Communism divided the world between them.

A world war constitutes the maximum possible concept of a global political crisis. Most states and populations of the world are involved; most social relations and state structures are more or less simultaneously transformed under the impact of a single set of closely related events. By this standard, contemporary crises fall far short. Major crises of the Cold War era—the Cuban missile crisis, the Second Cold War of the early 1980s—clearly held the potential for world wars but were contained. The wars in Korea and Vietnam, which directly involved the superpowers, their allies and surrogates, constituted global crises, although their potential to lead to more general East–West crises was also strictly contained. Other large-scale wars such as the Iran–Iraq war—while of global significance in affecting the balance of power in a key region and involving many other powers indirectly—were also of limited impact because their relevance to the East–West fracture was effectively controlled.

The post-Cold War years have seen many political crises, leading to the wars which form much of the subject matter of this book. Most have been, either exclusively or in large part, civil wars. Many of them have been wars of state reformation following the collapse of the Soviet and Yugoslav multinational states, with both civil and inter-state aspects. Of these, possibly only the Gulf War could be said to have constituted a global crisis in the old sense of a war involving several major powers and involving large parts of the world. In most other wars, great power interests have been minimally involved. Conflicts have been essentially local, and many in Western elites have argued against intervention on this ground.

We therefore have to ask whether post-Cold War crises are genuinely *global* political crises and, if so, what makes them such? The case rests on how far they are perceived to have global ramifications and whether intervention from outside the region of conflict, by the great powers or the United Nations, has taken place or become a serious possibility. Clearly, those crises which can genuinely be considered global are crises of a different order from the world wars or the superpower confrontations during the Cold War. It does seem appropriate, however, to consider some at least of the new crises in this light.

Why have some wars, such as those in Bosnia and Rwanda, been considered as globally significant? It is not obvious that they are qualitatively different from other wars, such as Armenia–Azerbaijan and the civil war in Angola. These too have involved huge death tolls and massive clearances of populations. The principal difference seems to be that some wars have been widely *perceived* to involve enormous suffering and violations of human rights, in disregard of principles avowed by the 'international community', and that this perception has been fostered by extensive global media coverage. Large-scale suffering and violations of human rights have been present in many other cases; perceptions of them have had, however, much less currency, and the obvious explanation is the relative weakness of coverage.

We may note two new criteria for global political crises. Global crises may still be constituted, as was the Gulf for the most part, by traditional criteria of conflicts of interests directly or indirectly involving major powers and areas of the international system. They may also be constituted, however, even where these are wholly or largely lacking, if there is a world-wide *perception* of a large-scale violation of human life and globally legitimate principles that is largely dependent on media coverage obtained. The existence of a global crisis can be confirmed by the occurrence of, or existence of significant pressure for, internationally legitimate *intervention* to resolve it.

In reality, traditional and new models of global political crises are not alternatives but indicate poles on a spectrum. Each crisis combines traditional and new aspects in different proportions. Although Bosnia and Angola, for example, no longer represent the sorts of geopolitical security interests for great powers which they did during the Cold War (which is, ironically, a reason for the eruption of new conflicts), there are still broad great-power interests in the regional security of the Balkans and southern Africa. Conversely the Gulf, the only post-Cold War war to appear as a pure inter-state conflict, entailed immense civil conflicts and human tragedies. The mediation of these in global communications quite changed the war's initial character and historic significance. We may conclude that threats to civil communities and their mediation are key aspects not merely of one kind of crisis but of contemporary global crises in general.

This shift in the definition of global political crises brings it closer to a broader concept of global crises in a social and humanitarian sense, to include famine, poverty, repression, natural disasters, epidemics and environmental catastrophes. Since these are most commonly produced or exacerbated by political crises, and especially wars, such a shift would seem to be appropriate. Indeed there may be a case for seeing social crises largely as aspects of political crises. Perceptions of humanitarian crises may be changing: for example, whereas in the 1970s and 1980s famine was often understood as a product of drought, now media coverage has publicized its roots in wars.

The West in contemporary global crises

The roles of Western states and societies in contemporary crises are different from those of others and also from the roles they played in earlier crises. Their current roles arise, first, from structural transformations of the state system in the last half-century; second, from the way that global crises are inserted into the relationships between Western states and society; and third, from the position of Western societies in global communications systems.

The dominance of the West in the world economic and political systems is not new but has existed throughout the centuries in which globalism has developed. Because Western states have competitively dominated the world, conflicts in distant places have long reverberated in Western societies. For centuries, most wars involving Western states have taken place in distant locales under the rubric of colonialism. Publics were accustomed to read of them in their newspapers long before television was invented.

Before 1945, however, distant conflicts ultimately held a menacing implication for Western societies. The rivalries they signified among European powers could, in the end, return to haunt Western peoples in a European or world war. In the Cold War period, this principle took even stronger hold. In a bipolar conflict, virtually any local conflict however remote could in theory endanger the stability of East–West relations. Although Western societies were in practice mostly free of direct threats from local Third World wars, there was always the danger that they would reach the West. People in Western societies—as in previous centuries— were onlookers in distant wars in which 'their' forces were sometimes also involved, but they feared the nuclear holocaust which might bring these local wars home with a vengeance.

Since 1989 this fear, in any specific form, has been lifted. Although the proliferation of nuclear arsenals means that nuclear war remains a background fear, there is no structure of conflict within which a nuclear threat to the West is credible ('nuclear terrorism' apart). War is now more than ever before something which happens to other people—in the former Yugoslavia or Soviet Union, the Middle East, Asia, Africa—but not to Western societies. Other than terrorism there is indeed no direct military threat to most Western societies; there is a remarkable asymmetry, greater than any in the past, in the involvement of society with war in different world regions.

The involvement of Western states with war has changed in another way. The collapse of the Soviet Union removed Cold War constraints on many Third World states and movements, enabling them to use military means more freely. It also removed many constraints on the West, the sole remaining bloc, and especially on the USA, the sole superpower, enabling them to intervene more freely in conflicts across the globe. The general acquiescence of Russia and China—the non-Western permanent members of the Security Council—enabled the West to mobilize the UN to legitimize its interventions.

In the 1990s the US-led bloc of Western states has started to act, with UN legitimation, like a global state intervening to regulate political and military conflicts across the world. UN-sponsored or -organized inter- ventions range from common small-scale monitoring, from relief and peacekeeping operations to the complex Yugoslav intervention and the

Gulf War. Although in most of the new conflicts intervention has been minimal, Western states increasingly view these in terms of whether the dangers to political stability and human life are sufficiently serious to require direct regulation. In principle, monitoring, regulating and intervening—by political if not military means—have become the norm. There is enormous variation in practice, mainly according to the extent that Western interests are involved.

These changes have been accompanied by great confusion among and within Western states. Politically, ideologically and militarily no clear guidelines have been formulated by any state or international organization, still less agreed by those involved. States have clung to old definitions of nation-state autonomy and national interest even as they moved into new political territory. Interventions have been increasingly confused and inconsistent. Crises have been marked by serious but poorly demarcated conflicts between major Western powers and reflected in an enlarged but uncertain new status for the UN.

The role of Western societies has also been transformed in this situation. Instead of fearing that distant wars will lead to East–West conflict, people in Western societies need no longer feel threatened, in the short or medium term at least, by their states' involvement in distant wars. The fate of Western personnel—civilian as well as military—is of course a central concern. Fear of the loss of Western lives has been a major policy consideration. Important as this factor is for those involved and their families, it is not a personal issue for the majority of people. The fact that virtually all soldiers in interventions are volunteers—Western states do not normally send conscripts into conflict—is another significant change.

Responses to global crises within Western societies are particularly important to the character of intervention. The fundamental reason is the way in which crises are inserted into relationships between states and society. Governments are electorally accountable and try to manage most activities so that they will, in the end, assist the cause of re-election. Global interventions may affect this task in contradictory ways; the polar positions are easy to delineate. A short, successful low-casualty intervention may be politically advantageous. On the other hand, a long-drawn-out, inconclusive or failed intervention, costly in lives, has been seen—since Vietnam—as a major danger. Steering a politically successful course while responding to issues actually posed by a crisis has become a major dilemma for Western governments.

A central difficulty is the essential unpredictability of public responses. Conventional wisdom is that international issues rarely have a significant instrumental effect on voting patterns. Such issues are likely, however, to have an indirect effect on perceptions of strength and weakness in the performance of an administration, party or leader. People are concerned about casualties among 'their own' troops or civilians; but they may equally become concerned about the plight of a threatened civilian population. When such concerns might arise is difficult to predict, depending on often unforeseeable events in the conflict. The concerns for Western military personnel and for civilian victims tend to be incompatible.

Governments cannot escape from these dilemmas. Interventions constitute limited operations, at most limited wars, and they have to be combined with normal economic, political and social life in the home society. There is no resort to the simpler certainties, censorship and control of a total war situation; the dilemmas have to be managed. States have to carry out international policy while satisfying the needs and the concerns of their electorates.

Even in the recent past, this was considerably easier than now. During the Cold War there was some restoration of the geopolitical privacy of elites, as international politics became a process of managing bipolar conflict. During this period, international and military issues were resolved behind closed doors and were rarely part of popular debate (although this was sometimes forced on states by peace movements). Wars like Vietnam and the Falklands were exceptions: the importance of mass media to modern limited war was first demonstrated in these cases.

There has been a significant shift in the character of international politics. While direct relationships between Western and other great powers are important, they are mediated even more by the problems of managing local crises. The centrality of this process, as we have seen, owes much to the way in which crises are configured, for the people as well as the elites, by mass communications. Western societies have therefore become central to international politics in new ways. The role of a specific crisis in international politics, and the nature of the international intervention in the crisis, depends partly on two societal factors. Media coverage directly affects state responses, and the responses of groups within Western society to the mediation of the conflict also have an effect on state policies. It is important to distinguish these factors in principle, but in practice it is often difficult to separate them. Governments often act on calculations about how coverage will affect public opinion, and media do not only report but also attempt to mobilize and represent opinion. In the era of expanded global communications and serial global crises, media and societal responses are part of world politics at every stage.

Society in the West is central to this process for a number of reasons. Society here has direct connections to and influences Western states. Global communications industries are rooted in Western societies and see them as their central markets, although others are growing in importance. Western politics has been most fully transformed by mass communications. Last but not least, states and social groups in non-Western societies are aware of the roles of Western societies in international politics and of media in setting political agendas. Groups in zones of crisis often appeal directly to society in the West by attempting to influence media coverage. As governments are uncertain about their proper roles in global crises, the influence of society increases. The domestic political significance of a global crisis is a large part of its significance for Western states.

The dilemmas of distance

Responses within Western societies to global crises are obviously affected by considerations of distance. Geographical distance between the Western and non-Western worlds has been reduced in significance because of global integration. Rapidly improving transport and communications mean that even the most remote parts are closer, and there are few areas without growing Western contact. Wars have also been getting closer: some, most notably the ex-Yugoslav but also some post-Soviet conflicts, are within geographical Europe.

Fundamental to establishing and maintaining distance is difference of experience. The bottom line is that wars are things which happen to non-Western people, not to us. The responses of Westerners are essentially those of the unthreatened to the plight of the threatened. This needs qualifying, however, because war—for example the bombing of civilians—is very much within the historic experience of Western societies, including personal memories of many still alive. Moreover physical threats to others in distant regions may be felt as psychological threats by Western people and undermine their sense of security. It is difficult for a city-dweller not to look on the destruction of a modern European city like Sarajevo and not to feel at some level a diminution of his or her own sense of safety. Not all media onlookers will have the geopolitical understanding which provides reassurance that this will remain another people's problem.

Distance, psychological or even geographical, is not therefore a straight-forward question. Distance is complex and relative and is constantly established, undermined and renegotiated in our responses. Distance is active, something which we create in our response: there is *a process of distancing*. Distance is also a question, of course, of openness—or lack of openness—in our attitudes to others' problems. We can open or close ourselves, either consciously or subconsciously, and we all move between different levels of awareness and responsiveness to a situation.

Distancing can therefore concern establishing or maintaining a degree of emotional, intellectual and practical closure to a situation, separating ourselves and maintaining our own ontological security. It has to be emphasized, of course, that by definition responses to others' situations contain elements of distance: we are separate individuals. Distance can be a condition for effective response: aid workers cannot allow themselves to share victims' plights completely or they might find it impossible to give effective support.

Emotional or psychological distance has no necessary connection with geographical distance, or even with difference of experience. We can (and all do) distance ourselves from those who are physically and emotionally close to us or who have similar experiences. We may, indeed, have good reasons to distance ourselves more from them than from people in faraway places. We may be more open—this is not exceptional but represents a pattern of response—to the problems of those faraway than to those of people nearby.

Distance is not purely a matter of individual psychology or how we deal with emotions. Distance is established, maintained and overcome in social relationships through concepts which are created, negotiated and shared within a given culture. While it is possible to look in depth, as psychological studies do, at individuals' responses in isolation, these always draw on a wider culture. If we look at responses in society in the West, we are looking at the ways in which individual responses are framed within this cultural context. We look at the main patterns of response and what they tell us about the society and culture in general.

Distance is socially established even in situations of physical proximity. The relations between parents and children involve culturally defined forms of distance. Of more relevance to this study are the ways in which people sharing a house, such as wealthy families and their servants (or even slaves), live by tightly defined concepts of a social gulf inhibiting or even banning feelings of common humanity. Or perhaps more appropriately to readers of this book, we may note how those in prosperous communities and secure occupations maintain a social distance from the poor, unemployed, homeless, mentally ill, etc. who inhabit the same Western cities. Social distancing may be acute even where geographical distance is insignificant.

Problems of distance are not exclusive, therefore, to global crises. They are compounded, however, where distances of geography and experience are as marked as they are in this context. Western people respond to global crises with these factors of distance built in; they share elements of culture, for example the legacies of colonialism and racism, which reinforce distance; and they respond to how states present issues to them. Media coverage of global crises both creates and undermines a variety of forms of distancing.

Distance creates dilemmas which we must constantly address in our responses to others' situations. These present themselves in many social contexts but are particularly acute in global crises. How much can we afford to expose ourselves emotionally to the plight of people in distant wars? How much should we get involved with situations about which we feel we can do little or nothing? How much should we feel responsible for situations which are not the result of our actions or even those of 'our' government? How much can we concern ourselves with the lives of others with whom we have no direct or personal ties compared to our own lives and those of the people to whom we are close? How these dilemmas are dealt with is a central concern of this book.

Responses and responsibility

To examine distancing in global crises, we need to look at the ways in which people in Western societies respond to them in a more general sense. It cannot be assumed that there is always a response. Some may so effectively insulate themselves from media and information about global crises that they have no basis on which to respond. The majority of people, however, do watch some television news, listen to radio or read some newspapers, and so are exposed to some coverage of global crises. To this limited degree they also make some response—even if only to shrug off global events as nothing to do with them.

Most responses are passive, limited to personal absorption of information or personal feelings, expressed no more than in odd remarks to family members or friends. Only at major turning-points are active responses made and then usually still by minorities: for example those who donated for British troops in the Gulf or to charities collecting for the Kurds. Those who make stronger, notably political, responses are even smaller minorities. It might be thought that people's responses are not very important. This is not the case if only because governments, as we have noted, know that responses to global issues can make a difference to national politics. Newspapers claim to express public opinion, opinion polls solicit and publish it and governments make calculations as to likely responses in deciding policies. People's attitudes, even if passive and silent, count in these senses.

Central to responses are dilemmas of distance, and at the heart of these lies the question of responsibility. There are different ways in which we establish distance from others. Some may be compatible with assuming responsibility for others, other sorts of distancing involve denials of responsibility. Being open to others' problems may involving assuming a degree of responsibility. This book is partly about how governments and people in the West take on or deny responsibility for people in distant global crises.

The concept of responsibility is extremely difficult to define and to apply to global crises. We may be responsible (or be held or hold ourselves responsible) for others' situations in many ways. We may be thought responsible because of things we have done or because of a pattern of social relationships in which we are involved. We may assume responsibility, even where such reasons are lacking, because of some general concept of responsibility for others.

There is a difference between accepting responsibility and acting responsibly. The assumption of responsibility may be relatively simple to establish objectively; agreement on what it is necessary to do to act responsibly in a situation may be more difficult to reach. The two facets are, however, intrinsically related. To be responsible means to fulfil one's responsibilities, while to assume responsibility means accepting a duty to act responsibly.

The meaning of responsible action is usually difficult to establish because responsibility may be defined in different contexts. This is particularly so in international politics. For whom, or what, do political and military leaders take responsibility? How we answer this question will determine our view of what it is for them to act responsibly in a given situation. The ideas of leaders will often centre around concepts such as upholding the national interest and assumptions about what this problematic notion means. More specific ideas will also be invoked, such as that of responsibility for the lives of soldiers sent into a situation. The actions of leaders may also be informed by other concepts of responsibility, such as for protecting their own political interests and those of their party.

It is difficult for leaders to take responsibility for victims of distant wars who are civilians of a different nationality. The instincts of most Western (let alone other) state leaders are almost always to deny responsibility, even where their own actions have influenced the fate of those at risk. Historically there has not been a strong concept of responsibility in this sense. Such a concept has been developed by other elite groups—critics in cultural and political life—and from the moral sensibilities of Western public opinion. It has been largely forced on leaders rather than chosen by them. The relationship between the different sources of this concept is another important aspect of this book.

I shall also be concerned with the relationship, in different groups, between particular and general concepts of responsibility for victims. When political and military leaders take responsibility—they often deny it in the cases with which we are concerned—they are usually accepting the consequences of their own actions. Others often hold them responsible in this sense. In the cases of elite groups such as doctors, journalists and academics, divorced from political decision-making, a specific responsibility arises from professional norms rather than from their previous actions. Among the population at large there is little likelihood of a specific responsibility, but nevertheless many feel themselves responsible and impute responsibility to governments on general grounds. (Of course, once people act on a sense of responsibility, however it arises, and advocate or support a course of action, then they share responsibility for its consequences.)

This book seeks to explore the sources of these wider senses of responsibility for the fate of others in distant wars where those people reacting could not have been ascribed any specific responsibility for the situation. I am particularly interested in where such ideas come from, what influences them, how they are expressed and how they in turn influence the policies of states. Such issues are the nub of the relationships among the population at large, civil society and the state in current crises. The violence of war is mostly distant to people in Western societies, and yet we increasingly take some responsibility for it.

Representation in global crises

The dilemmas of distance, responsibility and involvement revolve in a double sense around the question of representation. On the one hand, as we have noted, distant wars and the situations of those fighting and suffering within them must be perceived as significant and represented ideologically as such. For this to be the case, information about and images of people's predicaments and beliefs must be *shown* to the other members of global society. On the other hand, it is important that those fighting and suffering should be represented politically, in the sense of being able to make their needs and values effective in the arenas of global power. Their causes need to be *advocated* globally.

The representation of combatants and victims in distant violence is typically indirect. They rarely communicate their own information or create their own images: information about and images of them are produced by third parties who transmit these to wider audiences. Nor do they have a direct political impact: they depend on others, on institutions which they have not created and do not control, for the effectiveness of their representation.

The two forms of representation are mutually dependent: representation in the sense of knowledge requires political representation to become effective, and political representation requires information and imagery to inform it. The two forms of representation correspond to two major institutional contexts which are central to this book. Civil society in general (to be discussed in more detail below) is the sphere of broad cultural, ideological and political representation of society. Communications media are the principal arena of informational representation in which images are produced, transmitted and consumed.

The interrelationships of political and ideological representation are highly important. All institutions of civil society involve ideological representation, while media cannot avoid political representation. Media should be seen as one component of civil society, specializing in ideological representation, both informing and informed by the function of political representation in civil society at large.

The globalization of political and ideological representation is at the centre of the processes involved in this book. The unequal terms upon which globalization is occurring make it difficult for people involved in conflicts distant from the centres of global power to achieve representation in pivotal civil society and media institutions which are based in the national contexts of major Western states.

The representation of people involved in distant violence thus depends largely upon the representative activities of Western civil society institutions, including media. It depends on the intersection of their needs and demands with the interests, beliefs and agendas of groups in Western society. The nature of this intersection is important to this book. It is argued that the institutions of Western civil society are limited in their capacity to represent the needs of those fighting and suffering in distant contexts. Each institution is limited in a different way, depending on its political and ideological characteristics.

Defining civil society

In discussing representation, I have referred considerably to 'civil society'. There is much debate about this concept, and it is important to clarify it before we can develop an analysis of civil society in global crises. There are two principal issues of definition about which we need a preliminary decision. One concerns how far civil society can be freestanding from states. It is widely agreed that it comprises institutions of society outside the state; it is less certain whether it has nevertheless a distinct relationship to the state. The other concerns the range of institutions which are to be considered as the components of civil society. Does it comprise all of society outside the state or a narrower constellation of institutions which represent society in particular ways?

As in all issues of definition, we must decide which analytically is the most valuable. In this study, the two issues will be resolved as follows. It will be assumed that while historically the development of civil society has been closely related to that of the nation-state, this relationship is not fixed or immutable. Civil institutions may be more or less closely dependent on state institutions; the nature of civil society changes as does that of the state. The connections between these changes are empirical questions of socio-historical analysis.

It will be argued that not all non-state institutions are central to civil society. While in the broadest sense it includes economic as well as cultural, political and ideological institutions, economic institutions such as firms and corporations play mainly functional rather than representative roles. Although central to the actual organization and structuring of society—to the systems through which society works—their representative roles are a relatively minor part of their activity. Economic institutions do not generally represent themselves in a political and ideological sense, but rely on employers' associations, governments, parties, etc. to represent them.

Civil society is used here, therefore, in a more specialized sense than 'society minus the state'; it is closer to Gramsci's proposal: 'between the economic structure and the state with its legislation and coercion stands civil society'.[1] Civil society is held to comprise the institutions which have the specific role of *representing* groups within society, in broad cultural, political and ideological senses, both in the context of society itself and in relation to the state. Representative institutions in the economic sphere— trade unions as well as employers' groups—are fairly specialized components of civil society in this sense. They tend to confine themselves in the main to matters which directly concern the economic interests which they represent, leaving wider matters to other institutions. The central institutions of civil society are those which define the meaning and significance of events, representing social interests and articulating widely held viewpoints in relation to them.

Modern Western societies have developed a wide range of institutions of this kind—notably religious, political, educational and cultural. In the development of civil society, in the eighteenth and nineteenth centuries and the first half of the twentieth, these institutions have been predominantly national in character. Civil society, representing national society, has effectively constituted the nation which nation-states have claimed to embody in forms of legal, political and military power. In this period, with the nation-state the dominant form of state power, civil society has also taken mainly national forms; there has been a close relationship between the forms of the state and of civil society.

Towards global civil society?

During the Cold War, both state and civil society changed in the West. National forms were maintained, but they lost much real significance. There was a huge internationalization of Western military, economic and ideological power. Western states increasingly shared frameworks for organizing their monopoly of violence and their management of economic life. They created the conditions for massive processes of economic and cultural globalization. In this context, the old national civil society declined and with it many of the forms which were most characteristic of it in the mid-twentieth century—churches, mass political parties and trade unions —all of which have tended to lose membership and influence.

Civil society has been partially renewed in new institutions which are less formal, less tied to particular social interests and less national. Sociologists have given most attention to 'new' social movements (i.e. those based not on class but on other social axes or issue interests). Mass participatory forms tend to be episodic, but other institutions—single-issue campaigns and voluntary organizations, especially global development and human rights agencies—are more enduring if less activist. These non-governmental organizations (NGOs) are particularly important in that, although based in the West, they operate across the globe. They have been seen as institutional expressions of the emergence of global civil society.

Media should also be considered important institutions of civil society. There are key differences between media and other institutions to do with the informational character of much media activity and the quasi-instantaneous communication between media and audiences. Most other institutions largely take for granted the information which their members or audience possess and are more concerned with influencing the value framework within which information is evaluated. Media, on the other hand, are always heavily concerned with communicating information and have highly divergent relationships to evaluation. Much television broadcasting eschews open commitment to value-frameworks (except those concerned with information), while at the other extreme, many newspapers are highly committed to promoting particular values.

Frequency of communication between media and audiences is another key differentiator between them and other institutions. Many newspapers publish daily, and television and radio broadcast continuously, sometimes updating news and interpretation hourly or even more frequently. Political and religious leaders, educators, movement activists and others communicate with their audiences intermittently and update their analyses of specific situations episodically; they are not required in the same way to inform or comment regularly on any given situation.

A related difference is that media news analysis claims, implicitly or explicitly, to provide a total context of information relevant to given situations (whether or not media do this is, of course, another matter). The views of political and religious leaders, educators, activists and others are 'parts', while the media provide the 'whole' picture. In this sense media contextualize and relativize the outputs of other institutions.

Media and other institutions also have different relationships to the tension between the universal values (religious, political, educational, etc.) on which civil society institutions claim to be based and their essentially national character, based on the aim of representing nationally defined interests and viewpoints. Their responses to global events—and their capacities to represent, even indirectly, the needs and views of people involved in distant violence—are determined by the ways in which this tension is perceived and managed. In so far as media fulfil their function of providing information on the widest possible (i.e. global) basis, they inevitably tend to transcend the national limitations of state and civil society. It is for this reason that global crises have tended to bring out conflicts between globally oriented media (especially television) and nationally centred institutions (including sections of the press which define themselves in a strongly national sense).

Theorists of civil society have often seen the weakness of civil society as a key difference between the non-Western and Western worlds. Recently, however, economic and cultural development have laid the foundations for an expansion of civil society world-wide. In Eastern Europe and the former Soviet Union this has taken, to a great extent, national forms and has been linked to the creation of new or more genuinely independent nation-states. The same has happened, to a considerable degree, in parts of Africa, the Middle East and elsewhere. Although civil societies often appear highly national, they rest on the globalizing forces of education and cultural diffusion. The growth of civil society combines global and particularistic aspects—even the idea of the nation is universal.

These changes in civil society—its world-wide expansion, the decline of some traditional national forms and the rise of global (or globalist) social movements, NGOs and media—have led many to discuss a movement from national to global civil society. There have been few studies of precisely how global civil society is emerging or of its role in global crises. Few have asked whether institutions can adapt from the national context of Western civil societies to global roles or how Western-based institutions can represent those fighting and suffering in zones of crises. This is a study of how institutions in one Western society represented people in one set of distant wars. It asks how far the emergence of a global civil society, connecting those in zones of crises with people in the West, can be seen in this case.

Notes and references

1. Gramsci, 1971, p. 208. This is not, of course, the only concept of civil society which Gramsci offers.

CHAPTER TWO

Violence, genocide
and the Iraqi case

If the processes of representation of distant violence have changed, so has violence itself. The wars of the post-Cold War years have been referred to as 'new' global crises. Clearly, just as it is questionable to refer to many wars as 'global' in significance, so it is to describe them as 'new'. Local wars in the Third World have been the staples of warfare since 1945. While some have been inter-state wars or have involved the great powers militarily, most have been largely or wholly civil wars between local protagonists, even if outside powers have supplied or supported them.[1] Inter-state wars have been larger and more destructive, but civil wars have been far more common. Even inter-state wars often had major civil aspects, and most casualties were civilian. In this sense, wars since 1989 have merely continued well-established trends.

What is new about recent developments mainly concerns the contexts in which wars are fought—the overall pattern rather than specific features taken in isolation. The end of the Cold War altered the situation of local protagonists as well as of the Western powers. The crisis of the nation-state has accelerated now that Cold War disciplines have been removed; new forms of nationalism have fuelled new conflicts. The role of society is more critical even than in wars of the recent past. Civilian populations have not only been in the front line, but the local and global significance of the wars has revolved largely around their fates.

Throughout the twentieth century, of course, war has become increasingly genocidal. The Second World War saw the implicit genocide of the Allied bombing campaigns against Germany and Japan matched by the explicit genocide of the Nazi war against the Jews, which led to the codification of the concept.[2] Since 1945, however, although nuclear weapons completed the potential for mass-destruction total warfare, actual wars have been more limited than the world wars. Nevertheless, the pattern of civilian outpacing military casualties has continued in limited conflicts. Wars of national independence mobilized whole populations who were therefore considered enemies. Guerrillas' wars involved dependence on the civilian population of the areas they controlled, who have therefore been targets for the state or occupier. Even in relatively conventional inter-state conflicts, states have shown little compunction about attacking, either directly or indirectly, their enemies' civilian populations.

To find civilian society at the centre of war is therefore no novelty. Genocide is not at all new, but it has a particular role in post-Cold War wars. In many cases a major, deliberate aim of one or more of the protagonists has been to expel, kill and destroy the identity of a group (or groups) in society. Many wars have been about destroying social groups, not only as possible sources of opposition, but as components of society within a given territory. In the post-Communist wars of the former Yugoslavia and the former Soviet regions, the aim has generally been to establish new states or extend existing ones based on ethnic definitions of population. Wars have been about dispossessing people of their homes and land. The expulsion (often accompanied by slaughter) of the individual, family and local community from their living space has been linked to its incorporation into the political territory of the genocidists' state. Wars have also been about destroying the culture of opposed groups, including in Bosnia both the systematic burning of mosques and the attempt to destroy plural urban communities and the independent intellectual life which they contain.

The wars of the 1990s have therefore been as much about the composition of society and the structure of civil society as about the shape of the state and who controls state power. In these wars, culture and human rights have been not just casualties of war, as always happens, but deliberate targets of many combatants. In these senses, the character of the new wars has magnified the moral, social and political issues with which Western states and societies have been presented as well as the problems of responsibility in our responses. Because contemporary wars are wars of civil society, they raise particularly acute questions for civil society in the West and for the possibility of global civil society.

The Iraqi wars and issues of responsibility

The crises which began with the Iraqi invasion of Kuwait in 1990 are, at the time of writing, the most important of the post-Cold War years. They are distinctive as initially inter-state rather than civil wars in appearance; they are unique in involving the only war (rather than war-management or peacekeeping operation) fought by major Western powers and the UN since 1989. They are not typical wars but represent what is so far the maximum case. Since inter-state wars involving important non-Western powers represent the most serious likely challenge to world order, the Iraqi wars are the most important precedent of the early 1990s. Since the centre of this book is a study of British responses to these wars, it is important to provide a statement of what people and institutions were responding to and a preliminary assessment of the issues of responsibility against which to measure responses.

I call these the Iraqi wars, since they were initiated by, against or within the Iraqi state and resulted largely from its crisis and strategies. There were at least four short but destructive wars, closely interconnected, in the Iraqi region in 1990–1: the Iraqi invasion of Kuwait, completed in hours on 2 August 1990; the war of the US-led coalition to liberate Kuwait, from 17 January to 28 February 1991; the Shi'ite insurrection in southern Iraq and its repression, from the end of February to April 1991; and the Kurdish insurrection in northern Iraq in March–April 1991. Although there have been subsequent tensions between the Iraqi government and its persecuted subjects in the south, with liberated Kurdistan and with the USA, and between Turkey and the Iraqi Kurds, at the time of writing they have generated no further wars. The Iraqi crises have not been resolved, however, and new wars are possible.

Most studies of 1990–1 centre on the inter-state crisis and ignore the insurrectionary wars of the 'aftermath'. They present a highly truncated and one-dimensional view. The uprisings were not accidental features but expressions of the same crisis of the state, in its relation with society, which underlay its external aggression. The wars of 1990–1 were, moreover, continuations of the war which Saddam Hussein launched in 1980 against Iran which did not end until 1988 and in which over a million people died; and of his genocidal campaign against the Kurds in the late 1980s. The Iran–Iraq war produced only the smallest gains—which were surrendered to Iran in 1990—and led to economic and political crises in Iraq. Saddam Hussein made financial and territorial demands on Kuwait, which led to the invasion, as a way out of these crises.

The first arguments about responsibility centre on the background to the 1990–1 crisis. At the centre of the crisis of 2 August were the Iraqi claims against Kuwait: the manifest claims to financial and territorial compensation for Kuwaiti 'occupation' of the oilfields which straddle the Iraq–Kuwait border; and the latent case, only revived publicly after the invasion, that Kuwait was not an independent state but the '17th province' of Iraq. The border and oilfield issues had some substance, as the Kuwaitis were prepared to acknowledge in offering compensation. The larger issue revolved around the relative novelty of an autonomous Kuwaiti entity: the area had previously been included in the Ottoman province of Basra, corresponding to the southern part of modern Iraq. If Kuwait had not existed in the Ottoman era, however, neither had Iraq; and if the Kuwait–Iraq border was an arbitrary line drawn by British colonial administrators, so were other borders in the region. Kuwaiti national identity was a relatively artificial affair but not much more than identity in other Arab states including Iraq. By 1990, Kuwait had been an independent state, universally recognized and a member of the UN for almost three decades. The Ba'athist regime in Iraq had previously recognized Kuwait and abandoned its claim to it.

The Kuwaiti state was an autocratic dynastic apparatus which extended citizenship only to a small minority of the male population. The majority of the population consisted of non-Kuwaiti Arabs, especially Palestinians, and others who performed most menial tasks. Kuwait was, however, a more open and less oppressive society than other conservative Arab dynasties (including Saudi Arabia) and the dictatorial Iraq. Its huge oil wealth was very unequally distributed, but even workers without citizenship were materially better off than many people in other Arab states.

The Iraqi invasion, aimed at securing the financial wealth and oil revenue-generating potential of Kuwait, was first presented as the liberation of its people from oppression and their reunification with 'mother' Iraq. In reality it imposed a terroristic regime on all who remained and caused the flight of a large proportion of both the Kuwaiti and non-citizen populations. The former fled mostly to Saudi Arabia, where they lived better than most refugees; the latter were (ironically in view of the Palestinian Liberation Organization's support for Iraq) some of the worst losers: Palestinians ending up in miserable camps in Jordan, South Asians returning via transit camps to unemployment and poverty in their home countries. There is no doubt that the Kuwaitis who remained were subject to a brutal and often murderous regime (although some atrocities which were widely reported proved to be propaganda inventions).

Responsibility for the invasion and its effects clearly belongs to the Iraqi regime. The responsibility of others for the crisis of July–August 1990 concerns the extent to which they misread Iraqi intentions, and by accepting the legitimacy of Iraq's specific demands unwittingly gave Saddam Hussein the impression (as the US ambassador appears to have done) that an invasion would not be opposed. In this sense all governments concerned, including the Kuwaiti, were deficient.

In a longer historical perspective, responsibility for maintaining the regime in power and encouraging its military ambitions belongs to a wide range of states: the Soviet Union which had historically sponsored and supplied the Ba'athists; conservative Arab states, notably Saudi Arabia and Kuwait, which had backed Iraq as a bulwark against revolutionary Iran; and Western powers, including the USA and the UK, which had tacitly backed Iraq in its war with Iran and effectively resupplied its military needs after the Iranian war (as 'Iraqgate' in the USA and the Scott Inquiry in the UK have highlighted).

The responses of the West and the UN, leading to the war against Iraq, fall into two phases. From August to October 1990, two main policies were adopted: extensive economic sanctions to punish Iraq and pressure it into withdrawing and the sending of a military force to Saudi Arabia, initially for defensive purposes since incursions into Saudi territory were reported and Saddam Hussein, having conquered the oil wealth of Kuwait, might have had his eyes on the supreme prize, Saudi Arabia. Given the failure to pre-empt the invasion, these responses were understandable. The annexation of one sovereign state by another was a flagrant breach of international law; the occupation caused terrorization or effective expulsion of the population of Kuwait; and it threatened the emergence of a totalitarian regional superpower controlling the majority of Middle East oil reserves.

It was true that other states had carried out comparable invasions, condoned by the West. The strength of response reflected the coincidence of concerns (in states and in society) about the illegitimacy of the annexation and the violation of the Kuwaiti population with Western strategic interests in oil. This should not be surprising, since with no effective global authority the projection of global power depends on those states which have the greatest resources. In this case, moreover, the interest was neither a narrowly Western one, since many Third World states were more dependent on Middle East oil than the West, nor specifically American, since the USA was less dependent than Japan and Europe.

The policies of the first phase were successful in their immediate aims. Sanctions were more tightly controlled than in any previous case. While they did not threaten to reverse the invasion in the short term, they placed considerable pressure on the Iraqi regime. Fears were expressed that they also threatened the food and medical supplies for the civilian population, whose living standards had fallen catastrophically during the Iran–Iraq war. These fears became acute as sanctions were continued after the Gulf War, in which US-led forces destroyed much of Iraq's physical infrastructure. It is doubtful that the Iraqi regime intended to threaten the Saudis, but their situation was effectively stabilized by the military intervention.

The real significance of this intervention, which included forces from many Arab states—including Saudi Arabia—lay not in its defensive character but in its potential for offensive action. In the early months, the forces were too small for this: Iraq was estimated to have a million men under arms, with half deployed in Kuwait or the adjacent areas of southern Iraq. To dislodge them, even with the advantages of Western technology, would require a similar-sized force. Given the costs of mobilizing and maintaining a large army in Saudi Arabia, President Bush (who was effectively in charge although UN authorization had been obtained) faced an early decision of whether to adopt an offensive strategy or not. By October it had been decided to go to war against Iraq unless it voluntarily withdrew from Kuwait. This choice was not made explicit in the public arena, where Western strategy was presented as centring on sanctions and defensive force. In effect, however, from October onwards a new phase had opened, with a deadline of mid-January 1991, when military and climatic conditions were likely to be most favourable.

The period from October to January publicly involved diplomacy, designed on the Western side to provide time to complete the military build-up while assuring the UN and public opinion that everything had been done to achieve peace. Saddam Hussein's intentions were unknown and a last-minute withdrawal was possible, but it became clear that he too had chosen war. He apparently believed that Iraq could inflict sufficient casualties on the USA, as the Vietnamese had done twenty years earlier, to cause it to withdraw.

While preparing a military campaign against Iraq, Western governments and military leaders were preparing a propaganda campaign to convince

Western and world public opinion. Since the Vietnam defeat which, in official circles, was believed to have resulted from television coverage,[3] Western governments had tended towards tight control of mass media in times of war. The British government's highly successful manipulation of media during the Falklands war[4] had been a model for the subsequent US invasion of Grenada. The details of these limited island operations were inapplicable to the Iraqi situation, but the principle of controlled deployment of media was highly pertinent. In an unprecedented five months of planning, a massive media operation was laid out which was to be largely successful until the Kurdish conflict in the aftermath of the interstate war.

General responsibility for war thus belonged to both sides, for both had chosen it. Since the West attacked, its leaders also chose how the war was fought and must take responsibility for the consequences. US political and military leaders, who planned the campaign, aimed above all to minimize the casualties to Western forces. They aimed to use air power to destroy Iraq's ability to resist before launching a ground campaign to force it out of Kuwait. Air power, according to propaganda, was designed to be 'surgical', i.e. concentrated on strategic targets and minimizing 'collateral' damage to civilians. While there is no reason to believe civilians were directly targeted, inevitably both targeting and weapons were less accurate than propaganda suggested, and several thousand civilians (relatively, a small number) were killed in bombing raids on Iraq. Although these casualties were publicized a little, larger numbers of civilians died in subsequent months as an indirect result of the bombing of electricity and water supplies, which damaged the infrastructure of social life in central and southern Iraq—these deaths received little Western attention.

The main Iraqi death toll was almost entirely unpublicized: the heavy attrition among troops in defensive positions in southern Iraq and Kuwait who were intensively bombed throughout the six weeks before the land campaign opened. Here there was a conspiracy of silence between coalition and Iraqi forces, both of whom suppressed news of the killing. Only at the end of the war did estimates of Iraqi casualties, ranging from tens to hundreds of thousands, begin to leak from Western military sources to the media.

Issues of responsibility for the killing resulting from the coalition's attacks on Iraq and Iraqi forces arose publicly at two main points in the war: the bombing of the Amiriya shelter on 13 February 1991—the largest civilian casualty incident by far—and the killing of fleeing Iraqis by American air power at Mutla Gap. Both incidents became media controversies, as discussed later in this book.

While Iraqi losses from coalition attacks were considerable—even if they involved tens rather than hundreds of thousands of lives—the largest-scale direct killings of civilians were almost certainly carried out in the Iraqi regime's suppression of the Shi'ite and Kurdish revolts. Here there was a horrific meshing of inter-state and civil politics. The regime, while proclaiming its success in having withstood the world's greatest military powers for six weeks, was gravely weakened by defeat. The war had destroyed many of its forces, severely damaged its economic infrastructure and reduced its authority and control over society.

The attacks on the armed forces and infrastructure were greatest in southern Iraq, close to Kuwait, and it was in Iraq's second city, Basra, that insurrection broke out in the closing days of the war. The predominantly Shia population had suffered the brunt of Saddam's wars, first against Iran and then the Western powers. They rose in large numbers and anti-regime forces quickly took control of Basra and other centres in the south, just as US-led armies invaded southern Iraq in pursuit of the occupiers of Kuwait. When Bush ordered his troops to cease fighting, on 28 February, they were a mere thirty miles from insurrectionary Basra. Within a week, however, Saddam's forces had regrouped and, no longer fighting the coalition, he was able to concentrate sufficient armed might on Basra to crush the rebels, with widespread killing and great brutality, although fighting continued there and in other southern centres for over a month.

The Shi'ite insurrection and its suppression are a defining moment of the Iraqi wars. Responsibility can be attributed in different ways. The rebels suffered for their political *naïveté*. Their leaders clearly made colossal miscalculations, underestimating the continuing strength of the regime and overestimating the will of the coalition and Iran to assist them. They seized their opportunity but alone against the regime they were crushed, and tens of thousands died—women, children and old people as well as militants. The Iraqi regime clearly takes the blame for the slaughter which its troops inflicted on the population.

Coalition leaders, especially Bush, must however take a great share of responsibility for the disaster. They had deliberately stoked the fires of revolt, hoping that popular dissatisfaction would lead to a *coup d'état* in which new Iraqi leaders would sue for peace on Western terms. They had deliberately allowed ambiguity to exist about their war aims, so that while their manifest goal was liberating Kuwait, they appeared to have the covert aim of toppling Saddam. They could not express surprise when many of the long-suffering Iraqi people took the opportunity of the coalition victory to press their own cause. They were faced with a direct choice at the end of February, when it was clear that US-led forces could make the difference between success or failure of the revolt. Bush chose to halt the West's war and leave the people of Basra to their fate.

There appear to be several reasons for this decision. The West wanted a campaign limited in objectives, timespan and risk to its troops. Involvement in the overthrow of the Iraqi regime (of which the success of the southern revolt would only have been the first stage) was likely to be much messier. With Western protection, revolts would probably have achieved quick success in the Shia south and the Kurdish north, but the regime's defeat in its central Sunni heartlands and in Baghdad was less predictable. At the least, it would have involved further coalition military action and a presence on the ground for a considerable period. Establishing an interim regime could have been difficult, as the suppression of dissent meant that opposition groups were small and exile-based. The centrifugal forces of Kurdish nationalism and Shia links with Iran might have been difficult to manage. There was concern about the principle of intervention in the internal affairs of Iraq as opposed to the inter-state conflict between Iraq and Kuwait. Whether these difficulties, which partly explain US reluctance, actually justify it is another matter.

There were more particular reasons for the decision not to protect the Basra rebellion. Arab allies, especially the rulers of Saudi Arabia, feared the success of the Shi'ite rebellion and its perceived boost for Iran more than they feared the continuation of a weakened Ba'athist regime. The Turkish and Syrian governments (and also the Iranian regime whose neutrality had been an important factor in the war against Iraq) feared that the overthrow of Saddam would lead to the break-up of Iraq and the emergence of an independent Kurdistan, strengthening Kurdish independence movements inside their own states. Western governments, too, feared the unpredictable political effects of backing rebellion in Iraq. Western publics were largely uninvolved; media did not penetrate on any significant scale beyond the line of US advance into rebellious southern Iraq. Basra's agony went unfilmed, and a largely ignorant world raised few demands of its leaders.

The fate of the southern rising is put into sharp relief by the outcome of the Kurdish rebellion in the north. Kurdish groups began to take control of their towns and cities at much the same time as the Shi'ites, but they did not face the same overwhelming military presence as their southern counterparts (Iraqi forces were concentrated in the south and around Baghdad because of the war). It was not until mid-March 1991, when Saddam had largely crushed the southern revolt, that his full military might was turned against the Kurds. At the end of March and beginning of April, the regime's army attacked Kurdish towns and villages, and the great exodus began. Over a million fled, many of them to northern Iran where they received little international attention; more to the mountainous border with Turkey. Western and global media found them and put their plight onto every television screen and front page in the world throughout much of April. Here was the essential difference between the Shi'ite and Kurdish rebellions and their suppressions which is explored in detail later in this book.

Media pinned on Bush, Major and other Western leaders much of the responsibility for this situation, in view of their encouragement to the Iraqi people to overthrow the regime. Turkey did not wish to take in the hundreds of thousands of refugees, and something had do be done to protect them. There was a dramatic about-turn as Major proposed and Bush took up the idea of 'safe havens' for the Kurds. The UN could not be persuaded to give specific support, because of Soviet and Chinese fears over the precedent for the situation of their own and other minorities. The USA, the UK and France therefore acted unilaterally, claiming a mandate from previous general resolutions, and troops were sent in to protect Kurds in an area north of the 36th parallel, while humanitarian aid on a substantial scale was sent by voluntary agencies (who had mounted large public appeals in the West) and governments. The West was therefore forced to do in April precisely what Bush had turned his back on, in the south, at the end of February, and get involved in the situation within Iraq.

The Iraqi wars of 1990–1 were therefore civil as well as inter-state wars, and as much as Western leaders attempted to separate the two, they were eventually drawn into the civil conflicts. The responsibility which they accepted in the Kurdish case had to be maintained, effectively, until Saddam fell, with a 'no-fly zone' policed by NATO aircraft from Turkey. Within free Kurdistan, Kurdish institutions developed, including a democratically elected assembly; Kurdistan also provided a base for the Iraqi National Congress, an umbrella organization of opposition groups. Kurdistan's autonomy was however precarious, its economy restricted by Baghdad, its borders constantly threatened by Iraqi troops, and Western support diminished once the initial crisis passed and media and aid agencies' attention focused elsewhere. (In 1994–5 it was also threatened by civil war between the two main Kurdish parties.)

The Kurdish situation proved a precedent for wider intervention in Iraq. The Western powers imposed a no-fly zone over southern Iraq, too, although this had limited value as there were no free institutions on the ground to protect. Airpower proved no deterrent to further brutal campaigns by Iraqi forces against society in the south such as the Marsh Arabs whose very existence was threatened by planned environmental disaster and military extermination. The West and the UN were more interested, in any case, in the sorts of intervention (destruction of weapons of mass destruction, control of nuclear plants) which restricted Iraq's ability to wage inter-state war than in those which protected the population.

Western civil societies in the Iraqi wars

Western states which intervene militarily in global crises need to mobilize civil society in their support. Although armies are typically parts of multinational forces and often operate under the aegis of the UN, they remain essentially national forces, for which national governments are responsible and accountable to society. A, if not *the*, critical issue in every intervention is the safety of Western military forces. Governments need to strike an often difficult balance in responding to popular concern for the victims of global crises and for the security of a country's own troops.

Of all recent crises, the Iraqi wars highlighted the role of civil society most acutely. Because Western military action was vastly larger, more determined and more aggressive than in any other crisis, the participating governments had a much greater need to secure the support of society. This they did by a variety of means. On the one hand, they mobilized the traditional institutions of civil society and responded to challenges from them. On the other hand, they mobilized media and attempted to influence public opinion. This nexus of media and public opinion was strategically more important to states than any other institutions of civil society.

These parameters of the state–civil society relationship were common to all the Western states participating in the Iraqi wars. Within these parameters there were, however, significant differences among the states. These had to do with three main sets of relationships: the role of each state in the coalition against Iraq; the structural and cultural character of militarism in each state; and more general cultural and political peculiarities. The main part of this book concerns British responses to the Iraqi wars: this discussion provides an outline of the comparative context in which to view these responses.

The roles of Western states in the coalition against Iraq varied enormously. The USA was the organizing centre, main supplier of military personnel and largely orchestrated the relations among the coalition states, Western and Arab. US political and military leaders also organized the mobilization of media coverage and hence public opinion throughout the West and globally.

Throughout the Iraqi wars, all other coalition states were clearly subordinate to the USA. The UK, France and of course Saudi Arabia were its key military allies. Without Saudi support the USA could not have mounted the campaign against Iraq, and the two main European powers were both key military and political allies (undertaking the Kurdish intervention with the USA, as well as supporting it as permanent members in the UN Security Council). Other European states, notably Italy, Spain and the Netherlands, played significant military roles, and even post-Communist Czechoslovakia gave token logistical support. Alongside these were the contributions of Turkey, Syria, Egypt, Morocco and the Gulf states. The coalition depended financially on the Gulf states, notably Saudi Arabia and Kuwait, and on Germany and Japan, which were disbarred from military participation by their post-Second World War constitutions.

Clearly the Iraqi wars raised strikingly different issues in the Arab and Western worlds. In the Arab states—as among Arab and Muslim minorities in the West—there was considerable popular support for Saddam Hussein as a champion of Arab and Muslim interests. Saddam's propaganda partially succeeded in cloaking his regime in these mantles (including the religious one despite the secular character of the Ba'athist state). Large sections of Arab and Muslim opinion either did not know of Saddam's atrocities against the Iraqi people and Kuwaitis—although Arab coalition governments' propaganda attempted to publicize these—or they did not care. The plight of Palestinians forced out of Kuwait by the invasion was politically neutralized by the support Saddam received from the Palestine Liberation Organization. Visible support—which varied considerably among states—tended to fade, of course, after his defeat by the coalition and as his attacks on the Shias and Kurds became manifest.

Within Western states, the peculiarities of national civil societies clearly contributed to different responses. Some reflected historic cultural and political characteristics: Italy, for example, saw strong overt opposition to the war because of the coincidence of papal and Communist criticisms of the West's attacks. Such differences apart, public opinion in Western civil societies clearly followed, to a very considerable degree, the roles of national states in the conflict. In the USA, once the war began public opinion was overwhelmingly pro-war and there were active demonstrations of support for American troops, with the display of flags outside homes and shops a very widespread phenomenon. In the UK, in contrast, while public opinion (as we shall see in later detailed discussion) was equally overwhelmingly pro-war, flag-waving in this American-led war in no way matched the patriotic displays of the previous, strictly national, Falklands conflict. In states less pivotal to the coalition, public support was still strong but passive, and some of the relatively superficial nature of the support for military involvement is perhaps indicated by popular support in Belgium for its government's refusal to commit troops to the conflict.

A major differentiator of the responses was the role of military culture and institutions. Historic experiences of war were important: opposition in Germany was relatively strong, at least before the war began, due to hostility to any revival of militarism. Public debate about the wisdom of attacking Iraq was also much stronger in the USA, with its people's memories of the failure in Vietnam, than in the UK, which had experienced no military defeat in living memory and where national myths of war were uniquely positive.

Equally important was the nature of the national military force. Compulsory military service was actually a barrier to participation in the conflict. Young people everywhere—even in the UK, where the last conscript left the armed forces in 1963—feared conscription. In Germany, where it was extremely unlikely (because of the constitutional position) that the government would participate directly in the war, there was nevertheless a strong reaction to the danger of conscription for the war.

Everywhere, media were central to the responses of civil society. News management by coalition states, globalization of television news coverage and the emergence of global news organizations—especially Cable News Network (CNN)—meant that there was a great deal of common content to media in different states. However, for most viewers, coverage was filtered by nationally based television media, each responsive to its own cultural and political context. Other nationally based media, most notably the press, also coloured the way in which people were informed about and responded to the war.

Notes

1. For a demonstration that there have been roughly three civil wars for every inter-state war, see Table 2.1, 'Wars 1945–1980' in Shaw, 1991, pp. 59–60.

2. Genocide was defined at an international legal level following the Second World War, and was incorporated in the International Convention on Genocide of 1948 which stated that genocide comprises acts 'committed with intent to destroy, in whole or in part, a national, ethnical, racial or religious group' (Kuper, 1981, p. 32). Genocide includes cultural as well as physical extermination, it is not confined to ethnically defined groups, it does not necessarily involve the destruction of the whole of a group, and it does not necessarily involve the level of systematic extermination practised by the Nazis. The internationally recognized definition of genocide is the one employed in this book.

3. Academic studies have tended to discredit this belief: see Mandelbaum, 1982; Hallin, 1986. Nevertheless, it was undoubtedly held by many policy-makers, and thus was influential in the Gulf.

4. See Harris, 1992.

— Part II —

Limits of National Civil Society

In this part of the book I wish to examine how institutions of civil society within a national context respond to the challenges posed by global crises. I aim to discuss how far, in what ways and with what limitations major institutions responded to the problems of the Iraqi wars. My purpose is to see how far institutions located within a national civil society have begun to respond to global challenges and to become part of an emergent global civil society.

For most institutions of national civil society, distant wars represent indirect challenges. They raise issues of principle to do with violations of human life and freedom which impinge on institutions' ideologies. Since institutions' activities mainly concern state and society within the national context, distant wars represent tangential issues. In most wars, Western nation-states are not initially involved and issues are first posed in terms of whether anything can be done to help victims. It is implicit in 'doing something' that the national state and some members of the national society will be directly involved—this then becomes part of the problem. In the Gulf, on the other hand, in which Western nation-states and their forces were centrally involved from an early stage, issues were posed more concretely in terms of national policy and the interests of the state and the members of its forces.

In examining the responses to distant wars of British institutions, we must take account of the British state's role in the development of global state intervention. The UK is a major bulwark of Western-dominated world institutions. Its history as a world empire and co-victor in the Second World War has given it an importance in the UN and NATO out of proportion to its declining economic weight. In some post-Cold War political contexts Germany or Japan have more importance, but the UK (like France) remains a major military–political actor. The UK is a nuclear-armed state, a permanent member of the UN Security Council, a more reliable ally of the USA than France, and a state with historic global links and diverse military experience (including recent specialization in low-intensity operations in Northern Ireland). Although the country was the first to abandon the institutional basis of mass militarism (i.e. conscription), militarism remains strong in British culture.[1]

For all these reasons, British governments tend to have a high-profile role in formulating and implementing Western and UN policy in global crises. British policy debates on global crises have not merely a general but also a national dimension. In the Iraqi crises, of course, the UK state was the closest political ally and military collaborator of the USA (Saudi Arabia apart) at all stages; but it was essentially a secondary actor. Asked in Parliament if the war would end when Saddam Hussein left Kuwait, the Prime Minister, John Major, replied, 'I assume we shall conclude the existing conflict when that happens.' 'This,' the *Independent* rightly concluded, 'was a candid admission of the military reality—that Britain remains a junior partner in a US-run operation in which the critical decisions are taken not in London, but in Washington and by the US military command in Saudi Arabia.'[2] The British 'War Cabinet'—officially known as the Gulf Committee—decided the level of Britain's commitment, but it did not, as the Falklands War Cabinet did, dictate day to day strategy. Despite close political and intelligence links between Britain and the USA, 'Sometimes events in the Gulf have unfolded too fast for the Whitehall assessment to be fed fully into the secret side of Washington, but it is regarded as "value added" when it is.'[3]

Nevertheless, the British state and its relationship with its national civil society came centre-stage at a later phase of the Iraqi wars. When the plight of the Kurdish refugees was exposed, it was in Britain that pressure for international action to save them first became effective. At this point, when US policy was in the balance, the British prime minister, responding to media and public opinion, produced proposals to which the US eventually responded. An important turn in international policy resulted, with the precedent of 'safe havens' which violated the principle of national sovereignty. This example showed that, although the British state was essentially a junior partner, it could be important in certain circumstances, and the role of British civil society was correspondingly significant in world events.

In the remainder of this section I examine in turn the roles of major civil institutions to the Iraqi crises, in order to consider four major issues. The first is how far they were able to articulate coherent responses to the wars; the second is how closely their responses reflected the commitments of the state, or were independent of it; the third is about how the responses of institutions related to the concerns of individuals and groups in British society; and the fourth and final issue is about the extent to which institutions in civil society in Britain remained essentially national in scope or can be seen as elements of an emergent global civil society. These issues are all broached here, but the third and fourth, especially, continue into later chapters.

In this discussion I have selected for scrutiny three traditional representative institutions (political parties, churches and intellectuals); one functional institution involved with representation (schools); and three 'new' representative institutions (social movements, humanitarian agencies and Muslim community institutions). The role of media, the most critical of all civil society institutions, is saved for the following section. Within each group I have selected certain institutions for scrutiny to keep the discussion within manageable bounds.

Notes and references

1. See Shaw, 1991, pp. 109–62.
2. *Independent*, 20 January 1991.
3. *Independent*, 28 January 1991.

CHAPTER THREE

Traditional representative institutions

Certain institutions have 'traditionally' represented national society in its relationship with the state. I have selected three to examine in detail. Political parties are institutions through which society's relationships with the democratic state are formally mediated: their modern forms have evolved over the last hundred years. Christian churches are historic representative institutions, through which members of Western societies have interpreted the world for well over a thousand years. They have been reinvented as national institutions in recent centuries and have found particular roles in twentieth-century nation-states. Intellectuals are a social group with a more discursive ideological role than parties or churches, but they also attempt to represent national society. In the last century, as the role of churches has narrowed, intellectuals have played a larger role, partly through a variety of more formal institutions from universities to press and television.

These institutions are clearly traditional in different senses, but they all evolved in earlier stages of modern Western society (churches even earlier) and have been reinvented in modern times.[1] All clearly involve, however, traditions and ideologies which, while claiming universality, have been articulated in the national context. For our purposes, the important point is that they are traditional in this sense: that they have emerged in the national context rather than as responses to the globalization of society in the late twentieth century. They are not, as Gramsci put it, 'organic' institutions of the new period. How they respond to new global challenges, particularly of representing people involved in distant violence, is the first stage of our discussion of civil society's response.

Parties and distant violence

Political parties exist to articulate the interests of social groups to the state; they also reflect the state's interests and policies back into society. Their *raison d'être*, however, is the control of executive state power itself through winning elections. The interests of governing parties, therefore, come to be identified with those of the state, although they also continue to reflect their constituencies—there may of course be tension here. The interests of opposition parties, in contrast, are more distinct from those of state power, but they also experience the pull of state interests which they would respect if they won power and which they must therefore respect if they are to win power.

In recent global crises, few interests of groups within the national societies of the West have been directly engaged, except for powerful interests in avoiding casualties among service personnel and other nationals in the zones of crisis, their families and the communities to which they belong. Parties are affected, in their responses to global crises, by these interests, but otherwise chiefly by their conceptions of state interests, by the ways in which crises impinge on their ideologies and of course by their conceptions of how they impinge on their own (chiefly electoral) interests.

At the outset of the Gulf crisis, Margaret Thatcher was still British prime minister (she was ousted two months before war began). She was credited with having encouraged the strong stance against the Iraqi invasion adopted by President Bush. (Thatcher, the 'Iron Lady', had of course utilized previous international crises, during the Cold War and especially the Falklands War, to bolster her position and that of her party.) Once the USA had decided on military intervention, the British government quickly lent its support. After the election of John Major as Prime Minister in November 1990, the UK shadowed the American position closely, taking no independent positions or initiatives—unlike, for example, the French government, which carried out its own diplomatic manoeuvres up to the outbreak of war. British troops were committed early to the coalition, so the Conservative government had a substantial investment in its success.

Major's public stance, for example in the Commons two days before the coalition attacked Iraq, was not overtly warmongering:

> We do not want a conflict. We are not thirsting for war, though if it comes I must say to the House I believe it would be a just war. However great the costs of war may be ... they would be less than those that we would face if we failed to stand up for the principle of what is right ... . Those who caution delay because they hate war—as we all do—must ask themselves this question: how much longer should the world stand by and risk these atrocities [in Kuwait] continuing?[2]

A liberal paper suggested that 'in the first test of his Premiership, Major has struck the right note about the war in the Gulf, one in keeping with the sombre public mood—flat, factual and sincere. It is a relief, not only from the mindless jingoism of parts of the popular press, but from the triumphalism of his predecessor.'[3] A critic could only complain that 'at no stage in his speech did he explain why he believed sanctions could not and would not work. All he would say is that they had not worked yet. Ergo, they would not work later.'[4]

Major and Douglas Hurd, the foreign secretary, were determined to maintain cross-party support for military action and ignored advice to attack Labour's urging of longer reliance on economic sanctions. There were sound reasons for this: casualties in the war could have created a difficult situation in which it was useful to have the Opposition on board, and their leaders were fully briefed by Downing Street during the crisis. The government's refusal of jingoism was symbolized by Major's rejection of 'a ritual backbench harangue about the BBC's decision to refer to "British troops" rather than "our troops"'.[5] Of course, to others, he didn't look or sound like a war leader:

> Try to imagine Winston Churchill declaring, as Mr Major did ... : "Saddam Hussein invaded Kuwait. There was no need for him to do it. It was a unilaterally nasty [pause while the British Prime Minister searches for a new word] piece of nastiness." He sounded as aggressive as a rather timid curate delivering a sermon.[6]

Throughout the war, Major quietly followed the American line, for example calling the bombing of the Amiriya air raid shelter 'tragic' but claiming there was 'legitimate reason to believe it was a military target'.[7] British political unity came under strain over the issue of war aims, notably after Tom King, secretary of state for defence, claimed UN authority for the destruction of Iraq's military might. King warned that forcing its armies out of Kuwait, without removing its capacity to mount a future threat, would be a 'betrayal' of the allied forces.[8] Hurd, on the other hand, avoided any clear indication of the point at which the war would end: 'There is a clear line being adopted: we'll fudge it', said one ministerial source.[9] (This ambiguity fed Labour unease about a wider war, as discussed below.)

The Conservative Party in Parliament was not a serious source of difficulty to the government. A few backbenchers 'indulged in tabloid-style enthusiasm for the war', while the former prime minister, Edward Heath, and a few others expressed reservations.[10] Heath, who had long pursued a maverick line, played an independent role in securing the release of British hostages from Baghdad and opposed the quick resort to military means: 'Everyone knew at the time that sanctions cannot be effective in five or six months, but all the indications are that sanctions are bound to be effective. It is the one case in the modern world where a country has been cut off.' He conceded however that 'there is always the ultimate point where force may be necessary', but until then sanctions should be kept up.[11]

In general, Major's strategy worked: by the later stages of the war he was the 'most popular Prime Minister for 30 years' according to one poll—74 per cent thought he was doing well.[12] During the year before the war, Labour had led polls; just before the war, they had shown the main parties level pegging;[13] a month later the Tories were leading and Major was reported to have 'instructed ministers to deliver election manifesto sub-missions' by the middle of the following week as part of contingency plans for an election as early as May 1991.[14]

The viability of such a strategy depended first on winning a by-election in the Conservative-held seat of Ribble Valley (7 March 1991, a week after the end of the war). A related obstacle was 'deadlock within the Cabinet about whether to scrap the community charge [or 'poll tax']; this was reported to be putting Major's option of an early election in jeopardy.[15] An

NOP survey in the by-election constituency showed, indeed, that 57 per cent said the poll tax was influencing their vote and only 2 per cent said 'foreign policy' or 'the Gulf crisis', even though 87 per cent were satisfied with the government's handling of the war, and 79 per cent with Major.[16] In the event, the Liberal Democrats convincingly defeated the Government in the by-election, mobilizing public opposition to the poll tax.

In the wake of this defeat, John Major moved quickly to abandon the poll tax and no more was heard of a 'khaki election'.[17] Attitude research carried out for the author and his colleague during the Ribble Valley by-election confirmed that opinions about the Gulf War had played a small part.[18] The Conservative defeat at Ribble Valley transformed the political landscape, with the Tory lead over Labour in opinion polls quickly disappearing, to be replaced by late March by a Labour lead.[19]

Despite the failure of the 'Gulf factor' to affect the by-election, Conservatives were quick to bank the political capital of the war, as this anecdote illustrates:

> The Labour Party ... suggested ... that Neil Kinnock [the then Labour leader] might speed out to Kuwait to congratulate our lads... . "Oh, no," said the modest Neil, anxious not to exploit the forces' triumph. Imagine the horror when the very next day the party bigwigs turned on their TVs and saw John Major ... standing heroically in the sand surrounded by Desert Rats.[20]

This film was to turn up again in the Conservatives' final Party Election Broadcast in the general election campaign a year later.

The political success of Major's war was quickly overtaken by the Kurdish crisis in April 1991. With over a million starving Kurds at the Iranian and Turkish borders, Major announced aid of £20 million plus two planeloads of blankets and tents, but when questioned about the way the Kurds had been 'incited' to insurrection, he replied: 'I do not recall asking them to mount this particular insurrection.'[21] This comment drew the caustic comment that

> It used to be Margaret Thatcher who was seen as deficient in human emotions ... John Major was the man with a heart... . Now, suddenly, it is Mrs Thatcher who speaks out with true feelings about the Kurds, while Mr Major responds to this enormous human tragedy with the prim detachment of a desiccated bureaucrat.[22]

Before long, Major had reversed his stance, and put forward the proposal for 'safe havens' in Kurdistan. 'I may end up with egg all over my face because they fail,' he remarked. 'But I will tell you this, I would rather end up with egg all over my face than not having put forward solutions to this problem.'[23] When the US administration agreed to back the havens proposal, the government chief whip was reported to have telephoned editors to make sure Major's contribution was not overlooked. Tory managers were doubtless relieved to discover that Major's reputation had recovered: his poll rating improved although his party's did not.[24]

During the 1992 General Election, the Conservatives sought to extract further mileage from Major's success. After what the Tories called 'Red Wednesday', when three polls showed clear Labour leads, Kenneth Clarke, a senior minister, referred twice in one interview to Major as the man 'who led us through the Gulf War'.[25] Film of Major's post-Gulf War visit to the troops was screened as part of the party's final election broadcast.[26] Major's reversal of the tide was due in part to his presentation of a strong stance on constitutional issues (the integrity of the UK state, electoral reform), and images of the Gulf success were clearly seen as an important symbol of his party's 'strength'.

Afterwards, the Gulf was a source of embarrassment for the government in three main ways. First, the 'friendly fire' incident in which British soldiers were killed in error by US airmen became a political issue because the families wanted to know 'why their sons died and wanted someone to accept responsibility'. But Major 'refused to accept or attribute responsibility—even though the government had the information to do so. The reason is to do with the "special relationship" and Whitehall's subordination to Washington.'[27] More seriously, the government was continuously embarrassed by its encouragement of arms sales to Iraq before the war. The government had eventually to establish the Scott Inquiry to investigate the matter, and senior Tories were paraded before it, with a potentially difficult report due in 1996. Last but not least, the government, like its allies, faced the continuing problem of the survival of the Saddam Hussein regime, its threat to the Kurdish enclave and the failure to resolve the political problems of the region.

Among opposition parties, the minority Liberal Democrats maintained a relatively low public profile during the war, although not for lack of trying. The party gave loyal support to the government while trying to adopt a larger policy perspective. As party leader Paddy Ashdown put it: 'The conduct of the war lies with the government. We cannot influence it, and maybe while the war is going on, we cannot freely criticise it. But it is the job of the opposition parties to look through the war to the peace which is to follow.'[28] (Later, during the UN operations in Bosnia, Ashdown was to take a very different stance as the most radically interventionist of the main party leaders.)

The position of Labour, the major opposition party, was more sensitive. Critical gestures by party leaders over the 1982 Falklands War had been exploited by the Conservatives, and it was widely believed that radical policies on defence, notably opposition to nuclear weapons, had been electoral liabilities in 1983 and 1987.[29] Labour's leaders faced a dilemma: they had learned from these experiences to be cautious on military issues and not to stray far from the patriotic consensus fostered by the Conservatives and media; and yet their party and constituency included most of those in Britain who had misgivings about war against Iraq, misgivings which many of them shared to some degree. The former Labour deputy leader, Denis Healey, a staunch right-winger and supporter of

NATO, was one of the most forthright opponents of war (mirroring the stance of Heath in the Conservative Party). The party's traditional left-wing (led by Tony Benn and Eric Heffer) was opposed, and the 'soft left'— sections of the left who accommodated Labour's 'modernizing' leadership and including members of the Shadow Cabinet—had strong misgivings about the drift to war.

Opinion in the party outside Parliament, so far as it can be gauged, seems to have been generally in favour of sanctions rather than war, and reluctant in its acquiescence in the war once it had broken out. MPs who stood out of line on the war, such as John Prescott, received support from their local constituency parties.[30] Most dissatisfaction with the national party line, however, was muted, and it was relatively rare for it to receive public expression.[31]

In these circumstances, the leadership's policy, as expressed by Neil Kinnock and Gerald Kaufman (foreign policy spokesperson), was primarily one of damage limitation, achieved by skilful balancing of support for sanctions as a means of dislodging Iraq from Kuwait, with support for war once the coalition had launched its attacks. This policy had the advantages of satisfying the pacifist and pro-UN instincts of many MPs and party members while placing Labour in the patriotic camp once British troops were at risk.

The policy placed party unity above any serious attempt to influence the Gulf situation, presumably on the calculation that while Labour's influence on the Gulf would be at best modest, the effect of handling it badly could be highly detrimental to Labour's election prospects.[32] Accordingly, the leadership played the issue quite cynically, remaining virtually silent during the build-up to war and making no challenge to the implicit choice of war already made by Bush. Kinnock saved his most impassioned appeal for sanctions to be allowed more time until his speech in the debate of 15 January—as the UN deadline to Iraq expired and just two days before air attacks began—when it was coupled with a clear commitment to support war.

Labour's strongest stance on sanctions was thus made when it was least meaningful and understood (by the government, for example) as a necessary sop to party opinion which did not seriously compromise its support for the war.[33] It followed the abstentions of frontbenchers Jo Richardson, Clare Short and Joan Ruddock and others in the parliamentary debate of 11 December 1990,[34] and it represented a superficial softening of the position previously expressed by Kaufman in order to prevent any serious party divisions when the war actually began.[35]

Labour's support for the war was carefully nuanced. Kinnock stressed that British troops would be engaged under UN authority and support would not be given 'in a drum-banging way', but 'because we understand why our forces are there, and the fact is that they require our solidarity and they will get it.'[36] He argued, on the one hand, that 'To make concessions before withdrawal would leave him with great strength. It would mean no more than war postponed'—but on the other that 'Part of the reason for arguing for the longest-possible use of sanctions, and it is no sense a concession to Saddam Hussein, or appeasement, is to try to ensure the killing rate is as low as possible.'[37] Once war had broken out, Kinnock was a consistent supporter, even complaining that the lack of instinctive European Community co-operation over the Gulf called into question plans for political union, let alone a community defence policy.[38]

There is no doubting the sincerity of some leaders' distaste for war and war-hysteria—Roy Hattersley even took to task William Deedes (a former Tory cabinet minister) for misquoting Rudyard Kipling, arguing that the British are not a warlike people and Kipling was not a warlike poet, and attacked Tory intolerance of dissent from the war.[39] But such arguments, like Kaufman's for sanctions,[40] were often articulated quietly in the pages of the liberal *Guardian* while in Parliament and on television the party stood four-square by the war.

Labour's distinctive input was to emphasize the need for limited war aims (being consistently opposed to their broadening to include the overthrow of Saddam Hussein) and a wider Middle East peace settlement including justice for the Palestinians.[41] These aims nuanced Labour's position *vis-à-vis* the government's—'Labour's Gulf policy is designed to be nearly, but not quite, that of the government'.[42] They were also aims around which the party could unite, but there was nevertheless repeated friction as those unhappy with the war struggled to make this clear.

In the Shadow Cabinet, Prescott got into trouble for signing a pro-sanctions motion after the war had begun and for subsequent attempts to block any shift of position on war aims to include the toppling of Saddam Hussein.[43] Robin Cook (then Shadow health spokesperson) challenged the bombing of Iraq's infrastructure which he argued would hit civilians harder than the Iraqi military. Both were credited with nimble footwork, 'anxious to voice widespread Labour unease about the war without splitting their party or the anti-Saddam camp.'[44] Like a number of frontbenchers in a so-called 'supper club' (an informal gathering of 'soft left' politicians which became notorious in the tabloid press), they tried to influence policy from the inside track.[45] Others like Short, however, resigned over the war. On the backbenches, of course, there was more outspoken criticism.

In retrospect, Labour's dilemma seems more difficult than it did at the time. The post-Gulf War experience suggests that Saddam Hussein's regime was more resistant to sanctions than Labour politicians believed, and the subsequent success of Slobodan Milosevic in using sanctions to bolster political support for his regime in Serbia is hardly encouraging. At the same time, both of these cases provide evidence of the harmful effects of sanctions on civilian populations. Of course, the effects of war were also terrible, in the slaughter of Iraqi conscripts, the direct civilian casualties (even if numbers were not large by historical standards) and the effects of bombing on living conditions. Labour was right to be cautious about endorsing a war policy, and sanctions appeared to be the only serious alternative. If Labour was to have had any serious influence, however, it should have expressed its views vigorously between August and October 1990, before the US had committed itself fully to the war strategy. After this, Labour's protests were expressions of concern rather than actions which were likely to influence events.

Labour's contribution to the war aims debate was, in a way, more revealing. Statements by Kaufman and much of the agitation by Prescott and others focused on the undesirability of extending war aims to include overthrowing Saddam. Kaufman argued: 'An invasion of Iraq for other purposes [than their removal from Kuwait] over the bodies of a defeated Iraqi army would not only go beyond the UN resolutions but would created [sic] insoluble problems. To defeat Iraq's war machine may turn out to be necessary. To occupy a defeated Iraq would be another matter entirely.' He unequivocally endorsed the public stances of the American and British governments, quoting with approval first Bush—'Who then should govern Iraq? Much as we may loathe Saddam, much as we would welcome his being deposed, that it is not for us to say'—and then Hurd—'We have to be very clear on our objectives and not add new objectives as we go along.'[46]

Despite such apparently clear positions, critics expended much energy on blocking what they feared would be concessions by the leadership. Seen as an extension of opposition to the war, this is understandable, but considered as an argument about war aims it is surprising that a party of the left should be so keen to prevent the overthrow of one of the worst dictators of modern times. It was more appropriate for the Conservatives than for Labour to see the war strictly in terms of restoring the international status quo ante and with it the corrupt Kuwaiti regime rather than of liberating the Gulf region's people from oppression.

The contradictions of Labour positions were therefore exposed, perhaps even more than those of Bush and Major, by the war's aftermath. When the coalition halted the war, as Labour desired, with the liberation of Kuwait, it condemned the Shi'ite opposition, in revolt in Basra just thirty miles from the USA's furthest advance, to slaughter and repression and the Kurds to his attacks, which sent over a million people fleeing to the mountainsides. When media management broke down, television and the press exposed the awful situation to Western publics, Bush and Major were forced into a rapid policy reverse, but Labour, both leadership and critics, had little to say. As the Kurdish issue broke in the media, Labour was caught calling on the government to take action against Iraqi-front firms in London, rather than urging action for the Kurds, although it later backed Major's plan.[47]

Labour simply failed to keep up with the issues. When Kinnock did pronounce, his cautious, legalistic words hardly seemed to measure up to the situation:

I believe that there is a *prima facie* case for the United Nations to investigate and pursue its own genocide convention and to consider the justification of intervention to prevent the destruction of a people. It must be the case that the offence of genocide is so great that it supersedes the normal and necessary constraints of sovereignty.[48]

Long-term supporters of the Iraqi opposition such as Ann Clwyd MP were active in urging support for the Kurds, but most left-wing critics of the war were unable to do more than try to make capital from the USA's inconsistencies.[49]

This experience suggests that Labour's leadership, insider critics and backbench left were trapped in an over-simple neo-pacifist approach. However understandable as a response to modern war, this failed to address the key problem of the aftermath: how to protect a civilian population from a genocidal regime. This is a central issue of most global crises and international interventions of the post-Cold War era to which a policy of avoiding British involvement in war is not really an answer. In none of the subsequent crises, moreover, has Labour's involvement been even as thorough or consistent as in the Gulf. Despite the constant media coverage of the Yugoslav wars, Labour's leaders and foreign affairs spokes-persons have never made a sustained intervention to modify the British government's stance, other than occasional forays at times of high media attention and policy crisis.

In conclusion, this discussion suggests that both the main British political parties managed their responses to the Gulf War largely in the light of domestic political constraints. Although they differed, both had clear strategies for representing the Gulf War itself, but neither had a clear approach to the Kurdish crisis—Major's 'safe havens' plan was an impro-vization in response to media and public opinion, and Labour could only follow suit.

Christian principles and state policy

Religious organizations are traditionally of the highest ideological signifi-cance in national civil society. Although many Western liberal–democratic states are secular, religion still generally sanctions states and provides an officially recognized framework of morality. Although most people are not practising Christians and many are atheists or agnostics, the churches' pronouncements are still seen as important markers in public debate.

Wars have traditionally posed particular dilemmas for churches, caught between the universal character of Christian beliefs and the particularistic demands of national policy, particularly between prohibitions on violence and the realities of war. Doctrine has sought devices to resolve these dilemmas, such as the notion of the 'just war', which in practice have involved churches in justifying state power.

In the Gulf, Western political leaders cloaked themselves in Christian 'just war' doctrine, although they did not go to the lengths of Saddam Hussein and declare it a religious war. Bush addressed religious broadcasters and declared: 'We know this is a just war, and we know that, God willing, this is a war we will win.' At the same time he espoused the notion of proportionality: 'We must act reasonably, humanely and make every effort possible to keep casualties to a minimum.'[50] Bush generally ended his speeches with 'and may God bless the United States of America'; similarly, Major in a television address assured relatives of troops he was 'praying' for them, ending his broadcast with 'God bless'.[51]

[handwritten margin note: just like his son]

Among Christian leaders themselves, there was some distance from this state invocation of their beliefs. Pope John Paul II, leader of the world's Catholics, condemned the Iraqi invasion as 'a brutal violation of international law', but warned Western states against invoking international law to 'protect their own interests, and assert their hegemony over others'. He set the invasion in the context of the 'dislocated land of Lebanon' and the rights of the Palestinians, 'so gravely tried, so unjustly treated'.

The real object of papal condemnation was, however, war itself as a method of resolving differences: in this respect he clearly departed from the 'just war' tradition.[52] John Paul II picked up on the teaching of John XXIII's 1963 encyclical, *Pacem in Terris*: 'It no longer makes sense to maintain that war is a fit instrument with which to repair the violation of justice.' John's position concerned nuclear war; John Paul extended it to modern 'conventional' weapons. Even a limited war, he said, would be devastating and its 'ecological, political, economic and strategic consequences' incalculable. War was 'unworthy of mankind'; on the other hand, the Pope advised Bush, that sending a message to a despot was supremely 'worthy of mankind'. John Paul II argued that humankind had to 'move resolutely towards an absolute ban on war and towards the cultivation of peace as a supreme good.'[53] He made a last-minute appeal to both Saddam Hussein and Bush to avoid war[54] and condemned the 'deplorable' bombing of civilians, berating 'the terrible logic of war', raising the danger of nuclear escalation.[55] The Pope's 'unprecedented campaign' against war was the cue for an anti-war Catholic left in Italy to forge 'an extraordinary alliance' with Italy's Communist Party. Later in the war, the Pope backed the Soviet peace plan,[56] and, towards the conclusion of the conflict, called a meeting of bishops from countries involved.[57]

National Christian leaders in Britain, as in most combatant states, responded rather differently from the Pope. The leadership of the Church of England, like the Labour Party, was resolutely if somewhat agonizedly behind the war. The retiring Archbishop of Canterbury, Robert Runcie, the only Christian leader widely reported in the media, gave the government's policy his clear support, although he also expressed some anguish. He averred that

> If there were really a simple and uncomplicated choice between the continuation of sanctions for say six months, and war, I would plump for sanctions.... I firmly believe sanctions must be maintained and that we must continue to support

every diplomatic channel that has any reasonable chance of success, but we cannot avoid the fact that it may be necessary to resort to war in the interests of peace in the long term.[58]

Runcie also appeared on Radio 4 to deliver a 'Thought for the Day' backing the coalition's actions. 'It's true', he acknowledged,

> that a Christian has a built-in resistance to the use of force. We are to be the peacemakers. But to do justice sometimes compels us to use force... . This war is not with the Iraqi people, but with Saddam Hussein and those who surround him. Dietrich Bonhoeffer, the German pastor who was killed by the Nazis in the last week of the Second World War, once said that God is among us in our lives, but not on any side. That's another instinctive Christian insight which helps maintain our reserves of compassion and mercy as we seek to do justice.[59]

Shortly afterwards, he was even more explicit: 'All those involved need our support, those who give orders and those who obey them.'[60] The *Sun* summed up the political meaning of the Archbishop's carefully nuanced position in the simple headline: 'RUNCIE: WAR OK.'[61]

Many other Church leaders followed Runcie's lead. A statement by the House of Bishops accepted the necessity of war; only three of fifty bishops abstained from supporting it.[62] Richard Harris, Bishop of Oxford, expressed the dominant view in measured tones:

> We are all flawed and right is not wholly on our side. Nevertheless, in this confused, contradictory and tragic world, even sinful human beings have to choose ... however saddened and disturbed we are by pictures of the wounded and dying, our resolve to achieve a just peace must not weaken... . We cannot allow the high human cost of war totally to inhibit the use of armed force against aggressors.[63]

Where it mattered, Anglican representatives loyally backed the government's line. At the World Council of Churches, the Church's delegation opposed a resolution calling for an immediate ceasefire followed by an Iraqi withdrawal, proposing an amendment that the Iraqis should withdraw before a ceasefire.[64] The General Synod, in which laity and clergy as well as bishops are represented, refused to hold an emergency debate on the war—a decision called 'scandalous' by Rowan Williams, Professor of Divinity at Oxford, who argued that 'with weapons of mass destruction, the inability to control escalation and the intransigence of the Iraqi army, it is impossible to mount an effective response "proportionate in justice" to the injustice of the invasion of Kuwait'.[65] Critics of the war like Stanley Booth-Clibborn, Bishop of Manchester, were 'disappointed that there was not more support from Anglican leaders for the position of continuing with sanctions'; Runcie was 'too quick to accept the political arguments for the war after it had broken out'.

Liberal bishops expressed reservations at the end of the war. Hugh Montefiore, retired Bishop of Birmingham, wrote that: 'If we rightly condemn bacteriological warfare, how can we justify taking action [the bombing of Baghdad water supplies] which must result in epidemics of killer diseases?'[66] David Jenkins, the then Bishop of Durham and a noted radical, attacked the proposed victory celebrations as 'obscene', arguing that a service 'would have to be focused ... on repentance for having got into this mess, and gratitude that we were able to end it so soon. At the moment, there's all this euphoria over victory,' he stated, 'and we should never have got into it.'[67]

The victory celebrations were the focus of church conflict in Scotland, where the government decided that the national service of remembrance was to be held because of the number of Scottish troops. Robert Davidson, Moderator of the General Assembly of the Church of Scotland, an opponent of war before it began, was excluded from the ceremony in Glasgow Cathedral which was organized by the Ministry of Defence and Cathedral authorities.[68]

The leader of English Catholics, Cardinal Basil Hume, Archbishop of Westminster, took a stance closer to Runcie's than the Pope's (whose pronouncements did not bind Catholics and indeed left more flexibility of interpretation than they seemed to.)[69] Like Anglican leaders, he was careful not to be openly at odds with the Government. Hume laid down an interpretation of Catholic doctrine from the Second Vatican Council, concluding 'that going to war in the Gulf cannot be said to be immoral'.[70] His support, like Runcie's, was agonized—the war was 'at best a tragic necessity'.[71] Hume was for a humane war, writing to Major demanding immediate assurances of a ban on the further use of napalm on Iraqi trenches (the use of which had been admitted by the US).[72]

A few Catholic leaders echoed the Pope's position. Thomas Winning, Archbishop of Glasgow, was an opponent of the war before it began and was also excluded from the service of remembrance in Glasgow Cathedral. Archbishop Cahal Daly, Primate of All Ireland, argued that modern weapons make it 'impossible to apply the criteria of a just war'.[73] 'We begin to talk of "surgical strikes" and forget about the gore and the grime and mangled bodies on the ground.'[74] Within the Catholic church, there was considerable activity taking its cue from the Pope's stance: the *Catholic Herald* urged its readers to 'sign up with Pope John Paul', whose opinion, it noted, stood 'head and shoulders above the rest [of those aired by church leaders] for its clarity and unambiguity'.

Several Catholic figures were among the founders of the Christian Coalition for Peace in the Gulf, although as the *Herald* asked, given the Pope's stance, 'is it not more surprising to see that only two of the 40-plus Catholic bishops in Britain have put their names to the document?'[75] (There were two Anglican bishops too, together with two main Nonconformist leaders, the General Secretary of the Baptist Union and the President of the Methodist Conference.)[76]

Bruce Kent, a Catholic priest who had been General Secretary of the Campaign for Nuclear Disarmament, portrayed the Churches' response in

an anti-war light: 'The response from the church, apart from the Archbishop of Canterbury and the Bishop [sic] of Westminster, who have sat on
the fence so long that rust is beginning to set in, has been encouraging. And
since the Pope's declaration it will get even better.'[77] Although there was
clearly much unease about the war among church leaders, Kent's optimism
does not appear to have been warranted by their record.

Some idea of the responses of clergy in general is provided by a survey
we carried out of ministers of religion in a local area.[78] This showed that
clergy were less likely to 'strongly approve' of the war (16 compared to 28
per cent) and more likely to 'disapprove' (30 compared to 17 per cent) than
a sample of the general population polled in the same period with the same
questionnaire. They were also more likely to be in favour of giving sanctions longer to work, to be concerned about loss of life among Iraqis and in
other ways more 'pacifist' than the population at large. Nevertheless, the
differences (as in the above figures) were not very large.

What also emerged was a very clear pattern of differences in attitudes,
among members of different denominations in the general population and
among the clergy. Catholics in the general population were more likely to
be pro-war, but less likely to want sanctions to have been given more time,
to endorse cynical reasons for the war, to believe the violence of the war
unjustified, to be concerned about loss of life among Iraqis, and/or to see
television as glorifying the war, than members of other religious groups or
none. They were, in short, consistently the least pacifist group in the
general population. At the other extreme, Nonconformists and non-
believers were almost equally consistently the most pacifist groups. This
spectrum of positions, with Catholics at one extreme, Nonconformists and
non-believers at the other, and Anglican identifiers in a middle position,
held remarkably well for most issues.

The attitudes of the Catholics are the more interesting because of the
Pope's clear position against the war. It might be thought that British
Catholics were ignorant of the Pope's position, but in our second survey we
asked respondents to say which political and religious figures had been 'for'
or 'against' the war. The replies suggested that the Pope's opposition was
clearly perceived: 74 per cent saw him as 'against', only 4 per cent as 'for'.
(In contrast, Runcie's ambiguity was reflected in a divided verdict: 30 per
cent saw him as 'for' and 48 per cent 'against', with anti-war respondents
most likely to see him as anti-war.) British Catholic leaders took less
uncompromising positions than the Pope's, but it is still interesting that
Catholics in the population were the least pacific group. The Pope's limited
impact on British Catholic opinion underlines the comments of the editor of
the *Catholic Herald*, who observed that 'the Pope's condemnation of the Gulf
War did nothing to stop the fighting' and concluded that 'in global/political
terms the papacy is becoming the equivalent of the British monarchy—
colourful, busy but deprived of any real day-to-day influence'.[79]

Our study of clergy's attitudes showed that other social factors were
relevant to how religious beliefs were actually interpreted. Military

experience and links tended to incline clerics to be both Conservative and pro-war. Equally, those who interpret their Christian beliefs in an anti-war direction tended to interpret them as implying Labour or Liberal Democrat rather than Conservative politics.

These findings are important for the overall interpretation of the role of religion in determining responses to war. Clearly religious beliefs are not held in isolation from social experience, culture or secular political values. If religious beliefs—or for that matter a rejection of them—play a part in determining attitudes, this is because religious ideas are one way, articulated with others, of actively expressing a relationship with the world. The world, in this context, is the complex of social relationships in which people are involved.

The limited impact even of the Pope's strong stand, the deliberate ambiguity of the stances of the main national religious leaders, the shortage of commentary on the Iraqi revolts, the limited correspondence between the attitudes of clergy and national leaders all suggest that, among the institutions of civil society, the churches had limited significance in determining the responses of British people to the Iraqi wars.

Intellectuals and representation

Political parties and churches perform representative functions in a corporate manner: leaders speak for their institutions as collectivities. Intellectuals, in contrast, while operating in institutional contexts, speak as individuals. They 'represent' society not through formal representativeness but by articulating values which define society's. Their representativeness is thus far more nebulous and contestable. Intellectuals define ideologies—relatively coherent world views—which are important if they represent significant social tendencies. Critics of intellectuals, who are usually other intellectuals, often dismiss them because of their failure to speak for clearly defined constituencies and dismiss their ideas as 'mere ideology' because of this.

The roles of Western intellectuals have become more complex in recent decades. In the era of national and class polarization which came to a head in the mid-twentieth century, it could be hypothesized that significant intellectuals articulated the world-views of nations and classes. Marx and Mannheim saw ideology as linked to class; Gramsci saw intellectuals as 'traditional' or 'organic' representatives of classes in a national context.[80] In the era of globalization, postmodernity and ideological dealignment, the roles of intellectuals are at once more important, in articulating expanded diversity, and more difficult to define because of the decline of fixtures like nation and class. The Gulf War highlighted these issues because it posed new dilemmas while seeming to revive the situation of the nation at war.

If independence is characteristic of intellectuals' activity, however, the institutional contexts in which they operate circumscribe their responses. Patrick Wilcken analyses 'structural changes in the intellectual community' in which intellectuals, 'occupying ever narrower areas of expertise', have been absorbed via expanded university institutions into the state. Radical discourse circulates largely within the institutions and between academics:

> Intellectuals can no longer go straight to the public, but must bow to the demands of the media if they are to reach a wider audience than their immediate academic circle. This reorganisation of the production and distribution of ideas has relocated the sphere of public criticism and deradicalised the public voice of the academy.[81]

It is certainly true that academics (and students) were less vocal during the Gulf crisis than the Vietnam War. In part this may be due to increasing institutionalization and, as Edward Said puts it, professionalization of the academy.[82] But it was also due to major differences between the two wars and between the political contexts of the 1960s and 1990s. It is not clear, moreover, that the expanded roles of media restrict the scope of intellectual influence. A few intellectuals may have been able previously to reach wide publics, but they utilized media like publishing houses, press and radio, rarely going 'straight to the public' as Wilcken suggests they did.[83] In the diversified media world of the late twentieth century, more intellectuals have access to more channels in press and television.

In the Gulf War, the specific contributions of university-based intellectuals were difficult to locate outside the press. The French writer, Jean Baudrillard, gained notoriety with his articles, inflating the significance of mediation to the point where he argued that 'The Gulf War did not take place'.[84] For him, it was only a war of words and signs, waged in the media. No such viewpoint emerged among British intellectuals, with their most widely published representatives (a few academics in among the more thinking journalists) expressing support for the war. The verdict of one conservative historian was 'been pretty sound, I think, the country, except for the intellectual classes as usual',[85] but many of the latter had actually fallen into line. Another commentator who noted 'the paltry presence of any organised intellectual case against what is happening' was closer to the mark.[86]

The pro-war position was represented not just by the intellectual voices of the more conservative papers, such as Max Hastings and the military historian John Keegan in the *Daily Telegraph*, and 'defence intellectuals' like Lawrence Freedman in the *Independent*, but by many agonized writers in the liberal and left-wing press. Hugo Young was correct to observe that 'the passage of time seems if anything to be hardening liberal opinion in favour of military action against Saddam'.[87] Chief among the liberal supporters was the philosopher and critic Michael Ignatieff in the *Observer*, despite his realization that he had been misled in late 1990:

> Throughout the autumn, we poor suckers earnestly debated whether or not sanctions could work, not realising that, after the military build-up in November, this was no longer a relevant issue for our leaders. The real question was: how to destroy Saddam as a power in the Gulf region. Sanctions could not achieve this goal.[88]

Ignatieff argued that there was no choice but war 'to correct' our own 'errors' in previously supporting Saddam Hussein but stood out for limited objectives against 'the macho fantasy of total victory'. Freedman seemingly agreed with this: having judged that it might not be possible to overthrow Saddam without marching on Baghdad, he argued: 'That is why it is vital to be clear with regard to the limited objectives of military action from the outset.'[89]

Left-wing supporters of the war had sometimes to discount their former positions, as with Fred Halliday, Arabist and former member of the *New Left Review* board. Halliday's position was that: 'The West's policy has been rightly condemned for its inconsistency ... . It would, however, be mistaken to use criticism of Western hypocrisy to collude in what is a clear case of aggression by a fascist state.'[90] Halliday's support drew condemnation from Robin Blackburn, editor of the *Review*, that his logic was that 'thousands and thousands of Iraqis and Kuwaitis had been killed or displaced for their own good'.[91]

Halliday replied that this was a 'fourfold blurring' of reality. First it 'ascribed responsibility for everything that took place to "the allied action"'—as though the Iraqis did nothing. Second, 'by focusing everything on the costs of war, Blackburn obscured the fact that costs are not everything'. The Kuwaitis had a right to self-determination and had suffered atrocities: 'Is anyone entitled in the circumstances to the moral certainty, from a place of safety, that the Kuwaitis just had to endure this for another year, or possibly two years ... while sanctions ran their course, whether to success or failure?' Third, Blackburn overlooked the fact that the 50–100,000 Iraqis killed were 'members of an army of occupation'. (They were conscripts, but Blackburn had accepted, in the Vietnam war, the killing of US conscripts as necessary.) And finally, Blackburn overlooked the fact that the anti-war case often rested on inflated ideas of length and costs of a ground war. He concluded that imperialism was not the only reality—there was also 'the existence of unspeakably evil tyranny'.[92]

Halliday was unusual in coming to a pro-war view from a Marxist background, but he was in good company: the sociologist A.H. Halsey— 'we now have no option but to conquer and discredit Saddam Hussein'— and the political scientist Bernard Crick—'I think it has to be fought'—were two eminent social-democratic intellectuals who concurred. The ambivalence many felt was expressed, however, by the Sovietologist John Erickson: 'It is a just war in many respects: though there is a lingering reservation that it was rushed through and more time should have been given to sanctions.'[93]

These reservations were taken further by a small number of anti-war intellectuals. The Marxist historian Eric Hobsbawm wrote: 'One hopes that it will be quick, but it is still a deliberate descent into barbarism.'[94] (He drew a strong response from Ignatieff, remarking that: 'The nerve endings of those who are appalled at the Allied course remain strangely sanitised towards what Saddam has been doing to Kuwait.'[95])

Among artistic intellectuals, there was vocal dissidence, not all of which was easily expressed. The Royal Opera House director of public affairs, Ewen Balfour, and radio presenter Gilles Peterson, from the radio station Jazz FM, were actually sacked for publicly opposing the war.[96] Harold Pinter's poem, 'American Football' was rejected on grounds of taste by the *London Review of Books*, the *Guardian*, the *Observer* and the *Independent*. When it was finally published, Pinter attacked the irony that his use of language like 'fucking shit' had been found more obscene than the realities of the allied attacks against which his polemic was directed.[97]

The official war artist, John Keane, also aroused strong criticism for a painting entitled 'Mickey Mouse at the Front', which featured 'the grinning Disney character sitting on what appears to be a toilet in the sand next to a shopping trolley full of anti-tank missiles'. The Armed Forces minister claimed that the image trivialized an important event. The artist's explanation was that:

> The Disney image ... came to him on his last morning in Kuwait City at a marina used by the Iraqis, where he found a children's Mickey Mouse amusement ride surrounded by faeces in a room which had been used as a toilet. ... 'The paintings are my response to what I witnessed when I was there. I found it a profoundly disturbing experience.'

The painting was defended by Dr Alan Borg, director of the Imperial War Museum, where it is hung, as a painting which 'summed up the disaster that is left at the end of a war'.[98]

The intellectual case against the war was made by a few key commentators such as John Pilger, Paul Foot and Edward Pearce. Paul Rogers, professor in the Bradford Peace Studies department, was a rare academic critic. His emphasis on the danger of a lengthy war[99] provoked Ignatieff to the caustic comment that he 'should retire from our screens and think about why he was so sure on 12 February that "we will be lucky if the war is over within 6 months"'. However Ignatieff also entered a partial defence of the anti-war camp: 'They are being attacked for something more than error. They appear to be guilty of worrying, of counting the cost, of preparing for the worst, of asking displeasing questions ... the press, far from picking too many holes, picked too few.'[100]

Anti-war writers such as the indefatigable Pilger—mostly in *New Statesman and Society*—focused on this deficiency (of television as much as the press).

> Why have we not seen a single frame of film of the Iraqi trenches after they were cluster-bombed and napalmed? Why have we not seen the bulldozing of bodies into mass graves? This latter image is the one that those who prosecuted the war fear most. They know it will evoke the memory of bodies bulldozed into pits in the Nazi concentration camps.[101]

On seeing TV journalist Kate Adie in army uniform, he commented: 'In step, in word, in uniform, the media and the military march together.'[102]

Pilger saved his most withering scorn for the war's liberal supporters:

While an estimated 50 children die each day as a result of the deliberate bombing of Iraq's water, power and sewerage systems, the triumphalists claim their place in the victory parade. Some do not want to be seen in the streets shoulder to shoulder with the 'boys'. They prefer to march gently in print, not as Worsthornes and other Kitcheners incarnate, but as liberal shareholders of Just War plc.[103]

Pilger and other anti-war critics, while sensitizing the public to the massaging of violence, missed more than the Kuwait atrocities to which Ignatieff drew their attention. Like Labour's left-wing, they had little to say about the Shi'ite and Kurdish revolts which actually called for Western intervention. A Doonesbury cartoon summed up the situation in a fictitious White House exchange:

'Mr President, I should warn you, we're going to be hearing from your former war critics in the weeks ahead. A lot of them will say they predicted just this kind of outcome!'

'But they **didn't**! What they predicted was an outpouring of Arab anger against the U.S., Israel and Jordan being dragged into the war, and a rise in Islamic radicalism! They **didn't** predict Saddam still in power, a bloody revolution, two million starving refugees, and thousands of U.S. troops posted indefinitely in Iraq!'

'You're right, Sir. They missed by a mile.'
'It's not a told-you-so-type situation! Not at **all!**'[104]

While, as Doonesbury suggested, governments could not take comfort from the partial vision of their critics, there was a serious implication to the disparity between the latter's prognoses and the actual crises of the aftermath. Although writers like Ignatieff moved quickly with the issues, most anti- as well as pro-war intellectuals were trapped within paradigms which only partially represented the contradictory realities of the Iraqi wars.

Notes and references

1. Eric Hobsbawm and Terence Ranger develop this understanding of traditions; Hobsbawm and Ranger, 1983.

2. *Guardian*, 15 January 1991.

3. *Observer*, 20 January 1991.

4. Ian Aitken, *Guardian*, 15 January 1991.

5. *Observer*, 20 January 1991.

6. Andrew Gimson, *Independent on Sunday*, 20 January 1991.

7. *Independent*, 15 February 1991. As William Rees-Mogg argued, 'John Major has not had to take particularly difficult decisions in the Gulf War. The decision to launch the air attack was taken by President Bush, and he will also launch the ground attack. The Prime Minister is only required to concur. So far as the Gulf war is concerned, the style, therefore, has been the substance of his prime ministership.' *Independent*, 11 February 1991.

8. *Independent*, 28 January 1991.

9. *Independent*, 30 January 1991.

10. Wellman, 1991.

11. *Guardian*, 15 January 1991.

12. NOP, *Independent*, 16 February 1991.

13. NOP, *Independent*, 18 January 1991 (fieldwork 12–14 January), showed Labour on 44, Conservatives, 43, Liberal Democrats 8. Terry Jones later commented that 'between September 1990 and January 1991 Conservative support increased by 10.5 per cent... . There were only 1.7 Allied fatalities per percentage point rise.' (*Guardian*, 5 July 1991.)

14. *Independent*, 18 February 1991.

15. *Observer*, 3 March 1991.

16. *Independent*, 6 March 1991.

17. So called after the General Election of 1918, when Lloyd George appealed to the electorate on the basis of patriotic sentiment at the conclusion of victory in the Great War.

18. This research, planned by the author with Roy Carr-Hill, was carried out by Gerald Mirfin.

19. MORI, *Sunday Express*, 24 March 1991.

20. *Observer*, 10 March 1991.

21. *Independent*, 5 April 1991.

22. *Independent*, 6 April 1991.

23. *Independent*, 15 April 1991.

24. A Harris poll showed 77:10 approval for the havens policy, 61:30 in favour of British troops to guarantee Kurdish lands, 54:30 for using force to protect Kurds (*Observer*, 21 April 1991).

25. 'World at One', Radio 4, 28 March 1992.

26. BBC 1, 2 and ITV, 7 April 1992.

27. *New Statesman and Society*, 22 May 1992.

28. *Guardian*, 30 January 1991.

29. The thesis that anti-nuclear policies were vote-losers should not be sustained in a simple way. For a fuller exposition of my views, see Shaw, 1991; pp. 109–62.

30. *Guardian*, 30 January 1991.

31. Lambeth Council passed a Trotskyist-inspired motion calling for allied troops to be withdrawn from the Gulf, for an immediate cease-fire and an Arab solution to the Middle East problem. Shadow Cabinet member Jack Cunningham condemned the motion (*The Sunday Times*, 3 February 1991).

32. A cynical if approving view was expressed by Edward Pearce:

'Labour dare not be brave, dare not make a forlorn stand. This is for the moment, a nasty little country for whom the underpress truly speaks. The "Brits", as they deserve to be called, ache for war and take a jackal pride in the thing that we do. Against that one cannot criticise a cool cynicism designed to keep Labour's head down and to keep the votes of the lager-patriots' (*Guardian*, 20 February 1991).

33. 'Resisting the UN's deadline for the use of force remained Labour's policy right up to the bombing of Baghdad. But it was only pursued *sotto voce*. ... As a concession to MPs, Labour leaders agreed that they would back a motion calling for sanctions, not war, at a meeting of the Parliamentary Labour Party (PLP) which, quite deliberately, was scheduled for the morning after the Commons vote. Few MPs were impressed by this evasion and, for the first time, shadow cabinet unity began to crack. The shadow transport secretary, Prescott, put his name to an early day motion, signed by a dozen frontbenchers, emphasising that there should be no precipitate military action. His name was deleted by Party whips, and reinstated by him. Prescott insisted that, since the pro-sanctions motion was already shadow cabinet policy, it was open to every party member to sign it' (Sarah Baxter, *New Statesman and Society*, 25 January 1991).

34. 'The first signs of front bench dissent' were in this debate, 'when a number of leading MPs abstained. They had agreed in an earlier meeting to abstain in sufficient numbers to send a clear message to Kinnock—and prevent their sacking' (*Guardian*, 7 January 1991).

35. Kaufman's position varied in response to changing pressures. As Baxter pointed out (*New Statesman and Society*, 25 January 1991) just before urging that sanctions be given time to work, Kaufman had claimed that 'On the gravest form of action—the use of force to compel Saddam Hussein to withdraw from Kuwait—we have been especially firm.' RW Johnson argued, however, that there was a division of opinion between Kaufman and Kinnock on the eve of war: 'Kaufman is effectively arguing that we should delay military action long enough to ensure that it is anyway practically infeasible. Kinnock has, happily, refused to be towed down this path and has rejected the peace at any price blandishments of Benn and [Tam] Dalyell with the angry affirmation that the Labour Party "is not a pacifist party"' (*New Statesman and Society*, 18 January 1991).

36. *Guardian*, 11 January 1991. Observers saw Kinnock's balancing act as successful; Patrick Wintour (*Guardian*, 30 January 1991) reported that 'Backbenchers from the pro-NATO John Gilbert to the pro-Palestinian Ernie Ross have been delighted by Mr

Kinnock's speeches.' The numbers of Labour MPs willing to vote against the government's policy fell from 55 (about a quarter) in November 1990 to 33 (one-sixth) in January 1991. The Labour Party National Executive Committee (30 January) recorded 'overwhelming support for Kinnock's handling of the crisis' (*Guardian*, 31 January 1991).

37. Parliamentary debate, 15 January; *Guardian*, 16 January 1991.

38. Speech to Royal United Services Institute (*Guardian*, 24 January 1991).

39. Hattersley insisted Deedes misquoted Kipling: the poem in question

> begins with a bitter couplet. "I went into a public-'ouse to get a pint of beer, The publican 'e up an' sez, We serve no red-coats here." The poem is a complaint about the British habit of only treating soldiers with respect when there is dangerous work to be done. That is not the characteristic of a warlike people and Rudyard Kipling was not a warlike poet.

Hattersley then attacked Edwina Currie, a Conservative MP, who had invited Major to note 'the unanimous vote in the Iraq National Assembly backing Saddam Hussein and his efforts in the war'. 'She then asked the prime minister to agree that a similar vote in the House of Commons would demonstrate the British people's parallel, but conflicting, determination. And you thought that we were against all that Saddam Hussein did and stood for. The idea that Parliament is the home of intolerance, like the notion that we are a warlike people and the libel that Rudyard Kipling was a jingoist, would well do with re-examination' (*Guardian*, 19 January 1991).

40. See for example *Guardian*, 7 January 1991.

41. The Labour NEC 'approved a statement seen by the party's soft left as clearly indicating that the war cannot be extended to deposing Saddam Hussein or the invasion of Iraq... . The NEC voted 21 to 3 for a policy calling for the disarming of Iraq's war machine, the denial of superpower status to any country in the region, and a UN conference leading to justice for the Palestinians. It rejected an alternative call from Tony Benn for an immediate ceasefire.' The resolution was a result of soft left anxiety about US intentions, and its attraction was described by Robin Cook as being 'that it sets out peace aims, unlike the government which simply has war aims. Our peace aims are regional arms disarmament and a settlement to the Palestinian issue' (*Guardian*, 31 January 1991).

42. Sarah Baxter, *New Statesman and Society*, 25 January 1991. A good example of this was Kinnock's support at a Parliamentary Labour Party meeting (20 February) for the Soviet peace plan, scorned by Major.

43. Other frontbenchers who signed this 'so that their opposition to the government's policy could be put on the record' were Clare Short, Marjorie Mowlem, David Blunkett and Harriet Harman.

44. *Guardian*, 12 February 1991.

45. The incident which most annoyed the leadership was the leaking of minutes of a 4 February meeting, revealing a plan to table a motion at the week's parliamentary party meeting to confine Kinnock to "the most limited war aims", a move abandoned after its disclosure (*The Sunday Times*, 10 February 1991).

46. *Guardian*, 30 February 1991.

47. BBC1, 1 pm, 2 April 1991.

48. *The Times*, 15 April 1991.

49. Letters from Maria Fyfe MP, Ken Livingstone MP and Marjorie Thompson, and from Dale Campbell-Savours, MP, *Guardian*, 12 April 1991.

50. *Independent*, 29 January 1991.

51. *Independent*, 30 March 1991.

52. Editorial, 'The Pope and the war', *The Tablet*, 2 February 1991.

53. Speech to diplomats, 12 January 1991; *Guardian*, 4 February 1991.

54. *Independent*, 17 January 1991.

55. *Observer*, 3 February 1991.

56. *Independent*, 25 February 1991.

57. *Independent*, 5 March 1991.

58. *Guardian*, 16 January 1991.

59. Runcie, 1991.

60. *Independent*, 21 January 1991.

61. *Sun*, 12 January 1991.

62. *The Times*, 16 January 1991.

63. *Observer*, 20 January 1991.

64. *Independent*, 21 February 1991.

65. *Observer*, 3 February 1991.

66. *Guardian*, 7 February 1991.

67. *Independent*, 4 March 1991.

68. *Guardian*, 4 April 1991.

69. Peter Hebblethwaite, 'How to read the Pope', *The Tablet*, 23 February 1991.

70. Cardinal Basil Hume, 'A pastor's reflections on the Gulf war', *The Tablet*, 16 February 1991.

71. *Independent*, 21 January 1991.

72. *Observer*, 24 February 1991.

73. *Observer*, 3 February 1991.

74. *Independent*, 21 January 1991.

75. *Catholic Herald*, 22 February 1991.

76. *Observer*, 3 February 1991.

77. *Observer*, 27 January 1991.

78. The survey covered all ministers of religion (of all denominations) listed in the Hull area telephone directory, and was carried out by this author together with Roy Carr-Hill during February 1991. Respondents were sent a questionnaire by post; just under 30 per cent replied (compared to about 40 per cent of a sample of the local population at large). While the response rate was not high, results do give some indication of the attitudes of different groups of clergy. While we must be cautious in claiming national representativeness of the clergy studied, there is no reason to think that this group of local clergy differs significantly from the national body. A fuller analysis is contained in Shaw and Carr-Hill, 1994. The following discussion refers to the more detailed analysis and tables in that chapter. Further discussion of the role of religion in the attitudes of the general population is included in the discussion of public opinion later in this study.

79. Peter Stanford, *Guardian*, 16 January 1991.

80. See Marx and Engels, 1965, and Mannheim, 1936. For Gramsci, traditional intellectuals were those like Italian rural priests and lawyers who represented institutional continuities with premodern society; organic intellectuals were the members of intellectual categories which developed with a new mode of production or phase of its development, e.g. accountants, personnel managers, social workers, teachers, party functionaries and journalists, among the many new kinds of intellectuals who have emerged in modern capitalism.

81. Wilcken, 1995.

82. Said, 1993.

83. Indeed Wilcken himself cites Régis Debray's model in which 'French intellectuals have been successively dominated by three institutions: the university (1880–1930), the publishing houses (1920–60) and the media (1968 onwards).'

84. Baudrillard, 1991. Christopher Norris, 1992, provides a useful polemic against Baudrillard's excesses.

85. Norman Stone, quoted *Guardian*, 9–10 February 1991.

86. *Guardian*, 14 February 1991.

87. *Guardian*, 14 February 1991.

88. *Observer*, 27 January 1991.

89. *Independent*, 19 January 1991.

90. Halliday, 1990.

91. *New Statesman and Society*, 22 March 1991.

92. *New Statesman and Society*, 29 March 1991.

93. *Observer*, 3 February 1991.

94. *Independent on Sunday*, 20 January 1991.

95. *Observer*, 24 February 1991.

96. *Observer*, 3 February 1991.

97. Pinter, 1992.

98. *Guardian*, 15 January 1992.

99. *Guardian*, 13 February 1991.

100. *Observer*, 10 March 1991.

101. *New Statesman and Society*, 24 May 1991. The full answer to Pilger's question was, of course, that the Iraqi government as much as the West wanted to keep these images off the screens.

102. *Guardian*, 18 January 1991.

103. *New Statesman and Society*, 15 March 1991.

104. 'Doonesbury', *Guardian*, 4 May 1991. © GB Trudeau/Universal Press Syndicate.

CHAPTER FOUR

A functional institution and representation

Civil society consists not only of representative institutions like political parties and churches but of functional institutions, which have tasks of elaborating and communicating information, images and ideas. These are often recognized and funded by the state to regulate intellectual formation. Mass media are such institutions, but because of their importance to my topic I consider them separately in Part III. The other main class of functional institution which is relevant are educational bodies, schools and universities. Wars throw up emotional, moral, ideological and political challenges to children and young people to which educational institutions must respond. This chapter will concentrate on responses to these challenges in schools.

Inevitably the Gulf War created tensions to which schools responded, often seeing them as problems to manage. Unfortunately there is limited evidence of how they did this. I attempted to organize, at short notice, a study of schools in one English county, but was denied access even to circulate a questionnaire to head teachers.[1] I then wrote to the educational press, asking for volunteers to reply; my letters were published in the *Times Educational Supplement* and *The Teacher* and a handful of teachers replied, most of whom completed questionnaires.[2] Discussion of these replies, together with press reports and a few Mass-Observation 'diaries'[3] must be considered as indicative rather than strictly representative of schools and teachers in general.[4]

The war's challenges were numerous. For children—as for adults—emotions were stirred by the orchestration of war-preparations and the coverage of the war itself. Reports included this about a six-year-old girl: 'for the first time in her life, Daisy wet her bed and woke up in tears. "Daddy's dead, and you're dead, and I can't find David" [her brother], she sobbed to her mother.' An eleven-year-old 'dreamt that the world was at war; he was at home; his father and I were dead'. A child psychiatrist reported another eleven-year-old afraid that poisonous gases released by the Iraqis might blow towards Ireland.[5] A nine-year-old girl asked: 'Will Dad have to fight? Will they drop a bomb on England? If we're evacuated would they bomb the countryside? Could chemical weapons spread across to Britain?' A seven-year-old asked her mother if they could invite some Iraqis to stay with them to save them from the bombs.[6]

Clearly these anxieties posed problems for teachers and schools, in different ways for different age-groups. A primary school teacher from Kent reported that 'some [children] were concerned that Iraq would bomb their town', and 'some spoke about a nuclear war'. Many children were 'more excited than usual, hyped up. There was a lot of aggression in the playground.' She also wrote that 'children talked about guns. Made machine gun noises and bomb explosion noises. Some had fantasies about their parents going to fight in Iraq. Made tanks. Dressed up in khaki desert uniform.' She thought that 'children were very excited by the technology' and this was how media coverage mainly affected the children.

This teacher, a Conservative voter and 'strongly' pro-war, dealt with the war 'once or twice' in a teaching situation, raising the issues of 'Saddam Hussein being a dictator. Invading a peaceful country. How would they like it if someone took over their house or bedroom and said "this is my house now". Linked Saddam with Hitler. Talked about oil issue.' The school's policy was 'to leave it to parents. We were concerned not to create too much anxiety in children.' This teacher sent a photograph of her own children, who 'unprompted, built a cardboard tank in the garden'. ('We do not encourage war type games so the idea for the tank stems from their own interest in the war. We did watch a great deal of News programmes on television.')

In contrast, another primary teacher stated: 'I knew the children would come in Monday worrying about the deadline and saying: "Will there be a war tomorrow?" We've done an enormous amount of mapwork. I've got children from Turkey and Cyprus and they become very anxious: they'd heard the phrase "the Middle East" but they hadn't realised it included their own countries.' This teacher confirms the fascination of technology: 'The boys are very keen on the B-52s. I asked one boy: "What do you think happens when all those bombs hit the ground?" His face changed completely. I find they don't just see the technology in a cowboys and Indians way: their feeling of humanity and sensitivity is very near the surface.'[7]

The confusing effects on primary children are also indicated in these comments of a housewife from Bristol who reported:

> My 7 year old is not yet worried about the war, but he doesn't know about its possibilities. Apparently in his school the children are worried about it—talk about the Gulf war disrupts the class of 5 and 6 year olds next door to him. I have heard parents complain that there is too much of it, it's too worrying for the children. I think if the children are worried they will need to talk about it.[8]

More proactive approaches are also indicated in the report of another parent from Plymouth who wrote that the head of her child's comprehensive school sent out a letter: 'This is to let you know that the staff of this school will do all we can to support students who show signs of stress or distress during this difficult period'; while in her son's primary school, 'children who had parents or close relatives involved were asked to come forward and share in the lighting of a candle for peace'.[9] A similar approach, aimed at parents, is indicated in another parent who writes that the liberal head of her children's infant school

> had the idea of an afternoon of meditation in the school hall, open to everyone of any faith or none who wished to give time to pray (only prayer was not mentioned, just meditation) about the situation in the Gulf. The turnout was remarkably high. Around the central lighted candle at any one time were to be found over one hundred people who comprised several varieties of Christian, two Jewish mothers and a good proportion of Muslims.[10]

A middle-school teacher reported little anxiety, although pupils with family members in the Gulf became quite withdrawn. The teacher 'let it known I was willing to listen but didn't push it and kept the classroom situation as normal as possible'. She also reported that many children, 'virtually all boys', participated in war games, and many, 'again boys, made very jingoistic statements'. She commented that the amount of television coverage 'meant the children thought of little else' and that 'press coverage tended to be quite jingoistic and this showed in pupils' attitudes. They found it very difficult to realise that there was another side of the conflict.'

This teacher, although pro-war, 'tried to make the children aware that not all Iraqis are bad. We also talked about what it was like for the troops and their families back home and sent letters to one regiment that one of the children had links with.' (The response of the children was 'excellent—they really did want to help'.) This teacher had taught in army schools 'and so was able to tell them about army life'. She found the advice of the National Union of Teachers on how to deal with the war 'very thorough and quite useful'.

A teacher in a Sussex secondary school reported only a few children showing anxiety at the outbreak of war: 'They expressed horror at the idea of being killed in a bomb shelter. I was forbidden to respond in any way.' Most treated the war as a game, used the war as an 'occasion for racist jokes', and 'did not think of the Arabs as people at all. Interestingly, not many of them know that the Kuwaitis (the good guys) were Arabs.' Few expressed opinions for or against the war, but the opponents 'had no audience' and 'learned to keep their own counsel'. 'Children who are normally sympathetic to people in need—contributing to Comic Relief, Oxfam, etc.— did not see the enemy as human beings and saw the war as a game.'

This teacher, who 'strongly disapproved' of the war, wrote in an accompanying letter that teachers 'who expressed support for the war and shared racist jokes about Saddam with their pupils ... were not prevented from expressing their views in any way', whereas he was banned from using an imaginative (but critical) worksheet he had produced or from dealing with the war in any way.

An alternative 'active' approach was to encourage practical support for service personnel, and later for civilian victims. A Welsh comprehensive teacher reported two English groups sending Christmas cards to service-men; one group adopted an RAF man as 'a special pen pal' (as the local paper described him), keeping contact even after he had returned to Germany, while another, who did not receive replies to their cards, 'turned their attention after the war to *HMS Battleaxe* which did serve in the Gulf'. They also wrote to a battalion to which an ex-pupil belonged that was serving on the borders of Iraq.

An English teacher in a Midlands inner-city comprehensive reported that 'most' pupils showed anxiety about the war, and 'most' expressed views against the war, centred on the moral issue of killing in war. This teacher dealt with the issue once or twice in a teaching situation, raising 'the human issue' of 'what it must be like to be far from home under military orders' and 'the morality of any war—especially after the bombing of the bunker in Baghdad'. She 'strongly disapproved' of the war and commented that it had 'made me realise how difficult it is not to be biased when one holds very strong views'.

Another English teacher in an inner-city London boys' comprehensive reported 'excited, even elated, rather "gung-ho"' reactions to the outbreak of war, although some were 'worried and disturbed whether this might lead to attacks on this country'. Children with family members expecting to be sent to the Gulf expressed fears, especially as 'media coverage of medical/hospital arrangements brought home to them that people were likely to be killed or severely injured'. The teacher observed behaviour difficulties as pupils became withdrawn, edgy, sullen, etc. He also noted war games among younger boys and that 'peer group banter' often had reference to the war. He felt, however, that 'pupils actually watched the news and cared about what went on in the rest of the world'; those who took time to watch documentaries often became well informed, although pupils were often unable to distinguish between tabloid opinion and facts.

This teacher, who approved of the war 'with reservations', reported oral work around 'jingoism, dangers; religious divisions; imperialism; balance between superpowers; whether we have moral right/duty to intervene', as well as an assembly about the victims of war. Unlike the other schools discussed so far, he reported that the school had a policy concerning 'the need for awareness, particularly identifying pupils from service families, support in classroom situations and in year groups, pupils encouraged to talk about feelings about war but sensitive eye kept on pupils who might have particular anxieties.'

An active approach was expressed by another English teacher in a Sussex rural comprehensive who, while dealing with the war only once or twice while it was going on, discussed it frequently afterwards through Literature and Media Studies. She described a performance of children's plays, poems, dance and music: 'All material was chosen from a certain platform of beliefs by the English teacher in charge (my husband) who allowed no pro-violence or war material to be used.' She dealt with the war as an issue of power and 'bully/victim' in discussion of *Waiting for Godot*.

She was the only one who specifically reported discussions with sixth-formers, referring to discussion of conscription (possibly because students aged sixteen to eighteen were worried about being liable).

This teacher wrote that her school had 'no policy' and 'largely ignored the war'. She complained, as an opponent of the war, that the 'lack of freedom for teachers to express opinion means that they, in effect, maintain the status quo.... If asked on a personal level by a pupil for an opinion on anything—I always give an honest answer.' She added that 'my choice of materials—the way I interact with pupils—my expectations of their behaviour—all show my attitudes daily—not *overtly* in verbal debate—by *action*'.

The London boys' school teacher quoted above also reported the issue which dominated press reporting of the war in schools, tensions involving Muslim pupils (although his school had only a small ethnic minority enrolment):

> Muslim pupils tended to be hesitant about supporting Saddam Hussein openly though some suggested he had some legitimate claims. However, many Muslim pupils felt that it was an issue which should be left to the Arab world to sort out. American (and British) involvement was seen as trying to protect our own interests rather than moral flag-bearing.

Only one teacher among our respondents was from a school, serving council estates in a Lancashire town, with a large Muslim minority (35 per cent). She reported that 'white students were very aggressive towards the Muslim students [whose] reactions were mixed but were mostly defensive, against the accusation of being Saddam's supporters'. Fighting between the two groups 'increased tremendously'.

This teacher also had more pupils with relatives involved in the conflict and reported girls worried that fathers would be called up. Worse, a seventeen-year-old boy who had left the school the previous summer was a victim of the so-called 'friendly fire' incident in which British soldiers were killed in an American attack. Many girls were distressed, a few hysterical and some had to be counselled after his funeral.

Press reports presented a mixed picture of the racial issue. Attacks by pro-Iraqi Pakistani pupils on Saudis were taking place in Hackney schools.[11] 'Muslim students chanted "Saddam" and "death to America" as they waited for a class.' The *Independent* concluded, however, that while

> many British schools reported increased excitement and tension among pupils when fighting began in the Gulf ... there has been no upsurge on racist attacks [in schools] as some teachers feared. There is little evidence linked to the war in sensitive areas such as the East End of London, Leicester and Bradford.[12]

A Tower Hamlets head reported Bangladeshi students feeling isolated when they read headlines like 'Bastards of Baghdad': 'We have done a number of assemblies in which we have talked about the obscenity of war. We think it is important to take a line that brings everybody together, to talk about the use of discussion rather than violence to settle disputes.' A

Portsmouth middle-school head, with children from both Asian and dock-yard/service families, said she received complaints about the school's stance:

> There is a lot of emotional response in the community and clearly parents are worried about the opinions their children might be hearing. We will ensure that a balanced viewpoint is expressed because we are aware that people have different views. Children can work towards understanding differences of opinion.[13]

A teacher claimed of a sixth-form debate in a racially mixed school in Harrow: 'The good thing is that we haven't had any awkwardness among the students over this; they've been able to discuss things in quite a mature way, without getting too angry.'[14]

It was largely up to schools to formulate policies for dealing with the crisis, and in many cases individual teachers were left to make their own responses. There was some nationally expressed concern about the consequences: a headmistress complained in the press, 'Children are picking up fear from everywhere, but nothing is explained to them.'[15] But among policy-makers probably 'the greatest fear ... was that if casualties mounted, some people would seek to take revenge on the Muslim community'.[16] Many local education authorities probably kept a low profile for fear of stirring the delicate emotions involved; even our own research enquiries were seen as potentially provocative.

The clearest national guidance for teachers came from their unions, for example in a National Union of Teachers' (NUT) leaflet which dealt with pastoral support and ethnic tension. This advised teachers to watch for signs of stress in children with relatives in the Gulf and to give emotional support. It argued that teachers, especially younger ones, might also need support built into schools' policies. It advised on how to deal with children frightened by news of the war: for example to 'alert parents to the advisability of appropriate discussion with young children to allay their fears, e.g. SCUD missiles cannot reach the United Kingdom'. It advised sensitivity and flexibility in providing either class or individual discussion.

In dealing with ethnic tensions, the NUT pointed to curriculum opportunities and argued for calm, a balanced approach and discussion:

> It should be recognised that pupils hold a wide range of beliefs and no attempt should be made to take a politically partisan approach or one which belittles a particular set of opinions. Teachers should be especially vigilant for any signs of name calling, abuse and bullying, especially of Muslim children. It should be pointed out that there are Muslims on all sides of the conflict .... Similarly there may be a tendency for all non-white children to be perceived as 'Arabs' and children should be reminded of the respect due to all ethnic groups.[17]

NUT guidelines were found 'useful' by several respondents, and an anti-war teacher remarked: 'It made me careful not to discredit soldiers in action in case pupils had relatives in action.'

This discussion shows education authorities, schools, teachers and unions both avoiding and taking responsibility for representing the violence of war to young people. It suggests how far, in the widespread absence of policies, individuals' beliefs and resources influenced the representation of the war in schools. It tells us little, unfortunately, about the response to the aftermath of the war, although, as the press reported, 'Children across Britain washed cars, arm wrestled and made collections at school in their resourceful efforts to raise money for the suffering Kurds.'[18]

Notes and references

1. I requested facilities for survey research from the Chairman of the Education Committee of the Labour-controlled Humberside County Council and also from teachers' organizations in the county, but none would co-operate.

2. The questionnaire is printed in the Appendix.

3. 'Diaries' were kept by some five hundred respondents of the Mass-Observation Archive at the University of Sussex. They are discussed more fully later in this work.

4. Only eight replies were received to the questionnaire, of which six were from comprehensive secondary schools and five from teachers who personally disapproved of the war, but other teachers wrote letters. In the following discussion, unreferenced quotations are from these replies.

5. *Observer*, 25 January 1991.

6. *Independent*, 24 January 1991.

7. *Independent*, 20 January 1991.

8. Mass-Observation Archive: Directive Respondent (M-O A: DR) 2128.

9. M-O A: DR 125.

10. M-O A: DR 1722.

11. *Independent*, 29 January 1991.

12. *Independent*, 20 January 1991.

13. *Independent*, 26 January 1991.

14. *Independent*, 26 January 1991.

15. *Observer*, 29 January 1991.

16. *Independent*, 26 January 1991.

17. NUT leaflet, 'GULF WAR / The Impact on Schools/ UNION ADVICE', February 1991.

18. *Observer*, 27 April 1991.

CHAPTER FIVE

New institutions of representation

The limitations of traditional representative institutions, in numerous contexts, have led to the creation of new modes of representation. Much sociological discussion has focused on 'new social movements', seeing these as critical societal actors in political issues. Social movements are, however, only one kind of new representative institution responding to new contexts. In this discussion I distinguish three distinct but related forms. Social movements involve mass mobilization or at least participation in often spontaneous and episodic protest. Campaigning organizations involve consistent, formal organization and not necessarily any active mass involvement. Community organizations represent distinct communities within society, organized around multiple dimensions of affinity rather than traditional class axes.

All new forms arise around 'issues', which typically have included both strong international or global orientations as well as local and national dimensions. How far can these institutions be seen as responses to the new 'organic' issues of the emerging global society? How much do they reflect the same limitations of national civil society as traditional representative institutions? How are they related to traditional and functional institutions? Are social movements the most effective civil society responses to global issues?[1]

Here I discuss three main 'new' representative institutions which were important in the Iraqi wars: anti-war movements (within the 'social-movement' mode defined above), humanitarian agencies (campaigning organizations) and the Muslim community (community organizations of a minority formed by global migration and transnational affinities). I shall look at each in the light of the questions above.

The anti-war movement

The Gulf War was too short, casualty-free on the coalition side, popular in its objectives and effectively managed in the media to create the conditions for an effective anti-war movement. A campaign took place but it barely developed into a mass movement. This limitation was widely recognized, even by the movement's members, as a cause of its problems. I shall suggest, however, that there were other difficulties which exacerbated its weakness.

The main focus of protests was the Committee to Stop War in the Gulf (CSWG), the main sponsor of which was the principal British peace organization, the Campaign for Nuclear Disarmament (CND), although there were other, often specialist mobilizations. Intellectual groups such as journalists and media workers (John Pilger and Paul Foot were among the sponsors of a campaign against war and censorship);[2] artists (Harold Pinter with other film-makers, musicians and theatrical figures signed a statement accusing the Labour Party of 'abject subservience to the Bush administration'); musicians and lawyers signed appeals.[3] And in a bold direct-action effort, the 'Gulf Peace Team' claimed 120 peace campaigners from 21 nationalities camping on the Iraqi–Saudi border.[4] The CSWG, however, was the umbrella under which classic demonstrative action was mobilized.

The CSWG was formed in autumn 1990 on a platform of supporting sanctions rather than war. After the coalition attacked Iraq, it redirected its campaign towards a cease-fire and a Middle East peace settlement.[5] Its co-chairs were Marjorie Thompson and Bob Cole, respectively chair and vice-chair of CND.[6] It claimed 75,000 people attending a demonstration just before war broke out, but only 10,000 (police estimate, 5500) for a rally shortly afterwards. The small numbers raised fears among CND leaders of a takeover by Marxist organizations like the Socialist Workers Party (SWP) and the Revolutionary Communist Group. It was reported that there were 2000 SWP placards amid 6000 demonstrators at a rally on 19 January 1991. Thompson outlined a perspective for growth: 'As casualties start to rise, there will be a groundswell of opinion, and we will be the natural recipients of that concern. ... The floods of new recruits will drown the lunatic fringe. ... But at the moment, the lunatics are making the running.'[7]

The fragile unity of the CSWG barely survived the non-realization of these pessimistic scenarios. Small demonstrations continued to be held in London and other British cities: by late January the movement's warning had switched towards environmental catastrophes, with the Labour MP Tam Dalyell calling the Gulf oil slick a 'mega-disaster' and a Green spokesperson claiming it was twelve times bigger than the Exxon Valdez disaster off Alaska.[8] In early February the CSWG claimed its largest demonstration of the war, with 30,000 participants (police estimate, 18–20,000),[9] but divisions continued.

Whereas influential peace movements have received extensive media coverage, the anti-Gulf War movement received only modest coverage. 'It is beyond doubt that the coverage of the anti-war movement as *news* was very limited,' concludes a study of dissent on television.

> In those programmes with a truly mass audience, namely the mass news bulletins, its presentation was very sketchy indeed ... it would be wrong, however, to argue that there was no debate on the justness, wisdom and morality of the Gulf War, but this debate was in general restricted to programmes seen by comparatively few people. There *was* a debate, but it was marginalised.[10]

Tony Benn was the only anti-war figure interviewed on BBC1 and ITN, but there was always one critic of the war on the BBC's weekly *Question Time* and regular representation of critical viewpoints on late-night, small-audience programmes such as Channel 4's *Midnight Special*. Bell argues that press coverage, of which there was some in the broadsheets early in the war, died away later.

The CND leadership attempted to 'purge' Trotskyist groups from the CSWG by asking all members to sign a fifteen-point position paper stressing that Iraqi withdrawal from Kuwait remained fundamental to a just peace. 'Those who did not sign would be asked to leave; it was hoped that groups like the SWP would be forced to withdraw.'[11] However, CND supporters were denied immediate endorsement of their plan[12] and activism remained stalled; when a vigil of 250 people was held over the threatened land war, 'most activists stayed at home to watch hostilities unfold on television'.[13]

The CSWG advertised in the press with the heading, 'STOP THE WAR. Hundreds more reasons for a ceasefire', over a picture of bodies from the Amiriya bombing. It appealed for support: 'If you don't want indiscriminate death and destruction, environmental catastrophes, nuclear or chemical war.'[14] CND also ran its own advertisements, for example: 'Now give peace a chance—join CND', with a picture of a child who appeared to be injured.[15] CND did indeed benefit from its campaigning, with subscription renewals up by 10 per cent and 400 new members per week.[16]

The Marxist complaint was that CND's

> readiness to take sides in an internal dispute in the Middle East, by sloganizing "Iraq out of Kuwait", contrasts with its equivocation about the role of the real force for militarism in the region—the armies of the Western powers. CND refuses to call for the removal of British troops from the Gulf.... CND does not so much oppose war as favour it by other means, such as economic sanctions. It supports the US war-aims, but quibbles over war-methods.[17]

This critique was a fairly accurate assessment of CND's position, but CND represented the view of many activists, one of whom reported that during a 24-hour picket outside the US embassy, '*Socialist Worker*'s placards have, without exception, been adapted by ripping the party's name off the top ... The majority of protestors ... mainly young people, are capable of working alongside these groups for peace, but will not accept their "leadership."'[18]

The CSWG and CND gave vent to the unease of a minority of the population about the methods being used in the war but were unable to mobilize more than a small number on the streets, especially after war broke out. The problem of their position was its dependence on a doom-laden scenario in which the war lasted longer, involved greater Western casualties and took worse forms (e.g. nuclear and chemical attacks or catastrophic environmental destruction) than actually materialized. It therefore partially missed the real targets such as the mass slaughter of Iraqi conscripts in their desert dug-outs and the destruction of Baghdad's water, sewage and electricity systems leading to death from disease.

The weakness of the CND/CSWG stance, like Labour's, became apparent during the Kurdish crisis. Although they had tacitly accepted the reality of Western intervention, their critique of Western military power had been relatively undiscriminating. Many activists responded to the Kurdish dilemma by fudging the issue of military intervention. Bruce Kent argued for the UN to come to the aid of the Kurds but in a vague, non-specific way; Tony Benn criticized 'the "non-interference" policy' as 'ridiculous coming from a power that has just laid waste to Iraq and still occupies a large slice of it', but his own proposal for intervention was limited to 'political and diplomatic support to the Kurds', opening the Turkish border for food, etc.[19]

Marjorie Thompson of CSWG went further and called for 'establishing a genuine peacekeeping force',[20] but this met with understandable surprise. 'What do Marjorie Thompson and CND actually want the UN to do?' asked an academic.

> Having been in the forefront of those who accused the US-led coalition of having a hidden agenda for destabilisation of Iraq during the build-up to January's hostilities, she now complains when the officially stated objectives, namely, the liberation of Kuwait, the whole liberation of Kuwait and nothing but the liberation of Kuwait, are shown to be genuine. The Americans are now accused of *not* wanting to remove Saddam.[21]

The anti-war leadership therefore suffered from political contradictions even as they struggled to arouse opposition and fight off sectarian critics. Given that the war did not take the 'worst-case' forms which they predicted, they probably had little scope to do more. There is little evidence that the 'peace movement' actually even mobilized its own core support, let alone moved beyond it and that of the political groups which attached themselves to the campaign. Local CSWGs in major towns were often dominated by far-left groups[22] and many local CND supporters were not involved. A poll among anti-war protesters in the USA also showed that the bulk were from the core anti-war movement, who had been against the Vietnam war in the 1960s and pro-'nuclear freeze' in the 1980s: 'The peace movement has shown little sign of being able to organise beyond this narrow and traditional base.'[23]

The anti-war movement's weakness can be largely explained by the circumstances of the war, but these were compounded by ideological problems. Its failure to grow is put in perspective, moreover, by the general absence of social movements concerned with global crises in the 1990s. The new issues which divided CND leaders in the Kurdish crisis were representative of a new agenda, to which the moral simplicities of the pacifist left, like the anti-imperialism of its Marxist critics, offered no clear answers.

Humanitarian agencies: representing victims

If social-movement activity around the Gulf War was weak, another sector of civil society came into its own and more obviously represented the responses of society in the West. Human rights campaigns and disaster relief agencies were closely focused on the kinds of issues which the war brought into focus, and many intervened actively to publicize issues, raise money and assist civilian victims. Nevertheless, examination shows that their responses had serious limitations.

Humanitarian organizations had their own agendas and much of their activity was designed to further these or even protect them from the distraction of the war. Oxfam's early adverts read, 'Don't forget Africa ... Oxfam hasn't'[24] and 'We are fighting a war against starvation... . This is a hidden crisis. Overshadowed by the Gulf War, the famine has been forgotten.'[25] Charter 88 sought to use the war to further its arguments: 'Dear Sleepy Britain ... The Gulf war should teach us something. It should teach us that there is also a battle or two to be fought at home.' Commenting on the lack of debate, the propaganda press and restrictions of civil liberties, it asked, 'If we are fighting for democracy, where's ours?'[26]

Amnesty International ran full-page advertisements under the heading, 'WITH ALLIES LIKE THESE, WHO NEEDS ENEMIES?' The text read,

> A man is half-suffocated, tortured, beaten senseless and his bruised body is dumped in the desert. Is this Iraq? Occupied Kuwait? No, the venue is Saudi Arabia and the victim from neighbouring Yemen. His crime is his government's pro-Iraqi stance. ... We are neither pro-war nor anti-war. ... We are solely concerned with protecting human rights. And human rights are under attack on all sides.

The advertisement referred to the UK government's arbitrary detention of Iraqis and Palestinians,[27] and the organization also concerned itself with the case of Vic Williams, a serving British soldier who refused to go to the Gulf.[28]

Agencies responded, however, to the human tragedies of the Gulf crisis, such as the plight of Palestinians and South Asians evicted from Kuwait. The Red Cross launched its 'Gulf Appeal'—'we will be at the heart of the conflict, caring for those who are suffering'.[29] Civilian victims were not the only ones to attract attention: the government launched the Gulf Trust to raise money for 'service personnel and families who had suffered as a result of the hostilities in the Gulf'.[30] Before long, the Royal Society for the Prevention of Cruelty to Animals was involved—their advertisement claimed, over a picture of a suffering bird: 'The RSPCA are flying into the Gulf so that others can fly out.'[31]

It was the Kurdish crisis which really got the agencies involved; it was such a big story that no organization could stand aside. For Oxfam, Iraq was no longer a distraction, as it launched a major appeal for the 'Refugee Crisis'[32] and for the 'Victims of hunger and conflict'.[33] Unicef UK claimed that 'Concern alone won't save their lives. £18 WILL.' Feed the Children asserted it was 'getting the aid to the Kurdish refugees now'.[34] The Kurdish Cultural Centre asked, 'Are we not human?'; a picture of a child with a bandage over half its face accompanied a long text which failed however to explain who they were or how money would be used.[35]

Kurdistan continued to be the agencies' major focus, although there were other disasters, not only in Africa but in Bangladesh, where the toll from a cyclone climbed quickly towards 250,000.[36] Concern for starvation in areas of Iraq still controlled by the regime was slower to emerge and was never given the same profile. Oxfam, however, did raise the issue, and was censured by the Charity Commissioners for being 'too political'. (Pilger claimed: 'This has had the effect of gagging Oxfam on the human disaster in Iraq'.)[37] With the Save the Children Fund, Oxfam reported that Baghdad had no uncontaminated running water, refrigeration, fuel or food processing: 'The unavailability of powdered milk spells nutritional and health disaster for children ... and the spread of diseases such as cholera and typhoid in the present conditions is inevitable.'[38]

Humanitarian organizations were not constrained by considerations of political advantage or offence in the same ways as parties, churches or schools. Their *raison d'être* gave them a remit to address human suffering as such, irrespective of political causes, and Kurdish relief was one of their finest hours. They not only raised very substantial funds for victims but also contributed to shifting governments' agendas. Nevertheless their focus on the Kurds rather than the defeated populations of southern or central Iraq reflected more than geopolitical constraints. Media coverage dictated agencies' agendas to a considerable degree. And, just like television (as we shall see), relief organizations represented Kurds only as victims, not as people fighting for human rights.

This reflects a general problem. While humanitarian agencies are able to act independently of—often authoritarian—local regimes, they also become 'preferred conduits for emergency aid from Western governments', and so, as de Waal argues, 'become more closely tied to donor governments'. In relief operations even more than development strategies, agencies are obliged to take governments' priorities into account. Similarly

> the majority of large agencies believe, along with most journalists, that only a certain kind of humanitarian story will elicit public sympathy and public funds. The story is stripped down to its barest essentials: helpless victims, evil bandit or warlord, and saviour—the latter inevitably white.

(Although de Waal adds: 'At least this is an improvement on earlier days [the 1980s] when the villain was the weather.')[39]

Humanitarian agencies, unlike almost all institutions of civil society which I examined, were able to switch focus quickly to respond to the Kurdish crisis. But even their responses were mostly limited to a simple humanitarianism which failed to represent many aspects of the struggle and suffering of people in the zone of crisis. Although the agencies were, in one sense, global civil society in action, they retained many traits of the national contexts from which they have emerged.

Representing Muslims

Another new sector of civil society dramatically strengthened during the Iraqi wars: institutions claiming to represent ethnic minorities. People in

Western Europe of Arab and Asian origin were greatly challenged by the wars. In France many of the large Arab population identified with the Iraqi cause, and French diplomatic activity was partly an effort to prove to them (as well as to French nationalists) that the government had not merely followed the American line—so as to minimize opposition once French forces were committed. In Britain, the Arab population was small, but of a total ethnic minority population of some three million about one million were Muslims, mainly of Pakistani, Bangladesh and Indian origin. Although South Asian communities had organized themselves on the basis of the countries from which they came, in the period before the Gulf crisis there was increasing public identification of Muslims by religion. This had been heightened by their campaign against Salman Rushdie's *Satanic Verses*, with angry protests in centres of Muslim population.[40]

Iraq posed complex issues for Muslims. The regime was secular and its attempt to mobilize Islamic sentiment was manifestly opportunistic. It had oppressed the Shia Muslim communities in Iraq and waged war against the revolutionary Islamic state in Iran. All the Muslim people of Iraq, Sunni, Shia and Kurd, suffered under the regime. By invading Kuwait, Saddam had terrorized Kuwaiti fellow Muslims and forced the expulsion of Palestinian and South Asian Muslims working in Kuwait. The government of Islamic Saudi Arabia had invited US intervention and most Muslim states, not only in the Arab world but in South Asia, had given military or political support to the US-led coalition. Despite all this, to many Muslims Saddam seemed, particularly in the aftermath of the Rushdie affair, like a champion of the Muslim world against Western and especially American dominance.

Saddam was strongly supported particularly among the young. One seventeen-year-old argued, 'Saddam Hussein is protecting his religion and his country. Kuwait belongs to him.' Another felt alone in admiring the British forces: 'Almost all of my friends at school are on Saddam's side—they think he's a good guy. I disagree with them and I think it's going to get me into a lot of trouble.'[41] Militant Islamic activity was reflected in anti-semitic slogans and attacks by pro-Iraq Pakistanis on Saudi children in Hackney.[42]

Many Muslims feared the consequences of this identification with the Iraqi cause. A nineteen-year-old restaurant assistant reported:

> My friend is getting a lot of trouble already because he's called Hussein. Lots of white people are anti-Muslim already. I think if a load of British men die in this war, people will turn on us and say, 'These Pakis killed our sons.' It'll never be the same again. Quite a few Muslims are allies and fighting Saddam as well: I don't really see him as a Muslim.[43]

A Nottingham greengrocer was quoted as saying that 'a minority of non-Muslims assumed that all Muslims supported Saddam Hussein and taunted them accordingly. They say "We'll beat you in the war" and things like that. I don't take any notice, but sometimes it makes me angry. We don't support anyone.'[44] The Commission for Racial Equality monitored racial violence nationally, reporting sharp increases early in the war, with attacks on mosques and racial attacks.[45]

Muslim fears and isolation were undoubtedly heightened by the arbitrary detention of Iraqis and Palestinians. Guilt by association was the justification for the detentions, according to lawyers, not hard evidence. Some were supporters of Saddam Hussein; some relatives of terrorists; some students paid for by the Iraqi government, studying subjects with potential military significance; and some had visa applications in progress, which may have brought them to the attention of officials.[46] Prisoner of War status was given to some students because their grants were administered by the military attaché at the embassy. Some 'students were treated as soldiers captured in battle and held because their names were on a list sent by the Iraqi embassy to the Bank of England'.[47]

The detainees included Palestinians such as Abbas Cheblak, 'an outspoken critic of Saddam Hussein for a decade, an organiser of conferences in defence of Arab human rights, and a passionate exponent of Arab–Israeli dialogue'. His supporters included prominent Jewish intellectuals, but he was denied a hearing by the High Court, which ruled that the Home Secretary, 'who personally ordered Mr Cheblak's removal, did not act unlawfully by failing to give proper reasons for his decision'.[48] Lord Donaldson commented: 'Those who are able most effectively to undermine national security are those who least appear to constitute any risk to it' and told Cheblak to 'try to have greater faith' in the 'Three Wise Men' tribunal and not 'rush off to the courts' to seek redress.[49]

Detainees complained of being strip-searched and separated from their wives who didn't speak English. There was no right of appeal against detention, only recourse to a secret three-man advisory panel (two of whose members had close links with the intelligence services), whose findings could be rejected by the Home Secretary. As the *Observer* commented:

> We are not engaged in total war, nor is the security situation so perilous that we can jettison normal judicial procedures. We went to war in the Gulf backed by a claim of moral superiority, but that is weakened by the way we are dealing with Mr Cheblak and his co-detainees.[50]

In this context, the equivocal positions of British Muslims are more understandable. Muslim leaders wished to manage the tensions within their communities and between them and the white British majority. As Istaq Ahmed, spokesman for the Bradford Council of Mosques, put it:

> Sadly, I think there will be increased tensions here and elsewhere. We as a community will find it very difficult to condone the British action, and that will be interpreted by the majority community as Muslims being disloyal or unpatriotic. We are very worried that Muslims will be provoked to acts of violence.[51]

The *Independent* commented that 'while the mosques endeavour to stay neutral, some Muslims say it will be difficult not to side with Iraq if the number of civilian casualties is high, or if Muslim holy shrines are destroyed'. (Ironically the Iraqi regime, in suppressing the rebellion in the south, eventually destroyed a number of Shia holy places.)

As the war continued, many leaders came out against the coalition assault, expressing sympathy for Iraq without crossing the rubicon of explicit support for Saddam. A Supreme Council of British Muslims, constituted at a conference in Bradford in January, urged the West to withdraw, leaving Muslims to sort things out themselves (in reality this meant leaving Saddam Hussein victorious). A resolution demanding that Iraq withdraw from Kuwait was turned down and its proposer barracked.[52]

The central committee of the Union of Muslim Organizations (UMO), representing 180 groups, passed a resolution at a national conference in early February, calling on Saddam to withdraw 'to remove the pretext for the stationing of non-Muslim troops in the area'. It failed however to condemn the invasion. Syed Aziz Pasha, UMO General Secretary, complained that 'people are always confusing our sympathy for the Iraqi people—and we believe women and children in Iraq are dying in their hundreds and thousands—with sympathies for their political leaders.' He didn't think Saddam a bad Muslim, 'but he had some weaknesses'; asked if his war was a *jihad* (or 'holy war') he was 'evasive', and stated that British Muslims should never break the law.[53]

A delegation of community leaders and academics from the Muslim Forum, led by Dr Zaki Badawi, Director of the Muslim College, had earlier met a Foreign Office minister, appealing to the allies to halt the war and promote human rights throughout the Middle East.[54] Badawi stated that, 'As British citizens, Muslims are of course entitled to express their views, but I hope they will not use a language which is offensive to the majority community.' He noted that Muslims' languages were ones of 'overstatement', English one of 'understatement', and hoped Muslims would join with other protestors such as CND rather than protesting alone. The Muslim Forum believed that the views of the majority had been largely ignored and that too much media attention had been given to extreme positions.

The war was a significant stage in the development of distinctively Muslim representation in British society. Both the Union of Muslim Organizations and the Muslim Forum aimed to establish an institution to speak effectively for Muslims, and Dr Kalim Saddiqui, Director of the Muslim Institute in London, proposed a 'Muslim parliament'—but 'moderates' and pro-Saudi Muslims would not be included. Saddiqui represented the radical view that the West was 'the force of all evil', seeking to defend its 'colonial' boundaries. According to him, Saddam was 'entirely to blame' for the war but was also a victim. Saddiqui expressed the dual position which most Muslim leaders were attempting to advance: 'No one should doubt Muslims' loyalty to this country: we are British ... But we are not going to accept the values of the establishment that are being thrust down our throats.'[55]

A fascinating account of Muslim responses is given by Pnina Werbner, who observed a meeting in Manchester in October 1990.[56] Werbner points out that British Muslims' opposition to Gulf-state rulers was partly a 'sectarian opposition to the Wahabbi movement' (the section of Islam dominated by the Saudis), but quotes a more representative opinion that 'the real crux of the Gulf situation is that there is a cultural conflict between the West and the Muslim world today'. There was a three-pronged attack:

> against the injustice of international law and global decision-making, both of which ignored Muslim national interests; against the corrupt illegitimate regimes of the Gulf states, denying the economic rights of ordinary Muslims; and against British legal discrimination which denied local Muslims their basic rights as citizens.[57]

The thrust of Muslim responses was the articulation of their own grievances as represented in the global context highlighted by the war. The linkages with Middle-Eastern issues were highly partial, often resting on a largely uncritical representation of the Iraqi regime and overlooking its manifold violence. British Muslims largely ignored the complexities of the issues and did not find it easy, in the light of their identification with Iraq in the Gulf War, to answer the pleas of Shias and Kurds. Muslim representation was largely the representation of British Muslims in their own tensions: despite their ambivalence towards the dominant nationalism, it was also a national response which failed to meet the global challenge and represent distant fellow-Muslims.

Notes and references

1. See also Shaw, 1994.
2. *Guardian*, 29 January 1991.
3. *Independent*, 19 January and 3 March 1991.
4. Leaflet in M-O A: DR1530.
5. *Independent*, 18 January 1991.
6. *Independent*, 17 January 1991.
7. *Independent*, 23 January 1991.
8. *Observer*, 27 January 1991.
9. *Observer*, 3 February 1991.
10. Bell, 1991; pp. 9, 15, 26.
11. *Observer*, 10 February 1991.
12. *Independent*, 12 February 1991.
13. *Observer*, 24 February 1991.
14. *Observer*, 24 February 1991.
15. *Observer*, 24 February 1991.
16. *Independent*, 26 January 1991.
17. George Nash, letter, *Independent*, 29 January 1991.
18. G. Flanagan, letter, *Independent*, 29 January 1991.
19. *Independent*, 5 April 1991.
20. Marjorie Thompson, letter, *Independent*, 4 April 1991.
21. Dr Mark Imber, University of St Andrews, letter, *Independent*, 5 April1991, which also asked: 'What is meant by a "genuine peacekeeping force"? There are only two kinds ... the crucial variable is whether the peacekeeping force has or does not have the *consent* of both parties. A force with a mandate from both parties (Iraqi and Kurdish) to supervise a ceasefire cannot be established because Iraq wishes to continue the slaughter. Does CND therefore want a UN force with a mandate to defend Kurdistan by force of arms or even fight its way to Baghdad? I thought this was what CND opposed.'
22. This was certainly true of the Hull CSWG, whose meetings I attended.
23. *Guardian*, 30 January 1991. One small new constituency was reservists and soldiers unhappy at being 'conscripted' into the war. In Britain, there was a high-profile campaign on behalf of Vic Williams, a soldier based in Germany who refused to go to the Gulf: 'I

was a keen soldier with a strong sense of duty ... but ... I did not think what we were being asked to do was justified. My conscience wouldn't let me take part in pure naked aggression. I felt let down by the politicians.' Many of the men, he believed, 'felt that this issue—between two Arab states—did not justify employing the British Army.' Williams's own position verged on racism, however: 'We don't speak the same language, have the same religion; it's an Arab problem—let them sort it out' (*Heart of the Matter*, BBC1, 9 March 1991). Williams deserted from his base in Germany and met anti-war people from a SWP-initiated group, Reservists Against War. In the USA, Amnesty International monitored several hundred cases of conscientious objectors—many of them black—and a sergeant jailed after refusing to go to Saudi Arabia was adopted as a prisoner of conscience.

24. *Observer*, 3 March 1991.

25. *Observer*, 3 February 1991.

26. *Guardian*, 23 February 1991.

27. *Observer*, 24 February 1991.

28. *Amnesty* (Campaign Bulletin of the British Section of Amnesty International), April/May 1992.

29. *Independent on Sunday*, 20 January 1991.

30. *Independent*, 2 February 1991.

31. *Independent*, 5 February 1991. A similar image was used in Green Party advertisements, 'Speaking for the Planet', *Guardian*, 8 February 1991.

32. *Independent*, 10 April 1991.

33. *Observer*, 21 April 1991.

34. *Guardian*, 16 April 1991.

35. *Observer*, 7 April 1991.

36. *Observer*, 5 May 1991.

37. *New Statesman and Society*, 24 May 1991.

38. *Ibid*.

39. de Waal, 1994.

40. See Husband, 1994; esp. pp. 95–7. Although Husband explicates the relationship between 'Muslim' identities and white racism, he curiously fails to explore the relationships between ethnicity, nationality and religion among British Muslims.

41. *Independent*, 19 January 1991.

42. *Independent*, 29 January 1991.

43. *Independent on Sunday*, 20 January 1991.

44. *Independent*, 22 February 1991.

45. *Independent*, 26 January 1991.

46. *Independent*, 13 February 1991.

47. *Independent*, 6 March 1991.

48. *Independent*, 24 January 1991.

49. Hugo Young, *Guardian*, 12 February 1991.

50. *Observer*, 3 February 1991.

51. *Independent*, 19 January 1991.

52. *Guardian*, 21 January 1991.

53. *Independent*, 4 February 1991.

54. *Guardian*, 31 January 1991.

55. *Independent*, 6 February 1991. Muslims' fears found an echo in the Labour Party, where many 'black' (i.e. mainly Afro-Caribbean) representatives and organizations, including black MPs and the unofficial Labour Party black sections, were involved in setting up a national campaign against racial violence, the detention of Arabs and Western intervention (*Observer*, 27 January 1991).

56. Werbner, 1994.

57. Werbner, 1994; p. 113.

— Part III —

From Managed Media
to Active Representation

Because of the limitations of other civil society institutions in the representation of global crises, mass media played an exceptionally critical role. There has been a huge amount of analysis of the media in the Gulf, but it has not been set in the context either of the limitations of civil society or an analysis of public opinion and individuals' responses. Nor, of course, has it examined the Iraqi wars together: it has been focused on the Gulf War, to the neglect of the other wars and even the Kurdish refugee crisis. The treatment of the latter is curious: it is widely recognized that the media played a strikingly different role than it did in the Gulf conflict, but all studies of media in the Gulf stop when Bush stopped, with the ceasefire on the 28 February 1991, and ignore the tumultuous two months of revolt, repression and human disaster which followed in Iraq. This study is the first to present a detailed account of the media coverage of this process.

Critical discussion has been focused, moreover, on one medium: television. It is beyond dispute that television was the central medium of communication in the war, and it is essential to understand its role. Many analyses have, however, merged the discussion of television and other media and have not distinguished between their distinct roles. Television's role was limited in important ways and we need to understand both these limitations and how far other media overcame them. In the discussion which follows I first summarize the role of television in the Gulf War;[1] I then present my analysis of television coverage of the Iraqi revolts culminating in the Kurdish refugee crisis; and finally, I develop a broader account of the media, arguing that newspapers played critical—and contradictory—roles in articulating and forming responses and representations of the Iraqi wars.

Notes and references

1. My discussion is based chiefly on Taylor, 1992.

CHAPTER SIX

Television as managed media

The televisual mediation of the war was one of its most striking characteristics; many responses of both institutions and individuals contain a commentary on this process. We saw in chapter 3 that for Baudrillard, the media war displaced the 'real' war. For the combatant states, the media war was undoubtedly an integral part of the war. Saddam Hussein appeared to believe that he could utilize the media to overcome his military disadvantage: that if he could inflict thousands of American casualties, pictures of returning body bags carried by television into American homes would force the administration to end the war. Conversely, the US and its allies aimed to limit their own casualties and to manage the media coverage so as to present a sanitized picture of the war.

In their approaches to media both sides reflected beliefs about the role of television in Vietnam. Iraq sought to emulate the supposed success of the Vietnamese in weakening America's resolve from within.[1] Bush aimed to exorcise the 'Vietnam syndrome' of military defeat and his media managers aimed to avoid the excess of unrestricted television coverage which was seen as having contributed to the USA's downfall. They aimed to build on the successes of media management by the British in the Falklands and the USA in Grenada and Panama.

These beliefs about Vietnam have been questioned by academic research on the media in that war[2] and were challenged during the Gulf War by Freedman, who argued:

> It is widely assumed that modern democracies cannot tolerate great loss of life in support of goals other than direct defence of the country. This is held to be one of the major lessons of the Vietnam war but it is founded on myth. ... It was not pictures of 'body bags' of which there was precious little footage, that made television's role important, but the continual questioning by journalists of optimistic forecasts from the local military command.[3]

In the Gulf, Freedman pointed out, the willingness to accept loss of life grew with the fighting: 'Public opinion can tolerate mounting casualties as long as there is real belief in the military objectives. ... The public can tolerate pain; it is less forgiving of futility.'

The USA was nevertheless taking no chances in the Gulf. The five-month lead in to the war created an unprecedented opportunity to plan media management, and when the USA attacked Iraq, they had created a 'controlled information environment'. Reporters were integrated with the military, either accompanying selected units through the 'newspool' system, or being fed selected information directly in briefings in Riyadh, Saudi Arabia (although there were also 'unilaterals', who operated outside the pool and were often credited with more objective coverage).[4] This system led to media mostly supplying controlled information which amounted to highly effective propaganda.[5]

In Britain, the government set up a propaganda committee, hired a public relations firm and agreed how to announce British casualties so as to minimize embarrassment.[6] Direct censorship appears to have been instituted voluntarily by broadcasting organizations, who cast their net widely. The BBC banned sixty-seven popular songs (some of them 'among those most often requested by the squaddies themselves')[7] and comedy programmes with a vaguely military theme. The banning by the minority Channel 4 of a series of Vietnamese films indicated a level of general cultural control that went beyond the political censorship evident in all the countries directly involved in the conflict.

'The Gulf War', Taylor points out, 'broke out on television. Or that at least is how television subscribers in many parts of the world will remember it.'[8] The instant coverage of air attacks on Iraq on 16 January 1991 was taken live from Cable News Network (CNN) by news organizations around the world, including both main British providers. Television coverage of the early phase emphasized high-technology efficiency: film was widely shown of American fighter pilots describing their assaults—'exactly like the movies', 'Baghdad was lit up like a Christmas tree. It was tremendous!', 'It was kinda neat'.

This was 'the video game war', in which the apparently remorseless efficiency of high-technology weapons combined with lack of evidence of casualties to match computer simulations. This was the war which later turned up as a computer game:

> On a moonless night, a huge C-5A Galaxy touches down in Saudi Arabia disgorging a large black object which unfolds its wings. You push the throttle to full forward. With a roar the two big turbo-jets hurtle the craft airborne. Another F-19 Stealth Fighter Mission has begun. A typical sortie from the Gulf War? Almost. In fact it is Micro-Prose's new flight simulation, *F-19 Stealth Fighter*. If the war, as replayed through the video nose-cones of aircraft on television screens looked, bizarrely, like a computer game, that is because it is. Except that the computer version is in colour.[9]

(This was one of several games, with names like *Desert Strike*, which came on the market.)

During this phase, many in the media 'failed to keep their distance from [the] terminological fog' involved in the 'high-tech' war: 'Like two sports commentators, David Dimbleby and [BBC] defence correspondent, David Shukman, were almost rapt with enthusiasm.'[10] Even more, they often reproduced the military's linguistic devices for masking the attacks' violent effects: 'It might appear that official coalition propaganda had not only dictated the overall picture but had even permeated the language of the media.'[11] The other side was, however, that 'television gives faces and histories and fears and weeping wives and children to troops. ... In this conflict, the latest airman posted missing might be someone who has just been speaking to us. ... The concept of cannon-fodder is harder to sustain.'[12]

The real cannon-fodder were Iraqi soldiers whose sufferings were completely unfilmed, victims of a conspiracy of silence between Iraqi and coalition governments neither of which wished people to know their fate:

> immediately after the war's outbreak, the coalition air forces began to concentrate on pounding the Republican Guard positions in southern Iraq and northern Kuwait. It was here that B52 bombers, some of which would soon be flying from Fairford airbase in Britain, concentrated their fire-power in their indiscriminate 'carpet-bombing' of the well dug-in, heavily protected and privileged 'elite' units. Similarly, thanks to immediate achievement of air superiority, allied planes were targeting front-line Iraqi conscripts.[13]

When the ground war began, the process was completed in some parts of the front by the extensive use of bulldozers to fill in Iraqi trenches, their occupants buried alive in the sand. This, too, never made television.[14] Nor, of course, did Iraqi atrocities in Kuwait, where cameras were banned.

After two or three weeks of the 'high-tech' war, with the war of attrition against Iraqi forces out of sight, there was 'a dearth of sensational new stories'. It was in this climate that attention shifted in early February to 'collateral damage', the effects of the bombing of Iraqi cities on civilians.[15] It was the destruction of the Amiriya shelter on 13 February 1991, killing hundreds of people, which really shook media management, creating 'precisely the kind of allied nightmare and the sought-after Iraqi propaganda opportunity which coalition media managers had feared since the outset of the air attacks on Baghdad.'[16]

The coalition had initially highlighted its avoidance of civilian casualties, but gradually shifted to stressing that they were regrettably unavoidable and that responsibility lay with the Iraqi regime: they were, for example, the result of Iraqis shooting down coalition missiles, deflecting them from their precisely guided targets and causing them to explode in unintended locations. The 'lofty pedestal' on which the coalition placed itself in the propaganda war, claiming not to target civilians, was 'always vulnerable to collapse when ... accidents occur.'[17]

This was what happened at Amiriya. The Iraqis lifted all censorship and Western reporters were able to transmit what they liked. Gruesome footage arrived in newsrooms and was censored by the broadcasters: 'The pictures were so horrific, and the filming of the corpses so graphic, that they would need skilful editing if audiences were not to be offended or alienated ... rather in the same way as television editors would treat pictures of a motorway or rail crash.'[18] Television reports overwhelmingly confirmed that there was no evidence of military activity: as the BBC's Jeremy Bowen put it, 'I think all the signs are that this was indeed what the Iraqis say it was—a civilian shelter ... I am as certain as I can be that this was a shelter.'[19] Nevertheless, this breach in the orderly progress of the war became a source of great controversy: 'Words turned out to be the sore point in the coverage; the pictures may have been self-censored but even the sanitised images were still so shocking that the commentaries of journalists became the focus of ire.'[20]

Although a British military official suggested it might have been a mistake, the co-ordinated official reaction was that 'it was a military bunker. It was a command and control facility. ... We have no explanation at this time really why there were civilians in this bunker.' It was plausible, the American briefer suggested, that Saddam might have deliberately placed civilians in this bunker for a propaganda coup.[21] This line was again indicated in later briefings and was picked up, we shall see, by the majority of the British press. Eyewitness accounts of television journalists clearly contradicted this line, and CNN, BBC and Independent Television News (ITN) continued to report their stories. The coalition line, meanwhile, was successful with public opinion: around 80 per cent of people interviewed in both the USA and Britain agreed that the shelter was a legitimate target, although sources at the Pentagon and in Riyadh were soon admitting privately that the bombing resulted from an intelligence mistake.[22]

The Amiriya incident also changed the British political debate about television and the war. In January, Major had

> dealt peremptorily with a Tory backbencher who criticised the refusal of the BBC to refer routinely to 'our' British troops ... [and] said that the BBC was trying to strike a balance in its coverage, and it was important that the Corporation's coverage was believed in countries other than Britain.[23]

After the Amiriya bombing the BBC was dubbed the 'Baghdad Broadcasting Corporation' by Tory critics, and Major's press secretary, Gus O'Donnell, intervened to complain over its failure to say that Iraqi censors had approved its film and the text of reports of the shelter. Whether Conservative protests reflected real viewer dissatisfaction is doubtful: the Broadcasting Standards Council received only twenty complaints over BBC and ITN coverage of the shelter bombing,[24] and polls showed television was trusted far more than the government, military or the press to tell the truth about the war.[25] Nevertheless, right-wingers were vociferous in their attacks on television, with suggestions that Brent Sadler of ITN was manipulated by Iraqi propaganda and a Freedom Association court challenge over two Channel 4 programmes which it claimed were 'one-sided propaganda'.[26] That minority programmes with a critical editorial stance should attract criticism, when the preponderance of stridently pro-war coverage in the press did not, says more about the politics of the right than about the real situation in the media.[27]

The other incident in which, to a lesser degree, television coverage departed from the smooth track of news management was at the end of the war. On 26 February, as television crews, denied serious access to the land campaign, homed in on liberated Kuwait, American planes were bombing a makeshift convoy of Iraqi troops and civilians withdrawing from Kuwait, on the highway to Basra near Mutla Gap. Bumper-to-bumper traffic—of civilian as well as military vehicles—was caught in what US pilots called a 'turkey shoot' and like 'shooting fish in a barrel'. Probably thousands were killed in or near their vehicles, in an operation of questionable military utility. It was only on 1 March, however, 'that the real extent of the carnage was brought home to television viewers around the world.' A CNN reporter called the event 'a massacre'. BBC viewers were treated to an item by reporter Kate Adie in which, as Taylor puts it, 'the reapers of carnage had turned angels of mercy' as one wounded survivor was shown being treated by the Americans, but British television still conveyed the horror. British soldiers interviewed expressed their disgust. Indeed television gave 'the impression that an ambush followed by a massacre had taken place. In fact it had been a battle. It may have been one-sided owing to the coalition's air supremacy but it had been a battle nonetheless.'[28]

This story was largely lost in the general relief at the end of the war and the horror at environmental damage caused by Iraq's firing of Kuwait's oil wells. There remains considerable suspicion about the reasons for the delay in transmitting footage of it. There is also the possibility that as John Simpson suggested, 'awareness of what the TV pictures of the slaughter at Mutla Gap might do to public opinion at home played an important part in President Bush's decision not to pursue the Iraqi troops any further, and certainly not to take the war to Baghdad',[29] although this has been discounted by others.

Coalition governments and armed forces won a stunning victory in the military campaign; they also won overwhelmingly in the television war. The war appeared to be virtually bloodless; fewer than two hundred coalition troops had been killed and the killing of tens or even hundreds of thousands of Iraqi soldiers had been conducted almost entirely out of sight. Propaganda had been largely successful, even if some of the claims for bombing accuracy were later shown to have been misleading. There was relative unanimity of media coverage, due to tight control of information at source. The fact that the war was fought mainly from the air produced distance between the bombers and the bombed which television then amplified.[30]

Notes and references

1. Iraqi 'media mismanagement' is analysed effectively in Taylor, 1992; pp. 87–133.

2. Mandelbaum, 1982; Hallin, 1986.

3. Lawrence Freedman, *Independent*, 30 January 1991.

4. Taylor, 1992; pp. 31–86.

5. Taylor, 1992; Introduction, especially pp. 23–6.

6. *Independent*, 17 January 1991. Casualties were to be announced by the defence secretary: the government wished to avoid repeating the Falklands situation when a civil servant, Ian McDonald, had become notorious for his wooden announcements. Statements to Parliament were to be avoided because they would give a platform to anti-war MPs (*Guardian*, 26 January 1991).

7. The favourite, according to British Forces Radio, was Barry McGuire's 'Eve of Destruction', followed by 'Nothing's Gonna Stop Us Now', 'Eve of War', 'Bang Bang' and 'Stop the Cavalry'. 'Reflecting the sardonic humour of the men who have nine seconds to put on their gas masks when there is an alert, the so-called "Saddam Hit List" also included "The Air That I Breathe".' *Independent*, 14 February 1991.

8. Taylor, p. 31.

9. *Guardian*, 2 May 1991. This was not the only exploitation of the war for commercial purposes: advertising also latched on to the war. Travel agents, Thomas Cook, were quick to offer free holidays for troops, over a picture of victorious soldiers on a tank—'As soon as they come home we want to send them away.' The clue lay in the statement, 'After all, the travel business suffered more than most as a result of the Gulf War.' During April 1991, as Kurdish refugees were barred from entering Turkey, its tourist office advertised in British papers that 'Now is the time to come to Turkiye'—'Turkiye, rich in history myth and legend, has 5000 miles of coastline, most of it untouched by tourism. There are mountains, lakes, plains, forests and vast unspoiled landscapes which Turkiye is determined to preserve. ... Come this summer!'

10. Philo and McLaughlin, 1993; p. 6.

11. Taylor, 1992; p. 47.

12. Mark Lawson, quoted, Taylor, 1992; p. 49.

13. Taylor, 1992; pp. 154–5. See also p. 221.

14. *Guardian*, 13 and 19 September 1991. Pilger claims, however, that film of this briefly formed the backdrop to a BBC2 *Late Show* discussion (*New Statesman and Society*, 19 May 1995). It also appeared in the BBC1 series *The Gulf War*, 16 January 1996. See too Maggie O'Kane, *Guardian*, 16 December 1995.

15. Taylor, 1992; pp. 163–4.

16. Taylor, 1992; p. 169.

17. Taylor, 1992; p. 185.

18. Taylor, 1992; pp. 188–9.

19. Quoted, Taylor, 1992; p. 191. The view that it was a civilian shelter was also endorsed by Dr David Manley, Civil Defence Adviser to the Home Office and an expert on military installations (quoted, Taylor, p. 209).

20. Taylor, 1992; p. 193.

21. Brigadier-General Richard Neal, quoted in Taylor, 1992; pp. 194–5.

22. Taylor, 1992; p. 212. However, according to Wafic-al-Samari, then Head of Iraqi Military Intelligence, part of the shelter was used by Iraqi intelligence services (*The Gulf War*, BBC1, 9 January 1996).

23. *Independent*, 17 January 1991.

24. *Observer*, 17 February 1991. CNN was also attacked at this time as the 'US Voice of Baghdad'.

25. *Independent*, 16 February 1991.

26. Independent Television News, 5 March 1991.

27. Another matter which attracted Tory protests was the BBC's removal of the National Anthem from the close of broadcasting on Radio 4. This was done, the BBC claimed, for practical reasons, because broadcasting continued into the night, but the Anthem was restored after protests. *Sunday Times*, 3 February 1991.

28. Taylor, 1992; pp. 251–6.

29. Quoted, Taylor, 1992; pp. 259–60.

30. 'The Gulf War may have appeared to have reduced this distance with the presence of video-cameras in the noses of smart weapons, but the fact remains that, once the bomb impacted, the pictures went blank.' Taylor, 1992; p. 275.

CHAPTER SEVEN

Television as active representation

If television during the Gulf War was mostly a highly managed medium, the aftermath of the war showed it in a dramatically different light. The changed role had been prefigured only in the moment of tension over Amiriya. Here the critical, even subversive potential of television had been clearly demonstrated, but it was largely smothered by the military propaganda campaign and, as we shall see, the willingness of most newspapers to reinforce it.

The preplanned work of media managers, as of the militaries in general, came to an end with Bush's ceasefire. The Iraqi wars did not end there, however, as the military intended and even most academic media researchers have implicitly accepted. On the contrary, at almost precisely this moment their most turbulent phases began and, with them, the most exciting, dramatic and influential period of media and above all television coverage.

Coverage of the Kurdish refugee crisis (which as we shall see was only one aspect of this period) has been much referred to but—unaccountably except in terms of the inability of researchers to adapt to unexpected events—has not been closely studied. This omission is remedied here by examining key elements of British television coverage of the revolts in Iraq, their repression by the regime and the consequent refugee crises, together with responses by Western states and civil societies.

The account covers the calendar months of March–April 1991, which include all the most active coverage. The focus on British television, rather than CNN or other US coverage, is explained partly by the availability of this material. It is also justified, however, because British television news programmes succeeded in generating such concern for Kurdish refugees that they actually precipitated an historic 'U-turn' by Major's Conservative government, which launched the virtually unprecedented proposal for Kurdish 'safe havens', established and maintained by Western powers, in northern Iraq. The British volte-face predated and influenced the American, which was required to make the proposal effective.

British television coverage thus played, I argue, a particular political role; there is, however, no reason to believe that it showed major qualitative differences from that of North American or other countries' television. In this sense, although there are national peculiarities, the analysis of British television's role may stand as representative until there are comparable international studies. This study is based, moreover, on a restricted sample of British coverage, concentrated on a viewing of one full-length (approximately half-hour) BBC bulletin, daily for the whole of March–April 1991, together with smaller samples of ITN bulletins. These are the two major national television news services reaching mass audiences; while study of minority channel bulletins would undoubtedly have revealed more sophisticated analyses, these reached fewer viewers. The study of ITN in two key sub-periods revealed only secondary differences of approach compared to BBC coverage. For this reason it was not felt necessary to replicate the latter with a full study of all ITN bulletins and the coverage of the two services is analysed together.[1]

Discussion is centred around three sets of issues to do with coverage, advocacy and political effect. The first set of questions concerns representation in the sense of what was *shown*: the extent and character of television coverage of post-Gulf-War Iraq; the coverage of the southern compared to the northern revolt; and the relationship between coverage of Shia and Kurds as rebels and as victims of repression. The second set concerns representation in the sense of *advocacy*: the degree to which Iraqi people were able to represent themselves in the television coverage or depended on British journalists to portray them; and related to this, whether television was as good at portraying Iraqis as rebels seeking to influence their own life-situation as it was at portraying them as passive victims needing outside concern. The third set, which it is of course difficult to answer from a content analysis, concerns *political effect*: the extent and ways in which coverage influenced the dramatic shift in government policy in April 1991 and why this effect occurred then rather than earlier at the height of the rebellions. This final set of questions is crucial and, even if answers are only tentative, it is important to suggest them here.

Bloodshed in Basra

With the end of the Gulf War, television coverage immediately broadened its focus. Alongside reports from liberated Kuwait and Baghdad 'returning to normal', the BBC on 1 March had film from the devastated road between Kuwait and Basra, showing 'rows of Iraqi corpses', a US soldier saying that the 'scene was apocalyptic', and commentary by Adie describing what had happened as an 'inferno' and remarking that it was an 'eerie and grisly end for a fleeing army'. Adie pointed out that many of those who fought and died were from minority communities persecuted by Saddam Hussein such as the Kurds. Her colleague Brian Barron had travelled a few miles further towards Basra and had been turned back by Iraqi troops. He was asked from the studio if there were signs of resistance in Iraq and gave a hearsay account of a tank commander in Basra splattering a portrait of Saddam with fire. ITN, however, had UN Secretary General Perez de Cuellar saying that the fall of Saddam was a matter for the Iraqi people.[2]

From the moment the Gulf War ended, therefore, revolt inside Iraq was a serious issue for television news—for the first few days it received repeated coverage—but television was also reporting the line being drawn between the 'international community' and this revolt. By 2 March, Basra was 'said to be in chaos' and people were reported to be trying to leave: 'The American military say that aerial photographs show a total breakdown of control, but no sign of revolt.' A US spokesman was shown speculating on breakdown in Iraq, and there was an Iraqi prisoner saying he hoped Saddam was killed. The newscaster pointed out in what was to be a constant refrain that 'conclusive information on what is happening in Basra is impossible to obtain'. Reporters were able to get around Baghdad, from which there was a story about a hospital in which children were dying because of lack of water, milk and medicines and the problems of sewage and disease in the wake of the bombing.[3]

Television kept the Basra story alive with indirect reports, although information remained sparse and film virtually non-existent. The BBC on 3 March was reduced to quoting from Teheran radio and noting that the 'US military, privately hoping for Saddam's downfall, today had little publicly to say'. It reported that Basra still seemed to be chaotic and disorganized: 'Reports of revolts against Saddam remain sketchy, but taken together, they strongly suggest that Saddam is facing revolts which he can't put down, as he always has done before.'[4] The following day it again carried reports from Islamic and US sources, on tanks attacking people: 'It looks like there is some anti-regime resistance going on.' The Shi'ites claimed control of Nasiriyah, there were reports of the Kurds taking Sulaymaniyah and that the military had moved two armoured divisions to Baghdad to protect Saddam Hussein. Unconnectedly, it was announced that 'Tom King [the Defence Secretary] has told British troops they will be going home'. It was left to ITN to put a particular political gloss on the revolts: 'Islamic fundamentalists say they control Iraq's second biggest city, Basra,' it told its viewers, while film from Iran showed, it said, a 'fundamentalist' ayatollah speaking. Over eye-witness accounts from refugees, ITN reminded viewers that: 'A major Western concern is that Iraq could literally split apart.'[5]

By 5 March, the BBC was already reporting the crushing of revolt by Saddam's forces. Justin Webb, from a US camp seven miles inside Iraq, said that just a few miles on, the Revolutionary Guards 'are saying there is no problem in Basra'. At the US forward position, there were first-hand reports from refugees of the chaos in Basra and other towns. A refugee, asked 'Who's winning?' replied optimistically: 'The people. The people want Saddam down.' The difficulties of reporting were again noted: 'These are dangerous roads for those trying to find out independently what is going on.' Two Austrian reporters had been held by government troops. ITN also interviewed Kuwaiti refugees returning in cars: 'All they want to talk about is the fighting in Basra and Nasiriyah.' It reported how anti-Saddam feeling was growing—there was 'a growing revolution outside Baghdad'—and that US satellite pictures confirmed the revolt. A US spokesman talked wisely about the political unreliability of defeated armies. Over film of Iraqi prisoners and aerial pictures of abandoned trenches, viewers were told that 'returning soldiers will decide the fate of Saddam Hussein'.[6]

Although there was clearly a life and death struggle going on in Basra and other cities, television had no film and no first-hand reporting. To the broadcasters' credit, the story was a major one, to which they returned virtually every day, but the difficulty of direct coverage meant that this dramatic conflict rarely made the main lead over more mundane issues with a domestic angle. On 6 March, for example, both channels led with Iraq's freeing of allied prisoners and the BBC followed this with Major's visit to British troops in Kuwait. Both channels reported that government forces appeared to have regained control of Basra, and homed in on a former British army officer, Brock Matthews, freed from a Basra jail by insurgents. The BBC told us that 'his fears are now for the rebels'. According to Matthews, the army were now 'beating hell out of them': they had only small arms, and although the uprising hadn't yet been crushed, it might soon be. ITN, on the other hand, showed Matthews returning to his Kuwait flat and telling the story of his treatment in captivity, but curiously had nothing from him about the revolt. Only Ben Brown on BBC finally raised the obvious implication for the West which both channels had avoided all week, reporting that 'refugees coming out of Iraq are appealing to the allies to intervene on behalf of the resistance, before it's crushed'.[7]

Although in some places the revolt may have been crushed, in others it went on. The BBC reported the Red Cross going to Basra to organize the release of Western journalists held there (none of these seem to have been British); refugees were fleeing 'fighting which by all accounts has now been quelled by the Republican Guard'. Edward Stourton on ITN, however, expelled from Baghdad (where there was no uprising), mentioned the Iraqi opposition's claim that it was still in control of nine cities and voiced Western governments' worries about the Islamic 'tinge' to the revolt in Basra, together with the worry that 'Iraq might become another Lebanon'.[8]

After the first week of March, as it became clearer that there would be no quick victory for the rebels, film from the affected areas remained as elusive as ever. The story, while not disappearing as it did in most newspapers, slipped down the bulletins as other events—the Ribble Valley by-election, riots in Belgrade, elections in Albania, as well as other Gulf stories, took increasing precedence. Clearly things were still critical in Basra, as the Red Cross was barred from going there; the Iraqis released Kuwaiti prisoners early to avoid Red Cross intervention.[9] As US Secretary of State James Baker visited Kuwait, it was reported that mustard gas had been used by the regime in four towns—'Mr Baker has warned Iraq about chemical weapons, although it is unclear what America can do about it'—and Iraqi opposition leaders met Douglas Hogg, the British foreign office minister—'the new fighting is more turmoil for a country still recovering from weeks of bombing, with Saddam Hussein still apparently in power', the BBC opined.[10] Baker's visit provided an easily filmed focus for Middle East coverage over several days, as he toured various capitals, more concerned with the position of the Palestinians than the insurgents and civilian victims inside Iraq. Mentions of Basra became less frequent, and although a united Iraqi opposition conference in Beirut received attention, 'their unprecedented political cooperation has come too late to stave off defeat', viewers were told.[11]

As the initial interest in southern Iraq faltered, new evidence of fighting emerged in the Kurdish north, with the crucial difference that access for journalists, while not easy, was freer than in the south. As early as 12 March, the BBC had a (second-hand) film report from Kirkuk, over which it detailed opposition claims of success in the fighting; indeed it told viewers that there was 'every indication that fierce fighting continues both in the Kurdish north and the Shi'ite south', and that Iran had claimed that napalm was being used by government forces.[12]

After this, although presumably fighting was going on all over Iraq, it was several days before the story resurfaced. On 15 March, the BBC reported that the government's victory in Basra was somewhat less complete than had been suggested a week earlier: refugees claimed that although the army was in control of the city, the rebels held the suburbs; there was confusion and 'in many cases it is impossible to tell who is in control'. A deserter appealed to the West: 'I only wish the allied troops would go into Basra, and help the civilians'; but this isolated comment was not picked up in the commentary. Only at the end of the month, when the plight of Kurdish civilians became a catastrophe, did this sort of comment become commonplace and receive back-up from both reporters on the ground and anchors in the studios.

On 16 March, news bulletins were able to use film of Saddam Hussein's appeals for unity on Iraqi television. The BBC's voice-over led with 'Rebels say the fighting goes on', and said of Saddam's claims to be crushing the revolts, 'It's wishful thinking.' The opposition claimed to hold Basra and to be advancing in the north; their spokesman in London dismissed Saddam's claims. It seemed the BBC agreed: 'Isolated from reality, it now seems that Saddam Hussein is planning to fight to the end.' The story was backed by a report from Jonathan Charles in Iran, with film smuggled out of southern Iraq which 'shows the scale of the uprising', and 'shows the revolt is moving closer to the seat of the Iraqi government'. A doctor was shown saying that outside help, food and medicines, was needed urgently. Iranians, however, were told at prayers that the overthrow of Saddam is a matter for Iraqis alone—this is 'no comfort for the rebels'. In a separate report, Bush and Major also 'agreed that Saddam Hussein should go, but there is still no role for allied military in his removal'.[13]

By now the poll tax, a crucial referendum in Russia and even rising conflict in Yugoslavia vied for the attention of the news, and still information was scanty and mostly without visual support. A report that 18,000 people had been killed by napalm bombs, which probably could not be corroborated and of which there was no film, made only a brief item in the middle of a bulletin.[14] But on 18 March the BBC had video film of Kurdish successes in Irbil, now under control of *peshmerga* guerrillas. A Kurdish Democratic Party spokesman claimed that despite the US threat that Iraq should not use its planes, it was doing so against the rebels. There was news of other rebel successes: towns were in rebel hands only sixty miles to the south of Baghdad and all over northern Iraq.[15] On 20 March, there was film of Karbala, south of Baghdad, 'said to be sheltering from air attack', and on the following day there were pictures by Japanese television of Kurdish forces in Kirkuk—'they appear to be in total control'.[16]

Film reports were still isolated items, however, and no British television reporter had yet made it to the areas of conflict. The nearest they had reached was still the southern border, where refugees continued to flee into American-controlled territory. 'Iraqi refugees curse their president and say the allies should oust him,' ran the lead into one such story.[17] Despite the fact that this seemed to be the sort of thing that refugees said whenever they were allowed to speak direct to camera, such coverage was episodic. The demand for intervention received no consistent expression and was never put to British or Western politicians. If concerned viewers picked it up, there was no indication from the bulletins that it was politically relevant in the West.

The Chancellor of the Exchequer's annual budget statement on 19 March totally squeezed Iraqi news, and for several days the story struggled to become important. Even claims that Iraqi helicopters had dropped sulphuric acid only made the final item in a 22 March bulletin, alongside Iraqi calls for the lifting of restrictions on the import of food (conditions of civilians in Baghdad, as a result of coalition bombing, were a much more occasional item than the revolts).[18] Only on 23 March, alongside unconfirmed reports of unrest in Baghdad, did the BBC again give prominence to the Kurds' gains and the first strong indication that 'the Kurds' hold on the north may not be secure'. US intelligence forces were saying that Saddam Hussein was preparing to move the Republican Guards against the Kurds. Saddam was also winning in the south—'everyone is being killed', said resistance fighters in retreat. 'Their revolution, they said, needed outside help', reported Mike Donkin, but still this was an isolated comment, although the situation sounded grim: 'Through sheer fire power, Iraqi armed forces are reducing rebels to a ragged band.' Film showed refugees scrabbling for food distributed by Saudi soldiers. Soon this was to become almost a daily image.[19]

The following day, Western news programmes could again use official Iraqi pictures. Film had been broadcast of the devastation of Karbala, as a warning to other areas. 'The damage to one of the Muslim world's holiest cities is immense,' the BBC announced, linking the story to a call from a rebel leader for the UN to intervene. A 'decisive battle' was reported to be pending between the Kurds and the regime.[20] Meanwhile there was film of more refugees fleeing Basra (from the Shi'ite rebels), of tanks and personnel carriers and towns in rebel hands, and of Iranians at prayer—'death to Saddam'.[21]

Finally, on 26 March, the BBC had a reporter in Kurdistan and the issue of the Western role finally made it into the studio, although still the fifth item in the bulletin (possibly because the reporter could only file over a phone link). Alongside week-old film of Kurdish forces in control of Zakho and the return from exile of Kurdish leader Jalal Talabani was a report that the regime's forces were preparing to attack them. Jim Muir told Anna Ford that the Kurds 'are appealing to Western governments not to let Iraq use chemical weapons against them; but America's policy is still that it won't choose sides in Iraq's internal struggles', and that the 'Shi'ite rebellion appears to be dying away amid horrifying reports of mass executions.'

In the first clear studio prompt for intervention, Ford asked Muir: 'Jim, are they asking for any help from the West?' Muir replied, 'They certainly are, and they are very angry that United Nations aid is going through the Iraqi government. They're disappointed at the failure of the West to come to their aid, after they encouraged them to revolt against Saddam's rule.' Muir stressed, however, that the Kurds were not looking for military aid but political and humanitarian support.

This story was followed by a strong report from Baghdad on the 'apocalyptic human crisis' there, with secret film from the International Gulf Peace Team of sewage in the streets, even untreated sewage in the basement of a hospital, and commentary stressing the danger of cholera, critically low food supplies and the grave shortage of water—'aid workers have said there is little time left to avert a major human tragedy'. But this story did not often get this sort of airing.[22]

After this, the crisis of the Kurdish rebellion and the issue of Western responsibility rose rapidly up the news agenda. Film of Kurdish artillery suggested the rebels' advance, but tanks shooting back indicated the expected counter-attack. Despite Kurdish accusations of the regime using weapons indiscriminately (over film of children in hospital), 'America has said it cannot use the cease-fire agreement to keep Iraqi helicopters grounded' so 'Saddam Hussein is expected to use them to the full'. This story was backed by more evidence of the plight of refugees in the south, and eye-witness accounts of atrocities, the use of chemical weapons and the destruction of holy places. At the same time the BBC showed new film of a soldier's-eye-view of modern high-tech weaponry in the Gulf War without raising the question, however, of why the power used then could not be used to support the rebels.[23]

As the following day's report was to emphasize, the Kurds were lightly armed and faced up to 150,000 heavily armed government troops.[24] Although fresh uprisings were reported in the south, and many government troops were deserting, it was an 'ill-matched battle', and there was 'no sign of the aid or the weapons coming into the region which the Kurds would need to stand up to Saddam Hussein's army'.[25] The Kurds had lost Kirkuk, and Iran claimed that the civil war was 'a barbaric massacre of innocent people'. 'Kurds', the BBC reported in passing, 'have repeated their call to the international community to help them in their struggle.'[26]

By the last day of March 1991, the first reports of the refugee exodus were coming in. The BBC had at last not just a reporter, Michael Macmillan, but also a camera crew in northern Iraq. 'Thousands of Kurds', he reported, 'have fled to the mountains of northern Iraq to escape from Saddam Hussein's forces. ... The Kurds have accused the Iraqis of massacring civilians.' Distressed civilians were fleeing from Iraqi helicopter gunships. 'This is the weapon the Kurds fear most. What they can't quite work out is that the Americans are shooting down Iraqi fixed wing aircraft, and yet they are allowing helicopters to fly. And this is the result of the Iraqi offensive': at this point the film showed a burnt Kurdish child. Macmillan stressed the weakness of rebels, with only rifles against tanks, the shortage of food and the Iraqi armies getting closer.[27] On 1 April, he reported that 'hundreds of thousands of people have fled their homes'. The 'faces of refugees told of a terrifying fear ... while the rebels claimed victory'. The Kurdish leader, Talabani, had in fact fled to the mountains, as Kurdish leaders had before, but: 'This time they thought they'd get the help of the Allies to succeed.'[28]

Macmillan's stories had many of the ingredients of the weeks of intensive coverage which followed: the flight, the fear, the defencelessness of the refugees, the innocent victims, the failure of the West. The story of the revolts inside Iraq, which had struggled to maintain momentum for much of March, was poised to take off and dominate the news for days and weeks on end, for most of April. So long as the Shi'ites and Kurds were *insurgents* against the Iraqi regime, their story never fully engaged the attention of British television news. Now that they were being transformed into pure *victims*, Kurdish refugees (but not their Shia counterparts) engaged it as maybe no similar group has, before or since.

Day by day, the story grew bigger and bigger. On 2 April, the BBC reported the French call for a UN Security Council emergency meeting to discuss the Kurds, over a film report stressing that thousands were fleeing, the revolt was collapsing, and amidst eyewitness claims that 'they are shelling the civilians'. Once again, the US responsibility was raised:

> The American decision not to destroy Iraqi helicopter-gunships may have been a factor in the failure of the uprising; but in any case the Kurdish rebels were ill-equipped to take on a dictator who had inflicted such devastating suffering on them before, and was quite prepared to do it again.

The bulletin stressed that the Shi'ite rebellion had also been crushed, making many people refugees and once again brought up 'the difficult position the Americans find themselves in—occupying as they do 15 per cent of Iraq. ... They're witnessing scenes of extraordinary deprivation.'[29]

ITN was a little slower to catch up with the story; its late evening news on 1 April did not even mention it. But by 2 April it too was upping the stakes and pointing the finger at the White House. It had American film of deserted Kurdish towns—'and fleeing to the Turkish border, thousands of refugees'.

> And everywhere, the same question to the American cameraman. 'And constantly I was asked, When will the outside world come to our aid? And of course, I really couldn't give an answer.' The State Department gave an answer today. The United States will give food to the refugees and moral support to the rebels, but that's all. ... President Bush, fishing in Florida, is keeping the whole matter at arms' length. No American lives will be risked. The United States does not recognize the Kurds' right to self-determination.

Bill Nealy reported that a CNN journalist swimming across a river to Turkey had been fired on by Turkish troops: 'They got through. Tens of thousands of Kurds are trapped. They have only the mercy of a vengeful Iraqi president to rely on'.[30]

The following day, 3 April, was when the issue totally took over television news. It occupied almost a whole BBC bulletin. The main lead was a story which baldly stated: 'They've no escape: thousands of men, women and children face famine and death.' Two million were on the road in

> the Kurdish people's desperate journey. At the foot of the mountains, they abandon vehicles and walk ... the only hope they have, the young, the sick and the old ... temperatures are freezing and the refugees have virtually no supplies. At the end of the journey lies heartbreak: Turkey has closed the border ... a human catastrophe ... some have already died.

Tom Carver, by phone, filled in the graphic human detail: families digging in the snow for water to make tea ... women in childbirth ... old women in dressing gowns ... children crying with no shoes on because their feet were frozen. 'Propelled by hope and fear,' he said, *'they blame America and the West for not intervening to help them. The question they keep asking is: Why did not President Bush finish what he started?'* Television was putting world leaders on the spot, linking them directly to the visible plight of the miserable refugees, putting the victims' accusations against the powerful.

In this light, the Security Council debate on the French resolution to condemn the persecution of the Kurds simply magnified the leaders' failure: 'Despite the allies controlling a fifth of Iraq, diplomats say the UN Charter means it has to steer clear of interfering in Iraq's internal affairs to help the Kurds.' And to make sure the meaning of this was utterly clear the report added: *'The best the Kurds can hope for are some kind words and some humanitarian assistance.'* This was followed by film of a demonstration in Washington attacking Bush for abandoning the Kurds; then Bush himself was seen golfing. It was mentioned that Major had promised help to the Kurds, but he was upstaged by former prime minister Thatcher, shown receiving a Kurdish delegation, who 'wants action now': 'They need help and they need it now,' she said. Then there was film of a London demonstration against Bush's double standards; the Kurds want military as well as humanitarian aid, it is reported. Meanwhile, the relief agencies were 'hopelessly short' of the means to help the Kurds.[31]

ITN's report was in a very similar mould: 'Relief workers say the situation is catastrophic.' A quarter of a million people were trudging to the Turkish border—it was 'an exodus of fear'. 'There is also anger and bitterness at President Bush's refusal to intervene.' Fleeing journalists were interviewed: *'It's a problem that we really must ... we have an obligation to do something about.* They've been let down very, very badly.' 'They're running for their lives ... They've had no water or electricity since the beginning of the bombing by the Americans. They're absolutely desperate.'[32]

These reports had the essential ingredients of what was, effectively, a campaign which lasted for several weeks, although within a single week it was to achieve a major change in Western policy. The graphic portrayal of human tragedy and the victims' belief in Western leaders was skilfully juxtaposed with the responsibility and the diplomatic evasions of those same leaders to create a political challenge which it became impossible for them to ignore. Television reporters and anchors never said, as their leader-writing colleagues in the press did, that Western leaders *ought* to help the Kurds. They did not need to: by simply showing what was happening, and putting on it a strong, clear and unequivocal moral construction, they created an unanswerable case without ever generating a single editorial statement.

What remained was to *show* what these reports described. By 4 April, although they led with a domestic story, both channels had copious film from the mountainsides. On the BBC, 'From the air the huddled masses can be spotted. They've run from a man who wants to kill them towards a country that wants to avoid them.' There were more refugees on the Iranian than the Turkish border, and the Iranians would let the Kurds in— 'a ray of hope in an otherwise bleak situation.' The BBC made it very clear why the Kurds were in this desperate position: *'They had no end of determination to fight. They needed help, but it never came.'* They also gave a very high profile to the only Western agencies actively working for the Kurds, the humanitarian relief organizations. Their opinions of the situation were regularly quoted with great authority, and spokespeople for bodies like the Red Cross and Save the Children were interviewed, calling for co-ordinated international action. Intermingled with footage of desperate Kurdish civilians, was a simple and powerful message: 'They escaped Saddam Hussein's troops, but now the Kurds face new enemies—cold and starvation. The weakest are dying—the old and the children.' Meanwhile, Kurdish representatives in London 'say all the aid is too little, too late'. On the diplomatic front, President Bush is described as 'caught between his own rhetoric ... and America's obvious interest' in keeping out.[33]

ITN's Andrew Simmons also piled on the agony: 'This is a place where all hope has been lost. A mountainside, with nowhere else to go, and little else but caves for shelter.' And then the appeal: *'Amongst the despair and fear,*

there is also a deep anger among these people. … "We need all of the world to help."'
This is backed up with a picture of a child 'burnt in a napalm attack'. The
report stressed that temperatures were below freezing and most had no
protection. 'Now here in the place where they wanted sanctuary, they
could face the prospect of death through starvation or exposure.' Norman
Rees took it still further:

> A human tide of misery and bewilderment … just some of the estimated three
> million Kurds fleeing from Saddam's slaughtering army. From the air, the scale
> of this human disaster becomes apparent. Makeshift camps strung across
> freezing mountain ridges … most of them women and children … little food …
> here an undignified, humiliating scramble over the carcase of a donkey … time
> running out for children weakened by cold and hunger. … The Kurds have lost
> the battle *urged upon them by President Bush* to unseat Saddam Hussein. Now they
> throw their guns aside as they try to persuade the Turkish authorities to let them
> in. Mothers still persuade their children to smile for the camera, *perhaps believing*
> *that if the world is watching, it must be stirred into doing something.*

Once again, a powerful and emotive case was followed immediately by
an exposé of Western leaders' political shallowness. ITN showed the most
damning film of the official British abdication of responsibility for the crisis.
After a lead-in saying that Britain was sending £1 million of blankets with
£20 million to follow, it reported that according to John Major, 'there'll be no
intervention'. Major, was then shown saying in his most pathetic tones:

> What is happening in Iraq at the present time is very distressing, and it is
> malignant, I agree entirely with that thought. But it is also wholly within the
> borders of Iraq, and we have no international authority to interfere with that. We
> did have international authority to remove the Iraqis from Kuwait.

But, asked a reporter, hadn't the West encouraged the Kurds to rebel?
Major responded with the classic: '*I don't recall asking the Kurds to mount this*
particular insurrection. There is a civil war going on. … We hope very much
that the military in Iraq will remove Saddam Hussein.'
This revelation of ineptitude was followed by an interview with a
spokesperson for Save the Children who stressed that helicopters were
needed and that the USA had them. As if to stress that Major's insensitivity
was not unique, Alistair Stewart (from the studio) interviewed President
Ozal of Turkey, accusing him of letting down the Kurds; the bulletin then
turned its attention to Bush, accused by Kurdish leaders of 'standing by
and doing nothing'. The way Bush was described made it absolutely clear
what ITN thought: 'President Bush set off for California tonight, *turning his*
back on the muted protests at his policy towards the Kurds, determined not
to interfere. Nothing is being allowed to interfere with his celebration of
victory. *A few say, that's a betrayal.*' As if to underline ITN's endorsement of
this view, there followed interviews with Senator Al Gore—'we encouraged them to rise up'—and a Kurdish leader who simply asserted that,
'The Gulf allies have brought this calamity on the Kurds.'[34]

This was only the beginning of the campaign. The following day ITN had 'four exclusive reports'. The two most highly emotive were from Kurdistan. Simmons reported from a refugee camp: 'Another day and one day closer to death for the families of the Kurdish exodus. Conditions have worsened. ... It may be difficult to believe, but these people are being described as the lucky ones.' (Others are kept on the mountains by the Turkish army.)

> We were the first people from the outside world to visit the mountain refugees.... *There was little we could do to them except to make promises that we would convey to the outside world the fact that time has already run out for them.* ...The situation here is desperate beyond belief.

He interviews a paediatrician, who has nothing to offer people but makes a heartfelt plea in broken English: 'We expect helps from France, from Britannia, from America, from any country. We are very need helps.' As if this was not enough to sum up this 'human tragedy of colossal proportions', a 'woman with a seriously ill baby tried to sum the situation up. "Tell everyone they either save us or kill us."'

The second film, from Dahuk, focused on a child victim with a burnt face. Pictures showed people fleeing the town; a man on the mountainside called out, 'George Bush why don't you interfere with this? God help us.' The 'stream of barefoot humanity ... chose to risk death in the bitter cold in the mountains rather than risk the troops of Saddam. But at the end of the long march *there was no safe haven*, just a makeshift camp on the hillside.' Thus a week before Major's about-turn brought 'safe havens' into political debate, ITN was already defining this agenda. Once again, the plight of the Kurds was trenchantly connected to the inadequate world response: 'Tonight, another delay at the UN, *more time for the Kurds to suffer unrelieved*.' The Soviets and Chinese were blamed for blocking the French resolution backed by the USA and the UK, but Bush's anger at charges of betrayal—'I have not misled anybody about the intentions of the United States of America'—was also unconvincing given the context defined by the bulletin.[35]

Reports from elsewhere in Iraq were less effective simply because the channels' own journalists were not on the spot to build up the emotive picture of suffering and Western callousness or because the victims could not be *shown* suffering in the same way. In the same ITN bulletin, there were pictures from an Iraqi cameraman in Iran of refugees from Basra, victims of napalm attacks. It was said the rebels fought with weapons which were practically useless and 'as many as 100,000 may have died in the uprising', but like the figures at the end of the Gulf War, this did not carry the same weight as the news from Kurdistan because no one could be shown dying and no correspondents could build up the story. For the same reason, although many more Kurds fled to Iran than to Turkey, the reporting of the former was intermittent, and the television campaign built up almost entirely around the latter where correspondents had daily access.

The campaign was incessant, with the overwhelming suffering of the Kurdish people described in strong, emotive language; the simple, heartfelt pleas of individual refugees: 'We are need peace ... survive ... do something, all countries'; the graphic film of both individual predicaments—women who had given birth, old ladies who could not even stand—and collective desperation—the daily scramble for food, the Turkish soldiers with their brutality. The voices over these scenes underlined both the human situation: 'These people reached breaking point long ago' and the imperative for action: 'Survival will depend on food and adequate shelter reaching them soon.'[36]

Frequently the news gave prominence to the warnings of the humanitarian agencies: on 7 April the BBC led with the news that the International Red Cross 'has just said the situation is drastically deteriorating'. Commentary often highlighted the visual images by linking an explicit message to a particular visual image: 'Many have lost their shoes, many never had any in the first place. *It is an image of suffering which demands help now, but still there isn't anywhere near enough.*' Although the Kurds on the Turkish border were the focus of this unremitting campaign, occasional coverage of their fellow-sufferers on the Iranian side, or of the refugees in the south, buttressed the main coverage. During film of a protest in southern Iraq, where '10,000 refugees are trapped in no man's land', and whose fate 'couldn't be less certain' as the Americans withdraw, a man was shown saying, 'They are as good as dead', and *'People ask, why did President Bush only liberate Kuwait?'* The political point was being pressed home on Western leaders, although only the Kurds would substantially benefit from its eventual success.[37]

By 8 April, the worms were beginning to turn. Major had announced his proposal to create 'safe havens' and overseas aid minister Lynda Chalker claimed 'we're going full guns' (although this was not to be taken literally, only food, blankets and medicines were on their way).[38] *News at Ten* showed US Secretary of State Baker spending 'just ten minutes' at a refugee camp and uttering Majoresque banalities—'It's really quite a tragedy, that's my impression'—which were quickly exposed as inadequate both by the commentary and the filmed intervention of a refugee. 'He seemed stunned. Whoever had briefed him had quite obviously understated the scale of it all.'

A Kurdish man appealing to Baker directly made the media's pitch to the statesman as well as his own: 'and we have been on the ice all these days, and we are suffering, our children are suffering, from hunger and starvation. So you have got to make for us something, to help us.' Baker could only agree: 'We know that and we're going to do that.' But the man hadn't finished: 'You see, the first thing we want now, we don't have enough water supply here. We are thinking all the nations in the world, just to help all these people here.' Once again, Baker could only concur: 'We are going to mount a very large international effort just to do that.' The commentary underlined the point: *'Mr Baker can now be under no illusion. The worst is not over, it is getting worse.'*

The remainder of this bulletin underlined the political point with more graphic visual and verbal reminders: Turkish soldiers had shot a little girl dead; there were dangers of cholera and typhoid; people had napalm wounds; the very young and the old were most at risk. 'We watched this three-year-old girl dying.' Aid, it was made clear, was too little and too late: it was distributed by people scrambling over each other for food. 'This is the disgrace. All this way they have come to find shelter ... when really it ought to have been brought to them.' Michael Nicholson repeated the political point from the Baker report: the aid so far 'really is a drop in the ocean. What really is needed is massive international aid, and now, *just as Mr Baker promised today.*'[39]

Television did not let up because Major had made his move and the USA appeared ready to follow, nor was it yet ready to give them much credit, even if Major's move was seen as a 'coup' in political terms. The following day, the first ten minutes of BBC news were again direct from the Turkish border, with graphic film and commentary: 'babies, already weak because their mothers can no longer feed them, are the first to die'. The immediate political context was still dire: refugees were stopped from crossing the border by Turkish troops, so they couldn't get food; and they 'fear that in two or three days' time, Saddam Hussein's soldiers will come to kill them. ... All they want is a place to live in peace.' A Kurdish engineer repeated the main political demand: 'We want from George Bush and John Major to save us, to help us,' and the commentary underlined the gap between Baker's promises and the reality: 'Yesterday, US Secretary of State James Baker called for a massive international effort to help these people. Today, that aid still seems a long way away.' The report then cut to an item showing an RAF Hercules on an aid mission returning to base because of severe weather, before returning to the politics of intervention. An academic expert underlined the limitations of Major's proposal: 'The government is stressing that it does not support the creation of an autonomous Kurdistan.'[40]

On 10 April, television could report that Bush 'has finally been pushed into reversing his hands-off policy in Northern Iraq'. His spokesman, Marlin Fitzwater 'even fought shy of supporting Britain's idea of supporting enclaves for the Kurds', but announced that US troops would defend refugees and aid workers. John Major and Douglas Hurd, it was said, over film of Kurds on the mountainsides, were 'defending plans for a Kurdish enclave in Iraq' although 'the British plan still looks like partition and could involve long-term military involvement'. The USA was willing to provide protection from the air above the 36th parallel, but Major wanted to protect all Kurdistan, including Sulaymaniyah which was in Iraqi hands. This political activity was underlined by commentary which emphasized the brutality of the situation on the ground: 'This is the attitude of the Turkish military to the Kurds' (they had stopped a mother carrying her dead baby through a checkpoint). Michael Macmillan reported: 'We have seen children dying here today from cold and disease ...

a week after these people arrived here, there is no effective aid for them. The much talked of international aid effort has not yet begun. And time is now running out.' Although some aid was getting through—the RAF Hercules aircraft prevented from flying the previous day were now accompanied on a successful mission—refugees were being injured in the dash for the supplies which were dropped.[41]

The days which followed showed the story remaining the main lead (or when some domestic issue pipped it to the top of the bulletin, the longest item), usually with the same pattern of the latest political developments backed up by lengthy film of the desperate situation on the ground. Gavin Essler, from Washington, neatly summed up the US (and British) position as that *'they want to help the Kurds to survive, without actually helping them in the civil war'* (by now, mention of continued fighting was becoming rarer). The emerging Western plan, it appeared, was 'drastically scaled back from John Major's original scheme and depends on Iraqi support'. The US reluctance to use force was set against the realities: 'children continue to die here of starvation and severe cold; yet another mother has lost her baby'; 'it is suffering on a terrible scale'; 'even at the bottom of the mountains, weather conditions are appalling'. In the end, however, the complexities of the political and military situation were not of central concern to the broadcasters, either: *'The task tonight is to save lives.'*[42]

By 12 April, the details of what the USA would back were becoming clearer: over film of refugees scrabbling for food, the BBC argued that it was 'the first step away from the daily fight for life for refugees'. While Major was 'still talking up Britain's plan', what the US proposed 'was much less than the Kurdish enclave he was proposing last week'. The USA, moreover, was withdrawing from the south of Iraq just as it engaged in the north. Nevertheless, the strength of American feeling was represented by Congressman Stephen Solarz announcing that: 'Fundamental American values are at stake. The principle of non-intervention in the internal affairs of other countries cannot be used as a rationale for paralysis when a government which clearly lacks legitimacy is engaged in the annihilation of its own people.'

Coverage on the ground was now shifting from the sheer misery of the people to the contradictions of the aid effort: people being killed by air-drops; the shortage of helicopters; the impassable state of muddy tracks; the desperate conditions of makeshift hospitals. Aid was coming, 'but it seems too little, too late. ... A woman in the hospital with a sick child mourns for another who's already dead. She says she's ready to tear her eyes out with grief. After days and weeks in the mountains, their strength has almost gone.' A spokeswoman for Save the Children, one of the agencies which received most coverage, claimed that the death rate was worse than Ethiopia at its worst and called for the Turkish government to allow more refugees down from mountains. A Turkish spokesman defended what the report called 'its apparently callous treatment' of the Kurds.[43]

As the large-scale efforts of the agencies were increasingly supplemented by governments, the plight of the refugees remained acute and the political situation, both in Iraq and among Western governments, uncertain. While most newspapers largely dropped the issue after Major's and Bush's eventual recognition of the crisis, television news continued to show dramatic film of the refugees' plight. Visits to Kurdistan by the overseas aid minister, Linda Chalker—who linked aid for the Kurds in Iran to Iranian help over British hostages in Lebanon—and her Labour Opposition counterpart, Ann Clwyd—who more daringly ventured into areas of fighting—gave a political dimension to the coverage. There were also reports of further fighting in Basra, refugees flowing into the demilitarized zone, and sit-down protests as refugees tried 'to persuade the Americans to stay'; but coverage of this downside to the reluctant US intervention in northern Iraq was much more limited and intermittent.[44] John Simpson also filled out the BBC's coverage with a series of reports from government-controlled areas.

In mid-April, the Kurdish refugees were still the main story and there was still harrowing and emotive coverage of their plight: 'At first light, the bodies of the children who died in the night are brought down from the mountain...'; 'people without hope, whose strength has gone, lie next to piles of human excrement and wait for death'; 'it was easy for a camera crew and a foreign journalist to get past the soldiers at the border. ... We left Ahmed with his mother, struggling for his life.'[45] There was increasing reflexive commentary on television's own role: the BBC showed a refugee family with dying babies but watching television: 'They watch the world they think has abandoned them' and interviewed an RAF man: 'Sitting at home watching it on telly before we came—you're so remote, you can't tell, but now, you just want to help.'[46] The critique of Bush was still strong:

> If Kuwait saw the best of George Bush, the Kurdish crisis has been far from his finest hour. *Day by day, the President has pursued other things ... fishing, relaxing, while allies and domestic critics have pushed his reluctant administration into action in northern Iraq ... at every stage he gives the impression he wishes it would just go away and he could bring his boys home.*[47]

Major, on the other hand, was getting some credit, at least from his own party.

Every day for three weeks, the refugees had dominated television news. In the last ten days of April, the coverage became a little less strong, although the story was still a major one. As Western troops and humanitarian agencies began to take control of the situation in northern Iraq, some of the political tension was going out of the issue. Occasional reports highlighted continuing contradictions: Chalker, for example, was shown visiting refugees, 'but they told her that they wanted more than food and shelter. *"We want some help to fight Saddam Hussein."*' Her prim reply highlighted the limitations not only of her government's response but of much of the television campaign: 'We understand that very well, but we *must keep you fed and clothed.'*[48] As British troops settled in, with predictable media attention, journalists also talked to the *peshmerga* who appealed for weapons to fight Saddam. There was also new attention to the neglected refugees existing 'in pitiful conditions' in Iran—'it's an exodus at least as twice as large as that near Turkey'—but this situation never became a major focus.[49] Too late, Simpson made it to Basra, to a landscape devastated by the allies, the rebels and the Iraqi army, and where 'the people who are left face a new scourge', cholera and typhoid. 'It's almost more than they can take.'[50]

In the last week of April, attention increasingly focused on Western troops' encounters with the remaining Iraqi forces in Kurdistan, Kurdish leaders' attempts to deal with Saddam Hussein (on which the BBC expressed considerable scepticism) and Kurdish fears (highly understandable in view of what the US had done in southern Iraq) of an allied withdrawal. There was conflict between Western troops and Kurdish militants who wanted the allies to extend their control southwards. 'The Royal Marines', the BBC pointed out 'are extending their control to reassure the refugees, not to create a safe haven for the rebels in Iraq's civil war.'[51] Moving hundreds of thousands of refugees down from mountains would be a 'daunting task'.[52] There were reports, too, which suggested the difficulty for refugees of returning to their homes, especially to a village destroyed by napalm and orchards ruined by chemical attack: 'Returning to this village will be a difficult, if not depressing experience.'[53]

It was time too for more reflective reporting. 'The President is defusing an issue which called into question his very victory in the Gulf War', Essler reported from Washington, while Simpson noted that: 'By comparison with the Kurds, the predicament of the Shi'ite people has had very little attention in the outside world. *That is not surprising; there have been no pictures of the suffering of the Shi'ite refugees;* the Iraqi government has seen to that.' But, Simpson pointed out, the Shi'ite rebellion 'was far greater and cost many more lives than the Kurdish uprising'.[54]

Notes and references

1. BBC1 and ITN (ITV, not Channel 4) bulletins were studied in the video archive of the University of Leeds Institute of Communications Studies. The ULICS archive on the Gulf, which is much more extensive for January–February 1991, contains all BBC1 and ITN bulletins to the end of April 1991. Italicized sections in quotations from these bulletins are my emphases, rather than emphases in the originals.

2. BBC1, *Six O'Clock News*, and ITN, *News at Ten*, 1 March 1991.

3. BBC1, early evening news, 2 March 1991.

4. BBC1, late evening news, 3 March 1991.

5. BBC1, *Nine O'Clock News* and ITN, *News at 5.40*, 4 March 1991.

6. BBC1, *Six O'Clock News*, and ITN, *News at 5.40*, 5 March.

7. BBC1, *Six O'Clock News* and ITN, *News at 5.40*, 6 March.

8. BBC1, *Six O'Clock News* and ITN, *News at Ten*, 7 March.

9. BBC1, *Six O'Clock News*, 8 March.

10. BBC1, 9.25 pm, 9 March 1991.

11. BBC1, *Six O'Clock News*, 12 March 1991.

12. BBC1, *Six O'Clock News*, 12 March 1991.

13. BBC1, late evening news, 16 March 1991.

14. BBC1, early evening news, 17 March 1991.

15. BBC1, *Nine O'Clock News*, 18 March 1991.

16. BBC1, *Nine O'Clock News*, 20 March 1991 and *Six O'Clock News*, 21 March 1991.

17. BBC1, *Six O'Clock News*, 21 March 1991.

18. BBC1, *Nine O'Clock News*, 22 March 1991.

19. BBC1, late evening news, 23 March 1991.

20. BBC1, early evening news, 24 March 1991.

21. BBC1, *Six O'Clock News*, 25 March 1991.

22. BBC1, *Six O'Clock News*, 26 March 1991.

23. BBC1, *Nine O'Clock News*, 27 March 1991.

24. BBC1, *Six O'Clock News*, 28 March 1991.

25. BBC1, *Six O'Clock News*, 29 March 1991.

26. BBC1, *Nine O'Clock News*, 30 March 1991.

27. BBC1, *Six O'Clock News*, 31 March 1991.

28. BBC1, early evening news, 1 April 1991.

29. BBC1, *One O'Clock News*, 2 April 1991.

30. ITN, *News at Ten*, 2 April 1991.

31. BBC1, *Nine O'Clock News*, 3 April 1991.

32. ITN, 12.30 pm, 3 April 1991.

33. BBC1, *Six O'Clock News*, 4 April 1991.

34. ITN, *News at Ten*, 4 April 1991.

35. ITN, *News at Ten*, 5 April 1991.

36. BBC1, late evening news, 6 April 1991.

37. BBC1, early evening news, 7 April 1991.

38. BBC1, *Nine O'Clock News*, 8 April 1991.

39. ITN, *News at Ten*, 8 April 1991.

40. BBC1, *Nine O'Clock News*, 9 April 1991.

41. BBC1, *Nine O'Clock News*, 10 April 1991.

42. BBC1, *Nine O'Clock News*, 11 April 1991.

43. BBC1, *Six O'Clock News*, 12 April 1991.

44. BBC1, late evening news, 13 April 1991.

45. BBC1, *Nine O'Clock News*, 15 and 17 April 1991.

46. BBC1, *Nine O'Clock News*, 15 and 16 April 1991.

47. BBC1, *Nine O'Clock News*, 16 April 1991.

48. BBC1, *Nine O'Clock News*, 19 April 1991.

49. BBC1, *Nine O'Clock News*, 22 April 1991.

50. BBC1, *Nine O'Clock News*, 23 April 1991.

51. BBC1, *Nine O'Clock News*, 28 April 1991.

52. BBC1, *Nine O'Clock News*, 30 April 1991.

53. BBC1, *Nine O'Clock News*, 29 April 1991.

54. BBC1, *Nine O'Clock News*, 26 April 1991.

CHAPTER EIGHT

Newspapers, ideology and representation

While television coverage tended to homogeneity and was not informed by highly distinctive editorial stances, newspapers editorialized and their coverage—despite homogenizing tendencies produced by media management and a common support for the war—was differentiated by the contrasting positions, styles and ethos of the papers. Differences between newspapers were consistently identifiable and were part of marketing and ideological strategies to maintain and extend readerships and influence.

While television played the main part in creating images of the war and disseminating basic information to the largest number of people, a thesis of this book is that the press had a very significant role in informing attitudes and responses in British society. In this chapter, I show how different papers dealt with the contrasting issues arising from the Iraqi wars, by considering their glosses on the television coverage and the attitudes they struck. To simplify the account, I concentrate on English national dailies,[1] not dealing with the Scottish, local, regional, Sunday and weekly press, although papers within each category made distinctive contributions. This analysis is linked in Part IV to evidence which suggests that newspaper readership was strongly and systematically related to differences in attitudes to the war in the population.

Down in the 'patriotic' gutter: the *Sun*, *Star* and *Sport*

At the lower end of the tabloid market were mass-readership papers which not only sensationalized and trivialized the war as entertainment but carried blatant patriotic propaganda. Britain's largest-circulation tabloid daily, Rupert Murdoch's *Sun* , fully lived down to its reputation during the Gulf crisis. The paper which won notoriety in the Falklands War with its 'Gotcha!' headline (over the sinking of the Argentine battleship *Belgrano*) adopted a highly stereotypical approach to Iraq. Saddam Hussein was 'THE DEVIL'S CHILD' who 'lusted for blood', was 'hooked on murder', was a 'mad dog', 'barking mad'; 'so crazy he is the most dangerous man in the world' according to 'a top psychologist'; the 'BASTARD OF BAGHDAD' who should be hung 'long and slow'.[2]

The *Sun*'s unique contribution to strategy was its advocacy of using nuclear weapons. A tasteless joke calendar for Iraq, headed 'DOOMSDAY', showed no dates after 15 January 1991. 'The use of tactical nuclear weapons in the Gulf will NOT mean the annihilation of Baghdad's five million people,' the paper reassured its readers in a calmer moment, and a 'readers' phone-in' on the brink of war revealed 49 per cent in favour of using nuclear weapons.[3] The paper returned to the theme as 'The *Sun*'s General Perkins' argued that: 'A series of shells could wipe out the entire 120,000-strong elite Iraqi Republican Guard.'[4] This nuclear cocktail was offered in a climate of fear, with the paper predicting that half of Britain's 35,000 troops could be hospitalized.

Although the USA dominated the coalition, for the *Sun* this was a patriotic conflict, a re-run of the Falklands. Its 16 January front page was a Union Jack with a soldier's head in the middle and the message: 'SUPPORT OUR BOYS AND PUT THIS FLAG IN YOUR WINDOW.' The flag became a daily masthead for 'THE PAPER THAT BACKS OUR BOYS'. The effect of this patriotic appeal was questioned: one observer reported that

> During the last three weeks I have been out and about in Southport, Liverpool and Manchester, in Hackney, Brixton and Bethnal Green. Scarcely a Sun Tommy Atkins poster celebrating 'our Heroes' have I seen blu-tacked to a window or wall. ... Could it be that the true mood of the people is not to Go Get 'Em Boys but to ask instead: What are we doing there? When will it stop? What good is going to come of it?[5]

If this was true, the *Sun* gave little sign of noticing. It backed 'brave' British 'lads', denouncing foreigners (French and Belgian appeasers and 'GERMANS HELPING TO GAS US AGAIN. They helped Iraq hit Jews'[6]) and all suspected of a lack of patriotism: Labour leaders, backbenchers and councils (although Kinnock, depicted as a 'British defector' in early January, had become a hero by late February);[7] minor royals like Prince Andrew and his wife, 'Fergie', accused of living it up while the nation rallied to war (although by mid-February, the paper was hypocritically urging the press to 'Get off their Royal backs');[8] and most unpleasantly, British Muslims. The *Sun*'s hate campaign focused on Muslim workers who objected to its flags posted in the workplace and 'FANATICAL British Muslims who have called for a holy war of vengeance after the shelter attack'.[9] In a full-page feature, the paper asked, 'WITH FRIENDS LIKE THESE, WHO NEEDS ENEMIES ... BRIT MUSLIMS PRAYING FOR SADDAM TO WIN.'[10]

The *Sun*'s contribution to patriotism was sexual titillation for 'our boys'. Starting with a 'Page 3 girl' wearing nothing but a *Sun* Union Jack T-shirt, the paper's regular scantily clad feature was devoted to patriotic sexual teasers until, in early February, the paper probably judged that readers were bored and dropped them (the war had generally left the front page by now). Although it also featured women soldiers, army wives and mothers with soldiers' babies, the sexual motif was predictably stronger.

The *Sun* was the most blatant of the papers in its distortion of the Amiriya shelter attack, failing to cover the actual events while telling its readers:

Saddam Hussein tried to trick the world yesterday by saying hundreds of women and children died in a bomb attack on an 'air raid shelter'. He cunningly arranged TV scenes designed to shock and appal. But the victims were sent to their deaths by the Iraqi leader himself. Hours later, Allied chiefs had shot down his story.[11]

The *Sun* was too busy celebrating US General Norman Schwarzkopf football-style as 'MAN OF THE MATCH' and attacking John Major for failing to hold a victory parade even to cover the Mutla Gap massacre.[12] The paper also ignored the Shia uprising and was slow to pick up on the Kurdish revolt, only mentioned once or twice in March. Finally on 4 April, an inside-page story told of 'Saddam blitz on freedom convoy' and a small editorial argued, 'Help them now', with tents, food, blankets, but not, the *Sun* argued, guns or troops. Patriotism had now become selfish as the paper proclaimed, 'If the UN decides to heed the French call to arm them, count us out. Britain has done its share in the Gulf.'[13] The paper then made matters worse by arguing 'Bush right to put golf before Gulf'—'President Bush and the West are NOT responsible for the tragedy of Iraq ... he never promised military intervention'.[14] After this, coverage was minimal until Major's U-turn, when the *Sun* was quick to claim that he had 'scored a triumph' with his safe havens plan. By this point, the paper had reverted to its more sophisticated position on Saddam: 'Bump him off.'[15]

The *Sun* was not alone in its approach. Its nearest rival, the *Daily Star*, responded in kind but with two political nuances: it was less consistently racist and did not advocate nuclear weapons—although it was not above this editorial comment: 'surely the latest Gulf joke is the sickest yet: Q: Have you heard the weather forecast for Baghdad on Wednesday? A: Very cloudy and 3000 degrees Centigrade. Like it, Saddam?'[16]

As the *Star* was targeted at younger, especially Northern working-class men, its coverage was if anything even more 'macho' and less 'serious' than the *Sun*'s. Its formula was simple: weapons on the front page, 'tits' inside. Its masthead showed a Union Jack with 'GO GET 'EM BOYS' over it; a silhouette of a warplane partially covered the word 'Star'. Its demonology of Saddam Hussein played the Hitler card: 'The changing face of evil Saddam' showed him turning into Hitler in four photographs.[17]

The *Star*'s secondary targets were familiar Europeans ('Why must our boys fight for these Euro cowards?'), Tony Benn and the Church of England (because the Archbishop of York urged prayers for Iraq). Like the *Sun*, the paper regularly used the sexual angle, with topless 'Starlets' selling giant *Star* yellow ribbons. A particularly nasty story exploited one soldier's children:

Little Christine and Rachael Wadeson are too young to know the real meaning of war—but they know their brave soldier daddy's got a job to do. Four year old Christine took just two sentences to sum up why the man in her life is so far away: 'Daddy's in the Gulf, he's got to kill that nasty man.'[16]

Not to be outdone on the Amiriya bombing, the *Star* proclaimed:

> SACRIFICED. Saddam herds his people to die in military bunker: Saddam Hussein pulled the cruelest con trick of the Gulf War yesterday. ... He knew the bunker was a top-priority military target and due to be hit by American Stealth bombers. He deliberately sacrificed them and then stage-managed a TV circus to convince the world there had been an Allied atrocity. He even arranged for 'grief stricken' relatives to be on hand when the foreign news teams were brought to the bunker by Iraqi publicity officers. The 'relatives' all spoke English and wailed into the cameras and microphones—but none of them wept.[17]

Like the *Sun*, the *Star* had no coverage of Mutla Gap.

While it headlined Major's remarks 'hoping that his own people will deal with him in the way he deserves'—RID THE WORLD OF THIS TYRANT. Angry Iraqis urged: Rise up and topple mad Saddam'[18]—the *Star* wholly failed to cover the uprising that actually occurred in southern Iraq! Only in late March did it give a front-page warning, 'GENOCIDE', repeated when Margaret Thatcher made her plea for the Kurds. The paper was easily impressed by the smallest gestures, believing that 'the dithering UN were shamed by John Major as he pledged £1m for the suffering Kurds'. It noted that 'those squawking loudest for us to make our lads fight for the Kurds were the same ones squawking for Stormin' Norman to stop when Baghdad was at his mercy'.[19] Stories about the Kurds were usually on page two, opposite a topless girl on page three, and they quickly faded out of the paper altogether.

The *Sun* and *Star* seemed like caricatures of tabloids in their sensationalizing and distortion of the war, but there was also a caricature of these caricatures in the sex-and-sport *Sunday Sport*. The flavour of its coverage can be gauged from these headlines: 'SADDAM IN GAY LOVER STORM' ('Furious Moslems last night accused America of a gay smear campaign'); 'SADDAM CABBIES INSULT TO BRITS' ('Fanatical Moslem cabbies have outraged a British town by pinning up pictures of detested tyrant Saddam Hussein in their taxis'); 'MAD SAD'S MUM ON GAME' ('Whoring Mum's past sent Saddam insane'); 'BUTCHER'S MEAT' (over a photograph captioned: 'Burning hell ... severely burned bodies line a Baghdad hospital—victims of the allied bombing raids and martyrs to sicko Saddam's quest for power'); and 'I'M GONNA SNUFF OUT MY DAD, SAYS MAD SAD'S LOVECHILD'. No wonder that the Imperial War Museum wanted a file of *Sports* for its Gulf War collection: as Dr Alan Borg, its Director, was alleged to have said: 'These papers are items of immense historical and sociological value and a priceless addition to the nation's cultural and historical heritage.'[20]

A rival in depth? The *Daily Mirror*

The *Daily Mirror* faced a problem as it tried to project patriotism while differentiating itself from its rivals. Its readership was older, more traditionally working class and Labour-voting than either the *Sun*'s or

Star's. The paper itself supported Labour and had to deal with the party's dilemmas as well as its own. Partly, doubtless, because a pose of moral superiority was more likely to be successful than trying to beat the *Sun* at its own game, the *Mirror* positioned itself on distinct political terrain. Although the *Mirror*'s patriotic indulgence of the war has led critics to dismiss its differences from the *Sun*,[21] taking its coverage as a whole it is clear that it was fighting a different campaign.

Editorials were quite clear on the need for the war: by January it was 'Too late for the Labour Party ... to plead for more time for sanctions to have an effect ... fighting to win in the shortest possible time is the only sane choice. ... This is what Mr Kinnock and Mr Kaufman should tell the Shadow Cabinet.'[22] Despite this strong stance, the paper gave space to the left-wing alternative, reporting Tony Benn's anti-war plea 'straight' the next day.[23]

On the eve of war, the *Mirror* matched its rivals in patriotism, with huge pictures of 'THE HEROES' (a 'young corporal'—'my biggest worry is if I see one of my mates get killed'—and a 'veteran RAF pilot'—'It would be a helluva end to my career to KO Saddam') and 'THE VILLAIN' (over a picture of Saddam Hussein with the quote: 'We will make them swim in their own blood'). Even so, inside John Diamond's column asked, 'Just what will our lads be dying for? It's hard to make a good case for one soldier's death.'[24] Like Labour, the *Mirror* was trying to have its cake and eat it. The paper's demonization of Saddam also reached down to its rivals' level—'He's as mad as Hitler' (quoting the same psychologist used by the *Sun*)—and invited readers to 'Make a mug of yourself', with a front-page cut-out 'ugly plastic mask' of Saddam Hussein.[25]

Its political line was otherwise quite distinct, however, stressing inter-party unity and reporting prayers and even protests for peace in a favourable light. Where the *Star* glorified weapons, a *Mirror* report highlighted 'a battlefield stocked with every diabolical device it is possible to concoct'. A double-page spread on the bombing of Baghdad stressed: 'Bombers drop twice as much explosive as it took to flatten Dresden. THE BIGGEST BLITZ MANKIND HAS EVER SEEN.' 'But the Baghdad blitz spared civilians' through computer targeting, the paper reassured. Coverage also stressed bomber crews' anxieties—'We went in as low as we dared, dropped the bombs and ran like HELL'[26]—and pity for their victims—

> 'Jesus God', whispered the young marine as the 155-mm howitzers roared and the desert earth trembled beneath. 'Jesus God, have pity on their souls. ... You want to damage the enemy, you want to kill him and destroy his might. But remember, those are human beings under that firestorm. Damn, I hate that man Saddam for leading his country to death.'[27]

The *Mirror* was up-front in attacking its rivals. Columnist Joe Haines argued that

> the gung-ho squad insult our soldiers: What they don't deserve is the tacky competition between the *Star* and the *Sun* to prove which is the most

nauseatingly gung-ho. ... The *Sun*, as ever, has the superior flair for the sewer. It is urging its readers to 'flash your knickers for Our Brave Boys' and inviting them to send a cheeky (geddit?) snap of themselves 'showing your knickers for the lads.' This is not only insulting to women, though some will be silly enough to accept the invitation. Even more, it demeans the servicemen in the Gulf. It portrays them as lusters after glimpses of the thighs of women they have never met, mindless, sex-mad morons whose morale can only be maintained by amateur soft porn.[28]

If soft porn was missing from the *Mirror*, however, this was only because its sexual appeal was more demure, its beauties in bathing costumes. Even before the war, the *Mirror* had sent pictures of 'Kerry, the eyeful on parade' to the troops.[29]

The *Mirror*'s 'home front' coverage was more balanced than its rivals'. It headlined 'Defiant Britons still fly the flag' (council chiefs ordering flags down so as not to offend Muslims) and parents criticizing a headteacher who banned Gulf War games: 'It's natural for little boys to play war games.' But it also reported the 'ORDEAL OF KIDS WHO FACE WAR HATE. Thousands of children with common Muslim name of Hussein are being tormented by their classmates.'[30] Political coverage included Labour criticism of the war, the role of Britain in supplying weapons to Iraq, cuts in troops' pay and criticism of 'victory' celebrations. The *Mirror* also continued Paul Foot's column, which was unashamedly anti-government, and made more than its rivals of the 'friendly fire' deaths in which British soldiers were killed by US planes. Bell notes, however, that Foot never used his column for an all-out attack on the war and speculates that he was kept in check by his editor.[31]

Certainly, the *Mirror* was trying hard not to appear too critical. Haines wrote, 'I don't want to appear unfeeling, but the constant harping on civilian deaths in Iraq verges on hysteria.'[32] (No stories of civilian deaths had appeared in the *Mirror* at this point.) The Amiriya bombing challenged the paper's balancing act: interestingly it was the *second* front-page lead. The paper led with a photograph of a victim under the neutral heading, 'WHOSE FAULT? "500 dead" in shelter; Slaughter, says Iraq; Military target, say US.' Alone among tabloids it corroborated television journalists' accounts: 'Whatever the truth, there was no disguising the horrific scenes of civilians incinerated in the worst incident yet of the Gulf War. ... *Correspondents said they could see no evidence of any military presence inside the wreckage.*'[33] The *Mirror* didn't follow up the story and even Foot's column failed to deal with it.[34]

The *Mirror* was probably the only tabloid to bring up (during the conflict) the Iraqi death toll: 'HORROR TOLL MAY NEVER BE KNOWN. ... The cost in human life in the conflict showed dramatic differences between the two sides last night. Iraqi casualties are of horrific proportions.' The paper estimated that possibly 20,000 soldiers had died and reported that the Red Cross 'has revealed that civilian casualties in Iraq are "far higher" than those announced by Baghdad. Even with the "smart" laser-guided weapons, some homes, schools and mosques have been hit.'[35] This was an important report, and the paper also had a front-page story on a British bombing error—'We hit a town by mistake admits RAF.'[36]

Mutla Gap, on the other hand, was mentioned only in a report entitled, 'SNATCHED BY THE BRUTES. Retreating Iraqis flee with 5,000 hostages on death road.' 'It was feared' said the paper, 'that some of the hostages would have been caught in the fire that rained down on the Iraqis.' Nevertheless the *Mirror* unusually gave some idea of the slaughter: a US pilot was quoted as saying, 'They were like sitting ducks. It was like the road to Daytona Beach on a holiday. Bumper to bumper.'[37]

The *Mirror* had a little more coverage of the Iraqi insurrections after the war than its rivals. A double-page spread, 'MOTHER OF REVOLUTIONS', dealt with the Basra revolt, but this contained nothing on the Allied refusal to intervene.[38] Only later did Foot comment: 'The US forces in Iraq drew back to allow the hated Republican Guard access to Basra to smash the insurrection there,' and quoted US and British official sources saying that the Shi'ite and Kurdish insurrections were not good for the West.[39] Since at this point the paper had had no reports on the revolts for twelve days, readers may have had little idea what Foot was writing about. It was an isolated comment, and for two weeks afterwards the *Mirror* reverted to silence.

Only in April did an editorial puncture this to proclaim: 'Britain should not allow the slaughter in Iraq to go on for one more day. ... Why must we wait?' This was followed by the *Mirror*'s only full front-page coverage of the Kurds which reported: 'YOU MEN. Do something for these doomed people, says Thatcher', with pictures of Bush, 'ZZZZ', gone fishing, Major, 'ZZZZ', gone watching football—contrasted with some Kurds: 'Help please, we're dying'. This time the editorial—'And STILL we stand by'—compared Saddam's massacre of the Kurds to the Nazis' murder of six million Jews.[40] The *Mirror* was certainly more assertive in its support for the Kurds than its closest rivals, but its coverage was minimal compared to television's. On 6 April the banner heading, 'WHO WILL SAVE US,' referred not to a picture of the Kurdish airlift but to a larger one of monkeys at London Zoo.

The mid-market tabloids

The mid-market tabloids, the traditionally Conservative *Daily Express* and *Daily Mail* and the newer, politically looser *Today*, faced fewer political dilemmas than the *Mirror*. They articulated the same nationalist ideology as the *Sun*, but their approaches, imagery and language were more restrained: chauvinist but not overtly racist and concerned more with the 'family bond' of male soldiers to women rather than the 'sexual bond' of the gutter press.[41] The violence of the war made occasional appearances, although these were only glimpses.

The *Express*, traditionally a Tory imperialist paper, was the most robust in its support of the war. Like the *Sun*, it attacked the Belgians as 'cowardly', the Germans for chemical deals with Iraq and Labour for 'turning soft on Iraq'. Not for it the government's 'understanding' approach to Kinnock's 'balanced' pro-sanctions, pro-war stance: 'Labour-split Kinnock faces both ways', the *Express* claimed, in 'an impossible balancing act'.[42] The paper made light of the plight of Iraqi and Palestinian detainees in Britain, headlining the '"Holiday camp" life-style of our Iraqi prisoners'.[43] Its war-prose was traditionally patriotic (Shakespeare's 'those at home now a-bed shall think themselves cursed', from *Henry V*) and its scorn for peace campaigners routine. Of all tabloids, the *Express* was most consistent in presenting the land war in narrowly national terms—'DESERT RATS HIT GUARDS'—as though it was a duel between the elite forces of Britain and Iraq.[44]

However, the *Express* defended the Royals from its tabloid rivals; avoided the overt racism which soiled the gutter press; and was the only tabloid to feature the West's unsung Arab allies with a rare feature on a 'Saudi dogfight hero'. The features on servicemen's spouses were more upmarket, with photos of a Brigadier's wife, and conservative coverage of women in the forces, asking, 'Should women be up at the frontline?'[45] Columnist Jean Rook even presented 'Hero Norman [Schwarzkopf]' as 'a wanting woman's fantasy conquest'.[46] Like all the mid-market papers, it pandered to environmentalism and animal welfare concerns with photo-spreads of oilstricken cormorants.

One report from its Riyadh correspondent pointed out that blood was the 'missing element' of the 'video games' and 'computer images hiding the real horror of conflict':

> Despite raids which can drop 5,000 tons of explosives on Iraq each day—more than the 4,200 tons dropped in total on Dresden in the horrific fire-bombing of 1945, more than Vietnam at the height of the US offensive—not a single body has yet been photographed, nor a single injured soldier seen on TV.[47]

It pointed out that the Republican Guard are targets 'of the 2000-lb bombs of the B-52s, that gouge out craters 36 ft deep and 50 ft across, send shrapnel flying 1500 ft, and blow out eardrums more than a mile away', aimed at demoralizing and forcing surrender.

This was however an isolated feature, suggesting that 'the unspoken battle to tell it like it really is', which the reporter argued occurred daily in briefings between military spokesmen and media, may have extended to *Express* editorial offices.[48] Early in February, the paper was hard on 'media fifth columnists', the television journalists in Iraq: 'Everything the broadcasters send back from Iraq serves Saddam's propaganda purposes. He would allow nothing else.'[49]

The *Express* had no difficulty, therefore, in proclaiming of the Amiriya bombing: 'IT WAS A MILITARY BUNKER', although its report more accurately noted that 'Saddam Hussein was last night *accused* [emphasis added] of deliberately sacrificing hundreds of women and children in a military bunker he knew was the target for Allied bombers.' Its editorial moreover posed the question, 'Was it a civilian shelter, as the Iraqis say, or a military bunker, and therefore a legitimate target, as the Coalition maintains?' only to conclude that 'it would be a brave individual who decided it was safe to take Baghdad's word. However, the BBC TV reporter on the spot assured viewers this was no propaganda stunt. Carefully chaperoned, how could he tell?' In reality Jeremy Bowen had neither taken Baghdad's word nor been chaperoned, as his reports made clear.

The paper conceded that 'either way, civilians have suffered and that is regrettable', admitting too that: 'Alas, even the awesome precision of the allied bombing cannot guarantee that all [civilians] escape. This is the price the innocent pay in war. The pity is that Saddam Hussein is making his people pay it.'[50] These were fair enough points in general, although in context they placed the responsibility for the coalition's killing on the Iraqi leader. By the following day, this position hardened in a full page headed: 'SADDAM ALLOWED FAMILIES TO BE SLAUGHTERED FOR A SICK PROPAGANDA STUNT: Facts and fiction behind the bunker blast,' with an editorial arguing, 'TV men should come home from Baghdad.'[51]

Coverage of Mutla Gap also neatly inverted responsibility for the killing: 'Slaughter of the innocent: Victims litter valley of death' turned out to be about how 'Iraqi troops slaughtered civilians in a last act of wanton destruction as they scurried from Kuwait. Horrific evidence of their atrocities lies along the main route from Kuwait to Iraq where the destruction and human cost of war can be seen at its most shocking.' The American bombing, it suggested, was only a response to this killing: 'the Allies took revenge on the Iraqi killers. Five dead Iraqi soldiers lay on one stretch of the carriageway within a 600-yard stretch alone ... a combination of Allied cluster bombing and Iraqi atrocities had reduced the trunk road to a slaughterhouse'. Only after this did it refer to 'unbelievable scenes of carnage' seen by a British officer, and reveal that 'as Iraqi troops fled toward Basra, Allied planes bombed their getaway route. Cluster-bomb cases bearing US marking littered the roadside and surrounding wasteland', and inform readers that 'civilians on the road were caught up in the bombing.'[52]

The *Express* provided some clues to Iraq's devastated condition, quoting a US official saying, 'If they can't raise the money, Iraq will stay at a primitive subsistence level for 20 to 30 years.'[53] Once the war had ended horrific estimates of Iraqi casualties (100,000) appeared. The paper reported only spasmodically on the civil wars, only once raising the question of Western responsibility: 'We let him escape by not wiping out all the Guards, say allied commanders: KO that could have finished off Saddam'.[54] The *Express* was rather more concerned that there should be a June election—'capitalise on Major's credit from Gulf'.[55]

Only after a month of revolt, although earlier than some, did it attack Western leaders' inaction: 'DESERTED IN THEIR HOUR OF NEED. Bush refuses to

halt Iraq's agony.'[56] The paper made official US and British positions clear—
'I WAS RIGHT SAYS BUSH. Britain backs "keep out" policy as Iraq revolt is put
down'—while editorializing on 'The shame of our silence':

> Amid the rising clamour for US intervention to halt Saddam's brutal repression
> of Kurdish and Shia rebels, one important voice has been missing—Britain's.
> Why the hesitation? ... Our reticence betrays those Iraqis whom the Allies
> encouraged to bring down Saddam and it mocks the sacrifice made in the name
> of liberty.[57]

For a while, the heroes were retired politicians like Thatcher and David
Owen who were calling for action, but it quickly endorsed Major's 'safe
haven' proposals and did not embarrass him by recalling his former
antipathy to intervention. Once the West decided to intervene, the Kurds
faded from the paper.

The *Daily Mail*'s themes were similar to the *Express*'s, but with
differences apparently related to its large female audience. It used the
psychological theme for Saddam Hussein (much more prominent at the
bottom end of the market), enlisting ubiquitous Oxford historian Norman
Stone to provide 'the final proof Saddam IS mad'.[58] Its attack on Germany
was over the rapid rise in conscientious objection during the war.[59] It
shared the *Express*'s ambivalence on women soldiers, but gave coverage to
'warrior wrens', featuring for example a US woman soldier who was given
a ten-day deferment due to childbirth and—the *Mail* equivalent of a *Mirror*
bathing beauty, perhaps—an attractive young Israeli woman soldier with a
gun.[60]

The *Mail* was more concerned than the *Express* about social aspects of the
war. Coverage of British Muslims actually acknowledged their dilemma: a
front-page feature posed a question, 'You are Muslim and British: what DO
you feel?', reflecting rather than condemning Muslim ambivalence.[61] Its
'expert on Arab affairs', John Laffin, wrote about the humiliation felt by a
billion Muslims world-wide; he also explained 'Why we can't just kill
Saddam'.[62] The paper's coverage of the environmental disaster was fuller,
but it tried to have it both ways, saying that while the Green warning on
the environment was justified, it was no reason to stop the war. 'Nature
does fight back!' after oil slicks: a claim backed up with pictures of clean
Brittany beaches and 'a healthy cormorant' twelve years after the Amoco
Cadiz disaster.[63] The *Mail* also plugged away at the Royals' roles,
commissioning a poll which showed 'a sense of unease running through
the country over the example being set by the Royal Family during the Gulf
conflict'.[64]

The *Mail* carried no reports of civilian casualties before the Amiriya
bombing: instead it echoed David Frost's criticisms of the showing of film
of injured children, with an ITN report singled out.[65] So it comes as no
surprise to find its coverage of the shelter bombing headed, 'Were civilians
deliberately put in bomb-target bunker? VICTIMS OF SADDAM'S WAR' and,
lower down, 'Shameful that the civilians were there, says US Army'

together with a diagram of a 'typical bunker' showing a military lower storey beneath a civilian shelter in the upper storey. (No such 'lower storey' was in evidence at Amiriya: it was the *Mail* which had a lower story.) A full-page inside article, 'Outrage as TV's bunker bomb bulletins "show bias to Saddam"', claimed that readers phoned the *Mail* to complain and that TV switchboards were 'swamped'.[66] (The number of calls was later shown to have been small.)

The *Mail*'s coverage of the violence of the war was limited. A 'world picture first' of the French bombing the Republican Guard mentioned only tanks being taken out, not men.[67] A report on napalm reassured readers that the USA would not use it on people, only to ignite oil in trenches.[68] On 1 March, a special twenty-four-page supplement included nothing on the loss of life: it was all weapons, heroes and the mistakes of Saddam. The next day, Mutla Gap finally merited an inside spread, 'On the highway to horror: a bottleneck of carnage as looters fled into an ambush', emphasizing the looting and making virtually no comment on the justification for the US action. (A British motorway pile-up made the front page twelve days later.)[69]

Mail reports on the uprising in southern Iraq tended to stress Iranian involvement and Islamic fundamentalism. On 16 March a front page headed 'BUSH'S TROOPS ON THE MARCH' pointed out that 'some are now within easy striking distance of Iraq's second city of Basra' and warned Saddam 'to end his war on rebels in his country'. Over the next few days the paper reported massacres in Basra with US troops quoted as observers, but the failure of any intervention to materialize (of which it had warned) went unremarked.[70] Only on 21 March did it criticize the USA:

> President Bush has the power to wipe out the Iraqi despot, but he does not want to take that responsibility. ... But what are the limits of non-intervention? ... We do not know. What we do know is that to stand by and allow such things to happen [Saddam killing his own people] would lie with leaden weight on the conscience of the world.

Within days, the paper was also picking up the Kurdish crisis, and soon it was castigating Bush—'Gone fishin' while Saddam slaughters the Kurds'—and praising Thatcher—'It takes Maggie to speak out for the Kurds. THE VOICE OF CONSCIENCE': 'As President Bush played golf and Prime Minister John Major watched football, it took former Premier Margaret Thatcher to stir the world's conscience last night over the genocide looming in Iraq.'[71] Over the next days there were many full reports of the Kurds' plight. When Major and Bush proposed 'safe havens', the *Mail* was still critical, headlining the 'Shame of the West in sending so little, so late'. Columnist Ann Leslie condemned the West for betraying the rebels, with a sideswipe at Edward Heath, Tony Benn and Marjorie Thompson, who had spoken out against military involvement before the war began: 'are they now protesting about our abandonment of the Iraqi people?'[72]

The third of the mid-market papers, *Today* (like the *Sun*, from the Murdoch stable), with an even stronger female audience, presented a generally more simplified view. Even during the launch of the air strikes, *Today* played the British card, with echoes of 1940—'THE FEW: 16 TORNADOS TO LEAD WORLD ATTACK'[73]—and constantly featured the 'Desert Rats'. It devoted much space to women and children: within five days at the beginning of the war it had three large features: a colour spread, 'WAR OR PEACE: THE GULF THAT SEPARATES THE SEXES' (picturing wives and a woman nurse reservist), a full-page feature, 'The children's voice' (the general gist of this was that war was bad, but we had to stop Saddam who was like Hitler) and a further double-page spread on women in war (featuring big colour photos of a woman doctor in uniform and a woman soldier together with a woman marrying a male soldier).[74] Likewise, it was quick to see the 'women and children' angle in Iraqi attacks on Israel and to give the full treatment to the 'agony of first woman PoW. ... Just 20 years old, she is threatened by every degradation suffered by womankind.'[75] *Today* did not bother with the *Express*'s and *Mail*'s political sniping at Labour.

By early February, as in most tabloids, the war was off the front pages. Inside, *Today* reassured its readers with the words of British spokesman Captain Niall Irving:

> The aim is not to destroy the people [in the Iraqi forces], it is to reduce their effectiveness by destroying their armour and wearing them down psychologically to the point where their will to fight is severely weakened.[76]

Not surprisingly, then, like most of its rivals, *Today* pinned the responsibility for the Amiriya killings not on those who aimed the bombs but on the Iraqi government. 'ENTOMBED BY SADDAM', *Today* asserted, not leaving the question open even to the extent of the *Mirror*, *Express* or *Mail*: 'He sent them to certain death, sheltering in the same camouflaged bunker in which the Iraqi military directed operations.' The inside story reinforced this message: '400 HUMAN SACRIFICES ... SADDAM'S VILEST WEAPON ... The "shelter" was hit yesterday ... as Saddam had calculated it would be, sooner or later.' Curiously, the editorial struck a different note, as though the leader writer had watched television but not seen *Today*'s headlines: 'It is no good even blaming [!] Saddam Hussein for apparently [!] moving civilians into a military target. We could expect nothing less from him.'[77] By the following day, he or she had caught on and the paper's attack on the BBC and ITN was strident: 'They presented their reports as though they were completely impartial. If they really feel like that, they are a disgrace to their country. ... The nation is at war. And the BBC and ITN cannot be conscientious objectors.'[78]

Today's hyper-patriotism and essentially unserious approach was reflected in how it covered the war's end. On 1 March it carried a front-page picture of a commando reclaiming the British embassy in Kuwait with the absurd caption: 'For 75 days it was part of a desecrated country where a tyrant swept away all semblance of justice. Now its liberation heralds a victory for the freedom of all mankind.' The paper simply did not cover either the Mutla Gap massacre or the uprising in southern Iraq, although it did manage a full-page colour picture of a British motorway accident two weeks later; its '80 mph road to hell' may have owed something to other papers' coverage of the Mutla slaughter.

Only on 28 March did *Today* wake up to the repression in Iraq.

> If the Allies restarted their war machine now there might be the same terrible loss of life that we saw on the road from Kuwait City as the invading forces attempted to flee. But if there must be deaths it is better that they should be of the Republican Guard rather than of women and children strapped to tanks or bombed with poisonous gas. It is not too late for the allies to act to even up the sides in Iraq's civil war. They should do so.

Once again, it appeared that leader writers had been watching the much-pilloried television news, as they would not have known about the earlier massacre from their own paper. This impression was confirmed on 4 April, when the paper noted that 'it makes it worse when we see harrowing pictures of the Kurds on TV intercut with President Bush on the golf course or fishing'. Interestingly, there was no mention of Major in this context; the paper later welcomed his 'plan to establish a safe haven for the Kurdish people' as 'a noble and practical act', but was quick to sound the alarm about the British input: 'how long does he propose to keep British troops there? ten years? twenty? fifty?'[79] *Today*'s coverage of the Kurdish issue was desultory, however, and the issue was not often on the front page.

The Conservative broadsheets: the *Telegraph* and *The Times*

The broadsheet (or 'quality') press provided substantially more varied information and comment on the Iraqi wars, not only than the more informative tabloids but also than television news. Most information which is in the public domain, including much on which this book is based, appeared in this section of the press. While in the tabloids the medium was often the message—coverage and opinion were difficult to distinguish—in the broadsheet press this basic distinction was largely viable. In the following discussion, rather than delineate coverage in detail, attention is given only to the most distinctive features of papers' coverage along with the main lines of editorial opinion.

There were significant differences among the broadsheets, particularly between the conservative *Daily Telegraph* and *Times* and the liberal *Guardian* and *Independent*. All had wide-ranging factual coverage of the Gulf War, and to a large extent of the subsequent revolts, but there were major editorial differences: the liberal papers' support for the war was more qualified and their criticisms of the coalition powers far stronger.

The *Telegraph*, with by far the largest broadsheet circulation, took a vigorously pro-war, pro-American and pro-government line, seeing Saddam Hussein as evil, if not to be compared with Hitler or Stalin.[80] Its version of the common Conservative complaint against 'Europe' was that 'Europe should not seek a role for the sake of its own misguided self-importance. It already has a role. This is to stand behind its American ally—indeed leader—amidst one of her greatest challenges for many years.'[81] 'Beware the peace-mongers', it editorialized; it criticized Labour for its 'weakening determination' but 'Why Labour hates England' by Roger Scruton turned out to be about the party's opposition to fox-hunting.[82]

The *Telegraph* had a clearer strategic conception than any of its rivals. 'For all the loose talk in the West about the prospect of allied air forces "flattening Baghdad," nothing of the sort will take place,' argued its editor, Max Hastings: 'no systematic effort will be made to terrorise or inflict casualties on the Iraqi civilian population, because such strikes would damage the moral basis on which this war would be fought'.[83] However John Keegan, the paper's defence editor, argued that the war 'would be like nothing ever unleashed on a battlefield before, since the Americans have taken to the desert the apparatus of the "Air Land Battle".' He concluded that the military balance was overwhelmingly against Saddam Hussein, who was 'moved only by inner voices, not intelligence appreciations.'[84]

Coverage included reports from a correspondent in Baghdad, giving 'on the ground' information; despite its strongly pro-war line, it interviewed CND's Marjorie Thompson and reported peace protests and the responses of British Muslims. Toby Young's analysis of the peace movement was surprisingly avant garde, recognizing that critics had no sympathy for Saddam Hussein, and arguing that protest resulted from the 'inauthenticity' of war, the end of certainty and commitment, and postmodernism.[85]

The *Telegraph* lead on Amiriya was 'Military HQ was in bombed bunker, says Washington' and its front-page story entirely about the political context. Inside, however, a full-page story gave no indication of any military use, and an 'Analysis' by Hastings failed to uphold official explanations, concentrating on more general reflections.

> After weeks in which this war has sometimes seemed to Western eyes sanitised, almost bloodless, this issue, squarely places cruel reality squarely in front of the public. ... The tragic truth is that it is probably impossible to bring this war to a reasonably swift conclusion, at tolerable cost in both allied and Iraqi lives, without accepting such episodes as that which took place in Baghdad yesterday as part of the price.[86]

The paper dealt with the Mutla Gap massacre on its inside pages and offered no comment.

Hastings noted that: 'Even if the Iraqi president's fall is not an explicit war aim, it is an outcome devoutly wished for in Washington and other allied capitals.'[87] At the end of the war the paper reported: 'The Prime Minister called yesterday on the people of Iraq to remove Saddam Hussein from power as the first step towards their country rejoining the international community.'[88] The following day's main headline proclaimed '"Saddam is finished" cries as Basra explodes in anarchy'. But the paper presented insurgents as 'fundamentalists' and 'Muslim rebels' and offered generally weaker coverage of rebellions than either the liberal broadsheets or television news.

Editorially the *Telegraph* was extremely sparing of comment on the Iraqi revolts. Its end-of-war comment celebrated Britain's 'decisive political attitude and unwavering military commitment ... in sharp contrast to the wavering or frankly feeble performance of all the other Europeans, with the marginal exception of the French'.[89] Keegan vented his spleen against the 'television grandees' whose commentaries had sold the pass on the real balance of forces in the war.[90] Bush, Major and Schwarzkopf were lauded. Only on 16 March did editorial comments notice the Iraqi revolts, pronouncing that: 'from a coolly geopolitical point of view, the continuation of a tough-minded dictatorship in Iraq might be preferable to the kind of chaos that would accompany the country's break-up.' There was, however,

> a moral factor to the equation. ... Mr Bush himself urged the Iraqis to rise up against their leadership in the closing stages of the war. ... For the Americans to sit by as Saddam's forces pound their own people is not an edifying spectacle. ... Even if direct allied military action in support of the rebels remains unlikely, there can be no question of an allied withdrawal from southern Iraq or an end to sanctions while a vengeful Saddam remains in power.

Stories about the revolts remained on inside pages until late March, and when on 1 April, as rebellion was crushed, the *Telegraph* finally returned to the issue, it was to firm up its opinion that 'there are good reasons for standing aside'. By 4 April, the paper admitted that the allies had badly miscalculated the damage they had inflicted on the Saddam regime. Keegan conceded that the assumption that he would be removed was wrong, but said there was no military option; Saddam was like Hitler after his 1944 defeats, wounded but not yet finished:

> Having rejected the option to occupy, we cannot physically get rid of him. The best option now must lie with the option correctly rejected while he occupied Kuwait, the maintenance of strict sanctions ... until Saddam's supporters no longer think his leadership is worth the candle.

As Keegan himself recognized, 'that may seem a tame recipe'; but it was acceptable because Saddam was not Hitler: he had 'so far oppressed only his own people and one small neighbour, not a whole continent'.

The paper acknowledged that the 'harrowing plight of the Kurds ... demands a response from the west', but its recipe was now restricted to sanctions. 'Western public opinion must accept, and harden its heart to the fact, that this course will inflict further pain and suffering upon the people of Iraq.'[91] By 9 April the paper was moved to criticize Bush: 'By pursuing even a marginally more active policy, the Americans could have much enhanced the prospect of deposing Saddam, without fatally engaging themselves.' The emphasis on disengagement was very much the centre of the *Telegraph*'s position: it made no active moral representation of the

Kurdish disaster. The limitations of Hastings' and Keegan's narrowly strategic views were very evident in the Kurdish crisis; as Keegan recognized, there was considerable irony in his and the paper's espousal of sanctions rather than intervention.

Interestingly, the *Telegraph*'s Sunday counterpart was far more forthright. Well before the refugee crisis, it argued that stopping the war when Bush did was

> one more example of shortsighted Western humanitarianism causing much later inhumanity. The allied armies had Baghdad and Basra at their mercy. Had the allies continued to wage the war, it would probably not have been necessary to occupy the Iraqi capital. The remorseless approach of the invader towards his gates could well have forced Saddam's overthrow or flight.[92]

'The road to hell,' it concluded, 'is paved with good intentions. But whose hell? It is always the same. Western liberal humanitarians do not suffer themselves. ... If the Iraqi war was worth fighting at all it was worth fighting to the finish.' The critique of liberalism would have been at home in the *Daily Telegraph*, but it reached radically different conclusions.

The Times, once Britain's premier journal of establishment opinion but by 1991 one (Murdoch-owned) broadsheet among others, carried a quantity of editorials fitting to its former station. 'Almost anything would be preferable to war', it agreed with Edward Heath, but 'appeasement would not'.[93] Like all Conservative papers, it took a superior stance towards French and European diplomacy, but it was sympathetic to Labour's dilemma, recognizing early that the party would back war when it came. Its leader on the outbreak of war held that it was about 'upholding international law': 'This is a war about peace, not just in the Middle East, not just in our time, but in tomorrow's world. That is why British soldiers are rightly asked to risk their lives.' It supported 'containing war', noting that the allies had decided not to conquer Iraq or topple Saddam; 'the moral essence of this operation is its strict conformity to United Nations resolutions'; and it approved the lack of 'mock heroics' by political leaders.[94] Its copious leading articles, continuing apace in the war's early weeks, said little that was remarkable given the paper's solid support for government policy. For one critic, however, this was '*The Times* clinging to power and its exercisers with the pattering and shaming reverence which has been its hallmark across the century'.[95]

The Times's coverage was broad and its policy on commentary liberal: editor Simon Jenkins could plausibly claim to have given 'plenty of coverage to the anti-war campaign' and to have columnists such as Anthony Parsons and Michael Howard who (while impeccably establishment) were certainly not jingoistic.[96] After Amiriya, the paper headlined the basic fact: 'Hundreds of Iraqis killed in shelter,' with a sub-heading, 'Allied leaders claim bombed bunker was legitimate military target.' It included an eyewitness report discounting a propaganda stunt and a Washington report emphasizing that behind the scenes there was a lack of confidence in the official line. Despite this, editorial comment avoided direct speculation that the bombing was a mistake.[97] The paper printed a pool report on the 'grim slaughterhouse' which 'Allied cluster bombing' created at Mutla Gap, but its editorial concerned 'Kinnock's good war'.[98]

The second week in March saw a build-up of stories about the Iraqi revolts. *The Times* had urged on 12 February that the allies think more about Iraq 'after Saddam' and give the Iraqi opposition 'a fair hearing in Western chancelleries'. It was not until 13 March that it acknowledged that allied success had caused the revolts, but now it urged caution and curiously concentrated on the danger of the regime's use of chemical weapons (which was not known to have happened) rather than responding to the actual pattern of rebellion and repression in Iraq. On 16 March it reported US troop movements inside Iraq, 'apparently designed to deter Saddam from crushing the rebellion'; but with no comment on the growing evidence that it was indeed being put down most brutally. *The Times* was more concerned about the Iraqi public health crisis and called for an end to sanctions, warning against the 'Lebanonisation' of Iraq and proclaiming that

> The allies' objective must be to withdraw all forces from Iraq as soon as possible. ... The longer forces remain in the area, the greater the temptation to use them to intervene. ... It is fanciful to think that the allies can set up a sanctuary in southern Iraq.[99]

By the beginning of April, of course, the paper was reporting Kurdish pleas for help, but it remained firm that Bush should resist the temptation to shift objectives and should 'withdraw from Iraq as soon as he can'.[100] There were no suggestions on how to help the Kurds. By 4 April, however, they were front-page news and a leading article proposed 'Saving the Kurds'. The text argued however that

> Military action that might have defended Kurdistan from the Baghdad regime existed only in the minds of those far distant from that benighted land, not in the realm of practicality. The urgent need now is for a huge humanitarian effort [and] ... feasible sanctions which might curb Saddam's excesses.

Soon, however, *The Times*'s line had to shift—the very 'sanctuary' it had deemed so 'fanciful' and the 'temptation' to intervene it had urged resisting were coming on to the agenda. The leader of 6 April saw the task as to define what the international community could do to give the Kurds back 'domestic security and to ensure them a measure of self-government'. This would involve 'intervention in the internal affairs of what ... is still a sovereign state, and an intervention well beyond the temporary occupation of a defensive zone next to the Kuwaiti border'. The paper saw this as setting aside a sound principle in the name of a higher morality, of 'protecting defenceless people against slaughter'. It failed, however, to argue for specific actions. It was even more cautious than other broadsheets on Major's initiative, pronouncing only that 'relief to refugees within defensible safe areas that stops short of unseating Saddam could mark the start of more effective collective policing'.[101]

The liberal broadsheets: the *Guardian* and the *Independent*

The daily liberal broadsheets produced very wide coverage, their readers treated to the fullest examinations of military, political and social aspects of the war and its aftermath of any media audience. They also obtained much information about the death toll, the carpet bombing of Republican Guards, everyday life in Baghdad and the attitudes of Muslim organizations and the anti-war movement in Britain—aspects which got cursory mention in the tabloid press and on television—and the most sophisticated analyses of the media themselves.

The *Guardian*'s coverage was distinguished by regular reports by Alfonso Rojo of the Spanish daily, *El Mundo*, who with Peter Arnett of CNN was one of only two Western correspondents left in Baghdad after the coalition air attacks began, and the only one whose reports were carried regularly by a British newspaper.[102] Rojo's 'Eyewitness' accounts of the effects of coalition bombing on the Iraqi people played a distinctive part in coverage from early February. When the Amiriya shelter was bombed, the *Guardian* was able to run Rojo's account, 'Bodies shrunk by heat of fire', alongside a political story, headed 'US insists it hit army bunker' which began: 'An unrepentant Bush administration courted a propaganda disaster yesterday, insisting in the face of televised evidence of hundreds of civilian corpses that US precision-guided weapons had struck "the legitimate military target of a command bunker" in Baghdad.'[103] The paper was thus the only national daily clearly to proffer disbelief of the military line in its coverage.

Rojo continued to file eyewitness accounts, for example of the RAF bombing, admitted to have hit civilians, at Fallujah.[104] The paper had to rely, however, on the pool for its Mutla Gap coverage.[105] It had very full coverage in comparison with other press of the Basra revolt and the rebels' pleas for allied support.[106] Correspondents Simon Tisdall in southern Iraq and Martin Woollacott and David Hearst in Kurdistan (and with Iraqi oppositionists elsewhere in the Middle East) provided unrivalled coverage of the revolts as they developed and then of how they were crushed with enormous suffering.

The *Guardian* was the only daily to argue editorially against war in January: 'There is no moral evasion in recognising that in the very specific circumstances faced in the Gulf, war could prove catastrophically counterproductive, and that reliance on sanctions may still be a far wiser course.'[107] It was consistent in opposing any extension of force to topple Saddam Hussein and the temptation to extend the war. Even when its correspondents exposed the disastrous situation of Shias and Kurds inside Iraq, it opposed Western military support:

It remains regrettably true that direct military intervention is both a dangerous precedent and—particularly when performed by the US—almost certainly counterproductive. ... The only pressure on Saddam consistent with international principles as well as the political realities of the region remains economic.[108]

Thus two *Guardian* journalists could claim it for the anti-war cause against left-wing criticisms:

True, the *Guardian* did not run big black headlines saying 'Stop the Gulf War'. ... But the *Guardian* did argue, alone in the mainstream national press, against force. Editorials continued to urge negotiations after the air war began on 16 January. On 5 February, the *Guardian* argued for a 'peace alternative', and said the allies should 'follow the French lead'. On 16 February it urged Mr Bush not to order a land war 'on the eve of fresh diplomacy'. On the 22nd it said that Mr Gorbachev had 'performed a service', and there need be no land war. The next day the *Guardian* criticised Bush's speech as 'an ultimatum, not a reply to the Moscow peace plan'. It is an easy myth to lump all the press together, but it just isn't so.[109]

The case was stronger because the paper's regular columnists, notably Woollacott and Hugo Young, often more impressive than its leader writers, had taken critical stances—and Edward Pearce was a trenchant opponent of the war. Its letter pages were also overwhelmingly anti-war.

If opposition to war had a fairly consistent national expression, it was— as it had been over the Falklands—in the *Guardian*'s pages. The paper's pacific message lost force, however, as these same pages provided so much evidence of the suffering of the Shias and Kurds. The *Guardian* failed to run a strong editorial campaign—even for humanitarian aid—to match its coverage, unlike (as we shall see) the *Independent*. Unlike some who had supported the war, who acknowledged a responsibility to help its victims, the paper seemed handicapped by its earlier stance. Only after the West had agreed to safe havens did it clearly move on:

The principle of non-intervention is still a substantial one, and to breach it is always a contentious course of action ... [but] there is no reason why international law ... should remain immune to changing public opinion and practice. ... The Bush plan can only be part of a much greater international effort which targets *all* the refugees, and *all* the civilian victims of the war.[110]

The broader perspective was commendable but pious in the absence of serious proposals to extend international action to other victims.

The *Independent*'s coverage was also wide-ranging and included the reports of Robert Fisk, perhaps the most enterprising and critical British 'unilateral', whose reports earned him a bouquet from the rival *Guardian*.[111] The paper's 'War Commentary' was provided by Lawrence Freedman, whose arguments were always sober and incisive. Unlike the *Guardian*, however, it did not stand out against the use of force in January. In endorsing the initial assault against Iraq it emphasized, however, the need for minimum civilian casualties and for political control of war, arguing that 'the way the war is won will shape the ensuing peace'.[112]

The *Independent*'s coverage of the Amiriya bombing was cautious: it headlined the coalition's claims in inverted commas—'Shelter "a military target"'—underneath an agency report interviewing survivors, while inside features argued that the bunker may have had a dual purpose. Fisk was more outspoken, arguing that military spokesman Richard Neal's obstinate insistence that the shelter was a 'legitimate target' itself came to 'the aid of the enemy'.[113] A follow-up editorial argued that 'horrible and tragic though the deaths in the shelter at Amiriya were, they should not obscure the untelevised horrors of murder, mutilation and torture that President Saddam inflicted' on Kuwaitis and Kurds.[114]

The *Independent* was also restrained in its coverage of Mutla Gap. On the day it was revealed, it had no coverage, except a short commentary piece, and its editorial, 'The doomsayers routed', attacked Labour's Denis Healey, Edward Heath and others who had prophesized disaster. It was several days later that it finally commented:

> Many did, quite understandably, feel shocked and distressed at the number of Iraqis who died, especially in the carnage on the road from Kuwait. However, this natural sense of horror did not invalidate the operation. War is always an ugly business.[115]

It was in the aftermath of the war that the *Independent* really came into its own. Fisk's stories told of Iraqi soldiers 'caught between bombs and death squads'—the executions of deserters, the impossibility of running away, what it was like to be on the receiving end of cluster bombs—and of 'wild dogs tearing to pieces the remains of Iraqi soldiers' on the Basra road.[116] Karl Waldron reported from Basra on Iraqi troops landed from barges after fleeing: 'Bodies and blankets rest under the shattered trees, perforated and torn by the shards of palm wood splintered by ordnance. ... There were not enough whole bodies left to count.'[117]

As the struggle inside Iraq grew, the *Independent* took a much stronger line than the *Guardian*:

> It is understandable that President Bush should be concerned at the consequences of allowing American troops to become embroiled in an Iraqi civil war. But to justify that policy by citing a supposed reluctance to intervene in Iraq's internal affairs is bizarre. An American-led coalition prepared the ground for the revolt by bombing Iraq for five weeks and by crushing President Saddam's forces. It has occupied about one-fifth of Iraq and called on its people to rise up and overthrow the leader, warning that United Nations sanctions are likely to remain in place until that happens. If that is not intervention, what is? With great courage the rebels are endeavouring to fulfil the hopes of the world, and they deserve some material assistance.[118]

The *Independent* consistently emphasized Western responsibilities:

The military conditions of the ceasefire should be strictly enforced. Not only fixed wing aircraft but also helicopters should be banned, since they are being used as weapons of terror against civilians as well as insurgents. If necessary, they should be shot down. Next, the current rebel leaders should be encouraged to set up a provisional government on Iraqi territory. ... The victorious coalition is liable to squander much of the credit it has earned if it comes to be seen as a passive accomplice of Saddam Hussein's intolerable regime.[119]

At its height the Kurdish crisis had constant front-page coverage, remaining prominent until late April. Editorials challenged fellow-supporters of the war in the name of responsibility:

Many people who strongly supported the allied role in the Gulf War, up to and including the annihilation of Iraqi forces at Mutla Gap, now feel outraged incomprehension bordering on shame. Our threshold for tolerating unspeakable horror in far away places is high. ... The situation in Iraq is ... a man-made human tragedy in which we are deeply involved and for which we bear much responsibility.[120]

Non-intervention, it suggested, was a very selectively applied principle: if it was acceptable for the US to intervene in Panama and Grenada, and justified in the cases of Tanzania in Uganda and Vietnam in Cambodia, so too for the Kurds. The *Independent* was less mealy-mouthed than the *Guardian* about the principle involved: 'What matters is that human rights should come to be considered to be as sacred as the sovereignty of nations. The Kurdish issue is bringing that day nearer.'[121]

Notes and references

1. Excluding only the *Financial Times*, an important elite journal but one with a largely economic focus, and the Communist *Morning Star*, which although a daily has a very small circulation.

2. *Sun*, 7, 17 and 22 January 1991.

3. *Sun*, 12 January 1991.

4. *Sun*, 22 January 1991.

5. Dave Hill, 'The patriot game', *Guardian*, 9–10 February 1991.

6. *Sun*, 26 January 1991. The editorial was entitled 'Menace of the Germans'.

7. *Sun*, 9 January, 25 February 1991.

8. *Sun*, 17 January, 2 and 12 February 1991.

9. *Sun*, 18 January, 15 February 1991.

10. *Sun*, 19 January 1991.

11. *Sun*, 14 February 1991.

12. *Sun*, 1 and 2 March 1991.

13. *Sun*, 4 April 1991.

14. *Sun*, 5 April 1991.

15. *Sun*, 18 April 1991.

16. *Daily Star*, 15 January 1991.

17. *Daily Star*, 28 January 1991.

16. *Daily Star*, 27 February 1991.

17. *Daily Star*, 14 February 1991.

18. *Daily Star*, 1 March 1991.

19. *Daily Star*, 9 April 1991.

20. *Sunday Sport*, 6, 20, 27 January; 3, 17 February and 3 March 1991.

21. Steve Bell, 1991; pp. 9, 15, 26.

22. *Daily Mirror*, 8 January 1991.

23. *Daily Mirror*, 9 January 1991.

24. *Daily Mirror*, 15 January 1991. Despite this sort of comment, Bell sees Diamond's criticisms as muted.

25. *Daily Mirror*, 16, 28 January and 7 February 1991.

26. *Daily Mirror*, 16 January 1991.

27. *Daily Mirror*, 30 January 1991.

28. *Daily Mirror*, 19 January 1991.

29. *Daily Mirror*, 14 January 1991.

30. *Daily Mirror*, 23 January and 1 February 1991.

31. Bell, 1991.

32. *Daily Mirror*, 9 February 1991.

33. *Daily Mirror*, 14 February 1991 (italics in original).

34. *Daily Mirror*, 15 February 1991.

35. *Daily Mirror*, 16 February 1991.

36. *Daily Mirror*, 18 February 1991.

37. *Daily Mirror*, 27 February 1991.

38. *Daily Mirror*, 4 March 1991.

39. *Daily Mirror*, 16 March 1991.

40. *Daily Mirror*, 4 April 1991.

41. This useful way of putting the issue I owe to Allan Shepherd.

42. *Daily Express*, 9 January 1991.

43. *Daily Express*, 26 January 1991.

44. *Daily Express*, 26 January 1991.

45. *Daily Express*, 1 February 1991.

46. *Daily Express*, 26 February 1991.

47. *Daily Express*, 21 January 1991.

48. Chris Buckland, *Daily Express*, 4 February 1991.

49. *Daily Express*, 4 February 1991.

50. *Daily Express*, 14 February 1991.

51. *Daily Express*, 15 February 1991.

52. *Daily Express*, 1 March 1991.

53. *Daily Express*, 26 February 1991.

54. *Daily Express*, 8 March 1991.

55. *Daily Express*, 4 March 1991.

56. *Daily Express*, 30 March 1991.

57. *Daily Express*, 2 April 1991.

58. *Daily Mail*, 15 January 1991.

59. *Daily Mail*, 6 February 1991.

60. *Daily Mail*, 7 February 1991.

61. *Daily Mail*, 26 January 1991.

62. *Daily Mail*, 18 January and 2 February 1991.

63. *Daily Mail*, 7 February 1991.

64. *Daily Mail*, 15 February 1991.

65. *Daily Mail*, 4 February 1991.

66. *Daily Mail*, 14 February 1991.

67. *Daily Mail*, 5 February 1991.

68. *Daily Mail*, 23 February 1991.

69. *Daily Mail*, 2 and 14 March 1991.

70. *Daily Mail*, 18 and 19 March 1991.

71. *Daily Mail*, 2 and 4 April 1991.

72. *Daily Mail*, 11 April 1991.

73. *Today*, 14 January 1991.

74. *Today*, 15, 17 and 19 January 1991.

75. *Today*, 23, 26 January, 1, 2, 7 and 11 February 1991.

76. *Today*, 7 February 1991.

77. *Today*, 14 February 1991.

78. *Today*, 15 February 1991.

79. *Today*, 10 April 1991.

80. Editorial, *Daily Telegraph*, 15 January 1991.

81. *Daily Telegraph*, 4 January 1991.

82. *Daily Telegraph*, 6 January 1991.

83. *Daily Telegraph*, 8 January 1991.

84. *Daily Telegraph*, 11 January 1991.

85. *Daily Telegraph*, 20 January 1991.

86. *Daily Telegraph*, 14 February 1991.

87. *Daily Telegraph*, 14 February 1991.

88. *Daily Telegraph*, 1 March 1991.

89. *Daily Telegraph*, 2 March 1991.

90. *Daily Telegraph*, 4 March 1991.

91. *Daily Telegraph*, 4 April 1991.

92. Editorial, *Sunday Telegraph*, 24 March 1991.

93. *The Times*, 2 January 1991.

94. *The Times*, 16, 17, 18 January 1991.

95. Edward Pearce, *Guardian*, 18 February 1991.

96. *Guardian*, 25 February 1991.

97. *The Times*, 14 February 1991.

98. *The Times*, 2 March 1991.

99. *The Times*, 22 March 1991.

100. *The Times*, 2 April 1991.

101. *The Times*, 10 April 1991.

102. Rojo's account of his stormy relationship with Arnett is described in 'Reporters at war', *Guardian*, 12 April 1991.

103. *Guardian*, 14 February 1991.

104. *Guardian*, 18 February 1991.

105. *Guardian*, 2 March 1991.

106. *Guardian*, 4 March 1991.

107. *Guardian*, 4 January 1991.

108. *Guardian*, 28 March 1991.

109. Victoria Brittain and John Gittings, letter, *New Statesman and Society*, 31 January 1992.

110. *Guardian*, 18 April 1991.

111. Philip Knightley, *Guardian*, 4 March 1991.

112. *Independent*, 18 January 1991.

113. *Independent*, 14 February 1991.

114. *Independent*, 15 February 1991.

115. *Independent*, 5 March 1991.

116. *Independent*, 2 March 1991.

117. *Independent*, 4 March 1991.

118. *Independent*, 12 March 1991.

119. *Independent*, 25 March 1991.

120. *Independent*, 4 and 5 April 1991.

121. *Independent*, 13 April 1991.

CHAPTER NINE

Media and representation in global crises

No one has doubted the importance of the media in the Gulf War. As numerous accounts have shown, media management was comprehensive and largely successful. Many critiques generalized, however, about 'the' media as though they were homogeneous, without differentiating sufficiently between media or between outlets within media. Even more sophisticated studies, while distinguishing *ad hoc* between different media, have not analysed systematically the relationships among them.

This book has attempted to show the differences between television and newspapers and among newspapers.[1] Television was central in diffusing information and images to the majority of the population. In Britain, over 90 per cent watched television compared to around two-thirds who read newspapers.[2] Non-readers and readers of tabloids would have obtained substantially more and certainly less-distorted information from television than from newspapers. At key moments and especially those unplanned by media managers—the initial aerial attacks on Iraq, the Amiriya bombing, the Mutla Gap massacre and above all the Kurdish crisis—television clearly led coverage and newspapers followed.

There is no doubt that readers of broadsheets could usually have obtained fuller information from these sources than from television (although this was not always true in the Kurdish crisis). Compared to the best newspaper coverage, television accounts, although occupying endless hours, were largely superficial and repetitive. Television, moreover, covered little of what was not filmed. The television war was fundamentally unbalanced—would Baudrillard have written that the 'Gulf war did not take place' if he could have *seen* the incessant bombardment of the Iraqi soldiers in their trenches on his television screen, seen the bodies of the estimated tens of thousands of dead? It was mainly in newspapers—even occasionally in tabloids—that he could have found a little information about the central killing field. Only through reading newspapers would he have realized that the debate over civilian casualties—although important in its own right—masked the reality that this was a war in which direct casualties (rather than those who died later as a result of civil war or disease) were overwhelmingly military.

Similarly, the uprising throughout southern Iraq, in which tens of thousands probably died, went unfilmed. It was, nevertheless, arguably more thoroughly reported on television than in all but the two liberal broadsheets. Considering the lack of film, television gave the Shi'ites considerable attention, but because of this absence never developed the sustained campaign which it waged for the Kurdish refugees.

At least as important as difference in coverage were differences in how media presented moral and political stances towards the war. Television news was formally neutral, referring to 'British troops' rather than 'our lads' and earning Conservatives' ire. In reality, during the Gulf War it largely purveyed the images and information desired if not produced by military managers—a fact that disturbed some journalists. During the Kurdish crisis, it played a very different political role, strongly and explicitly campaigning for Western aid to the refugees. Television did not just show what was happening: its linkage of human suffering with Western responsibility constituted powerful advocacy and achieved a remarkable and probably exceptional breakthrough, forcing a major policy change.

In the press advocacy was explicit and often supreme, to the point that much news coverage was dominated by propagandist values. The daily press was united in support for the war, with major reservations only in the *Guardian*. This fact does not take us far, however, in understanding the press's relationship to the war. Support in the manner of the *Sun*—with its incitement to use nuclear weapons and indifference to Iraqi victims whether of the coalition or Saddam Hussein—was very different from that of the *Independent*, foremost in drawing the conclusion that those who had launched war against Iraq also had a duty to protect its people from repression.

Badsey comments that

> The quality press may continue for some years more as a channel for elite political communication, particularly between government departments, although it is possible that in the US this function has already been usurped by CNN. The mass circulation press may be legitimately viewed as little more than a form of entertainment in all Western countries, at least in respect of foreign affairs reporting.[3]

This view neglects the fact that tabloids are purveyors chiefly of attitudes rather than information and have a particular niche in the propaganda war. The tabloid press was the home of patriotic hype which presented a war in which Britain was a junior partner as an overwhelmingly national campaign. It must have been the tabloids which Tony Benn had been reading when he claimed that Britain was 'experiencing the greatest wave of jingoism that I have seen in my life'. Others disputed this: according to the *Sunday Times*,

> Mr Benn was talking tosh; he cannot live in the same country as the rest of us. Britain has gone to war the way a mature democracy should when it has to fight.

No gung-ho jingoism. No histrionic gestures or speeches. No euphoria about easy victory. No war fever, despite the overwhelming support for waging war ... Those who would wrap themselves in the comic-book rhetoric of 'our boys' mistake the mood of the nation as much as Mr Benn.[4]

Despite this criticism from an upmarket rival, no tabloid was deterred from perpetuating stereotypical patriotism. It was inevitable that British papers would focus—as indeed did British television—on British soldiers and their weapons. But natural concern for one's own became, in the hands of most editors, instant denigration of (even friendly) foreigners and a distortion of the war in which Saddam Hussein was either mad or Hitler reincarnate, and the West's Arab allies—even the Saudis in whose country the West was based—were hardly mentioned.

The violence perpetrated in 'our' names was hardly acknowledged, as the tabloids mostly swallowed the military myth of a 'surgical' war in which weapons and buildings were destroyed but violence against people was absent. At this level we had 'a press edging towards the totalitarianism of inadvertence, a press which can be worn by the executive like a dress handkerchief.'[5] Moreover as John Simpson put it, 'We cannot explain such absences by government restrictions alone and it is not correct to see the British media as being simply forced along by politicians in the early stages of the war. Many of them, especially the popular press, were willing participants in a mood of patriotism and near euphoria.'[6] Or as another critic put it, the tabloids didn't 'stop at self-censorship; they hone and they select, they embroider and, where embroidery is not sufficient, they verge on outright fabrication.'[7]

Nevertheless, as we have seen, there were important differences between tabloids. Only the *Sun* and the *Sport* consistently indulged their patriotism in explicit racism directed intentionally at British Muslims. These and the *Star* were the only papers to link the war crudely to sexual exploitation. The rest of the tabloids mostly recognized, at least in occasional reports, the slaughter that was being carried out by the West. None, however, had the courage to emulate the television reports and clearly suggest that the Amiriya bombing had been a mistake. Nevertheless, there was a difference between those who simply asserted the military version and those who reported the question mark over the building's use.

The tabloids, especially the *Sun* and *Star*, represented much of the worst of British responses to the Iraqi wars. Their hyper-patriotism, racism and indifference to violence were more extreme than anything generated by the state or other institutions in civil society. On the other hand, the *Mirror* represented the only source of critical reflection on the war going into a large number of (largely working-class) homes, and even Conservative mid-market tabloids included some critical information which readers might not have gained from television.

Although much less than the liberal broadsheets, the *Mirror* and the mid-market papers campaigned for the Kurdish refugees, making explicit the message implicit in television news that something big had to be done to save them. With the exception of the broadsheets, the press jumped on television's bandwagon at a late stage. Its advocacy was nevertheless important to the campaign's political impact: its chorus was the final straw, the signal to Major that it could not be ignored. Although the tabloids generally denied 'our' responsibility when Western military actions had tragic human consequences (Amiriya, Mutla), they pinpointed Western responsibility when the West could do something to help Saddam Hussein's victims. Since Major's volte-face played an important part in Bush's, not only British television and broadsheets but even some tabloids can be said to have made a significant contribution to the change in Western policy on Kurdistan.

The political importance of the tabloids was, of course, their mass audience. The broadsheet papers had a different sort of significance: to set a standard of information—e.g. about the unfilmed wars of the trenches and the Shi'ites—which underlined the limitations of television. As Fisk put it,

> Print journalism has probably never been so important to the functioning of a democracy as in the age of satellite television. For however powerful and all-seeing a camera may appear to be, however 'live' a press conference, it is effectively superintended—piloted—by government authorities.[8]

Print journalism could challenge the demand of television news for 'immediacy, brevity, and, most pathetic of all, "sound-bites"—words that are both tasty and meaningless, a five-second substitute for human thought, the journalistic equivalent of junk food.' In a powerful critique of television, Fisk suggested that: 'Having therefore offered viewers war without responsibility, television ended the Gulf conflict by giving them war without death.' Whereas television reporters were interested in the present, not the past, and rarely held politicians to the record, print journalists alone provided the analysis, 'taking history books into battle.'[9]

It would be hard to argue that most print journalism lived up to a higher standard than television. Much of the broadsheets' coverage and discussion, however, including Fisk's own contributions, provided daily evidence, interpretation and comment of a sophistication not found anywhere else. Where politicians and religious leaders provided occasional comment at moments which suited them, where educators could choose when if at all to provide guidance or analysis, where campaigners could choose the issues around which they wished to focus, the press provided daily commentary and guidance.

For all the media's endemic failings and compliance with media management during the Gulf War, the Kurdish crisis was clearly a moment of great significance for the media as a whole. Even Fisk acknowledged that this was one of television news's finest hours, an 'obvious exception' to his general critique:

Videotape of the Kurdish catastrophe helped to shame George Bush and John Major into humanitarian involvement in northern Iraq. One had to read the dispatches of print journalists ... to appreciate the dimensions of the tragedy and political betrayal involved. But the satellite television pictures of babies and children actually dying on screen could not fail to be more powerful than the written word.[10]

Fisk over-simplified: it was not just pictures but authoritative journalistic commentary relentlessly pinning responsibility on Western leaders.

The media's flexibility and responsiveness to the Kurds' sufferings stand in contrast to the immobility of the other institutions of civil society. This was, as we have seen, a moment when the main opposition party was neutralized by its political compromise and its positions against 'extending the war'; churches, with their abstract messages, were slow to respond; and the anti-war movement was beholden to its anti-interventionist rhetoric. Those groups and individuals in British society who moved to act, notably humanitarian agencies and their donors, did so precisely because they were stimulated to do so by the media.

This was the media's finest hour, which brings into question some of the simpler, more general critiques of the media in the Gulf War. The public debate about media and warfare has been bedevilled by propositions of simple, unilinear effects: official doctrines which give too much credibility to the critical effects of media in order to maximize the case for control; and critical doctrines which give too much credibility to the manipulative successes of governments and militaries. The Iraqi wars show how the power relations between media and states can crystallize in different ways on closely related issues over short periods of time. The media which helped give Bush his Gulf War victory also almost snatched it from him in a matter of weeks. The very mobilization of Western (and hence global) media with the coalition's war against Iraq created their close involvement with the Iraqi crisis which exploded in the faces of Bush and Major.

Whether it was typical of the media's role in contemporary global crises, I shall discuss later in this book. First I examine evidence about 'public opinion' and how 'ordinary' individuals in Britain responded to the Iraqi wars and to media messages. I shall extend my argument about the significance of the press by showing how strong were the links between attitudes and newspaper readership.

Notes and references

1. Radio also gained importance during the war, although clearly less significant in terms of establishing images of the war than television and less significant in terms of attitudes than the press. I did not have the time or resources to incorporate radio into my study.

2. In our first sample 90 per cent regularly watched television news of the war, 72 per cent read the local evening paper and 65 per cent read a national (or regional) daily newspaper. For details of the surveys, see Appendix. Television viewing increased dramatically during the war: in the first

month, people in Britain watched 4.5 hours more per week than in an average week in 1990; the BBC's audience share, normally a minority, rose to over 50 per cent, reflecting the Corporation's authoritative reputation as a news-provider; and eleven of the top thirty BBC programmes were news (*Independent*, 18 February 1991).

3. Badsey, 1994; pp. 17–18.

4. Editorial, *Sunday Times*, 20 January 1991.

5. Edward Pearce, *Guardian*, 18 February 1991.

6. BBC2, 'Our war', 25 May 1991, quoted in Philo and McLaughlin, 1993; p. 13.

7. Steve Platt, *New Statesman and Society*, 22 February 1991.

8. *Independent*, 8 January 1992.

9. *Independent*, 8 January 1992.

10. *Independent*, 8 January 1992.

— Part IV —

Public Opinion and Individual Response

We have seen how the Iraqi wars were represented, first by a broad range of civil society institutions and secondly by mass media. In a democratic state, neither can assume that their images and opinions represent society unless the views of 'ordinary' members of society are taken into account. The positions of government and institutions must be seen to be representative of the majority of individuals in the national society and hence of society as a whole. It is necessary to validate institutional representations through representations of individual opinions.

This validation process typically centres on the idea of 'public opinion', which in late twentieth-century societies is represented through polling. The concept of public opinion is highly problematic: there is no single opinion, indeed no single public. How to discover what more than forty million British adults thought of the complex events of the Iraqi wars? Polling only reveals the patterns of diverse opinions. Nevertheless, polling has become increasingly sophisticated and accepted as representing public attitudes across a wide range of issues.

In specialized areas like voting behaviour, polling has become an important institution. In understanding how people respond to global crises polling is far less institutionalized, although considerable experience exists from Vietnam and in Britain from the Falklands. A study of the latter suggested, indeed, the role of polling in the mediation of the war: 'we have here a situation in which television selectively informs people's attitudes, then selectively reports on what those attitudes are, and finally ... uses this version of public opinion to justify its own approach to reporting'.[1]

Clearly, given the narrow focus and managed homogeneity of much television coverage of the Gulf, one might suspect that the conclusion would also hold in this case. It is important therefore to examine the polling data and their media presentation to consider their relationships to dominant messages. It is also important to look at alternative ways of representing individual responses to the Iraqi wars. In this part of the book, a critical discussion of opinion data is presented, alongside the author's own survey work and qualitative evidence of individuals' actions and attitudes, in order to provide more rounded ways of representing how people felt and thought about the conflicts.

Note and reference

1. Glasgow University Media Group, 1985; p. 143.

CHAPTER TEN

Deconstructing public opinion

Opinion polling is both a commercial activity and a political intervention staged within mass media. Political polling in the broadest sense is undertaken largely by specialist firms commissioned by newspapers and television, political parties and other interest groups. The polls which influence public perceptions and debate are those which appear in mass media. Whereas some policy as well as voting questions are asked regularly within polling series, global crises are episodic events impinging irregularly on political debate, and so taking a poll is a more significant intervention.

During the Iraqi wars, the most concentrated polling took place during the Gulf War. Fewer polls were undertaken between August–December 1990, and virtually none concerning the civil wars, not even the Kurdish crisis. Polling before the Gulf War showed strong majorities—larger than in most European countries—for the manifest objectives of the coalition's military build-up and for possible action against Iraq.[2] On the eve of the war, however, polls showed a sharp division of opinion over the immediate resort to violence—similar to that in the USA where a more sustained public debate had taken place.

Results depended as usual on the framing of the questions. ICM produced a 54 per cent majority for Britain doing all it could, including using force, to drive Iraq out of Kuwait, with 45 per cent for options short of using force. Men were for force in a ratio of 2:1, while a majority of women were against. The proportion backing force had risen from 50 per cent in favour, 41 per cent against in August 1990.[2] Gallup produced a slimmer majority: 49 per cent in favour of military action immediately, or within a few weeks, to 43 per cent who said sanctions should be given more time to work.[3] NOP, in a poll commissioned by the United Nations Association, found 47 per cent agreeing that allied forces should attack as soon as they were ready if Iraq did not withdraw, against 42 per cent who agreed that sanctions had not yet had time to work (it also found a majority of men in favour of force, and a majority of women against). Interestingly, among older men and women who had lived through 1939–45, 44 per cent were against war and only 40 per cent in favour.[4] In its regular polling, NOP found 71 per cent in favour, 23 per cent against sending troops to Saudi Arabia, 53 per cent for 'taking military action' after 15 January compared to 39 per cent in favour of 'waiting longer'. On a more loaded question, 62 per cent agreed that 'the West should insist on complete withdrawal from

Kuwait, even if this means going to war', while 32 per cent opted for 'the West should try to negotiate a peaceful solution to the Gulf crisis, even if this means that Iraq keeps part of Kuwait'.[5]

The narrow division over force—however widened by the questioning tactics—indicated a problem for the management of public opinion. It was suppressed in most polling during the Gulf War, but (our research shows) continued to manifest itself once a wider range of questions was canvassed. Published polls often focused on support for the principle of using force and, once force was a *fait accompli*, achieved much more satisfactory majorities, the more so the more general the question. Thus NOP's weekly polls for the *Sunday Times* showed 80 (rising over seven weeks to 88) per cent approval ratings for 'allied military action', but only 60 (rising to 79) per cent considering liberation of Kuwait 'important enough to justify the loss of the lives of British service personnel'.[6] (These exceptionally high levels of British support for the war were almost matched in the USA, France and even Germany, where support also hardened once the war began.)[7]

Polls showed all sub-groups of the population approving of the war, with men and Conservative voters more strongly pro-war but more women and Labour voters opposed. Around 30 per cent of female and 10–20 per cent of male Labour voters disapproved in the NOP polls compared to 6–10 per cent of female and 1–3 per cent of male Tories. Such differences were more striking on a wider range of questions. In a poll asking about war aims, a mere 9 per cent backed 'liberate Kuwait only', while 41 per cent also supported 'ensure that Saddam Hussein and Iraq are no longer a threat to the region' and 43 per cent also supported 'remove Saddam Hussein' as an aim. Support for these wider aims was greater among women and Labour voters—the groups who were least pro-war.[8] Indeed according to another poll, Labour women voters, the least pro-war group identified, favoured targeting Saddam Hussein himself by a 3:1 margin.[9] These findings indicated that attitudes to the war were more complex than simple questions about 'approval' of government policies, geared to newspaper headlines, would suggest. Yet pollsters barely explored these contradictions.

Our second survey (see Appendix), framed shortly after the end of the war, asked which one of several alternative courses of action should have been followed: while 7 per cent remained wholly opposed to the war and 29 per cent agreed that it was right to have ended the war, 48 per cent supported capturing Baghdad and Saddam Hussein and a further 13 per cent agreed that help should have been given to the rebels in Basra (a 'pro-interventionist' majority of 61 per cent in favour and 36 per cent against).[10] Support for wider aims including military action was manifest, too, in the limited polling evidence on the Kurdish crisis: a Harris poll showed 77 per cent to 10 per cent approval for the 'safe haven' idea, 61 per cent to 30 per cent for using British troops to guarantee Kurdish lands and 54 per cent to 30 per cent for using force to protect the Kurds.[11]

Rather than exploring such issues, the polls tended to correlate simple measures of support for the war with measures of approval of the government's handling of the crisis and of party support. Polling voting intentions was of course the staple of political polling, so it was natural that the polls would continue to register them and link them to Gulf findings.[12] Nevertheless the chain linking approval for military action, approval of the government's war record and the emergence of a modest Tory lead meant that published data focused on issues which benefited the government to the relative neglect of issues which might have shown a more contradictory aspect to public opinion. The purpose seemed to be to demonstrate, as the *Sunday Times* put it, 'an extraordinary degree of unanimity, unprecedented in modern times towards any policy'; but that this surface representation really represented unanimous opinion, let alone feeling, was not proved.

Active self-representation in the war

Just as the managed media coverage of the war generally minimized the violence used by the coalition, so opinion polling generally failed to probe the responses of people to the actual means of war as opposed to its ends or the principle of force. Polls also asked about 'attitudes' rather than experiences or feelings and in their eagerness to compose a representative 'public opinion' failed to represent the diversity of actual sentiments. In order to understand the responses of individuals to distant violence, it was necessary to undertake different research. First, it was important to discover the active responses in which people themselves represented their feelings and opinions in actions which had a significance for others—whether for those involved in distant conflict or other members of their national society or both. Second, it was necessary to explore more fully the responses of those who did not become active in a visible manner.

Research into active self-representations was based largely, due to resource constraints, on published data. The group from British society which was clearly and directly involved in the war—service personnel themselves—represented their own needs and feelings, if not in a formal or public way, then in family and wider social contexts. Despite all that was written about the 'surgical' character of the war, and although coalition casualties were relatively very low, members of the military clearly had mixed responses to their experiences. While on the one hand there was a celebration of violence—'Bloody brilliant, I can tell you' was one airman's comment on seeing bombs strike home—on the other there was anxiety— 'This was the first time for me. I was just relieved I was out of it. Just off the target there was a lot of flak. It was the longest moment of my life.'[13] There were difficult feelings to come to terms with about what they had actually done to other people: a helicopter officer's wife said,

> He's not aggressive and yet I see an aggression in him that I never saw before. Sleepless nights are spent trying to come to terms with the knowledge that he

has actually had to kill people; even the sound of [his son's] toy Jumbo Jet can upset him.[14]

The press reported soldiers finding difficulties, too, with what they saw that other troops had done, most notably from those who visited Mutla Gap:

> Why did this happen? Saddam's forces are nothing to be reckoned with, are they? They didn't want to go to war. They just wanted to put their hands up. They are our enemy but they didn't want to be in the war in the first place. They are a sorry sight to see.[15]

Or from a soldier burying the dead, including women and children, 'Iraqis or perhaps Kuwaiti or Egyptian refugees': 'The Iraqis who died on this road were stripping Kuwait City. But I shudder to think what it would have been like in their position.' One British officer, 'his face a mask of disapproval, said his men were angry about the continuing bombing of the Republican Guard as it retreated. "The boys don't like it", he said. "Those men have had enough. That's not war."' On the other hand there was a denial of responsibility from some soldiers: 'A British colonel, asked if he knew the number of casualties the Iraqis had suffered, said stiffly: "We are not in the business of keeping score. Their body count is their concern."'[16]

Families of the soldiers also represented great anxiety. A mother of three soldiers described the night war broke out: 'I was on my way to bed. I took one last look at the television and I couldna' believe it. We watched all night and the tears flowed.' Families often found it difficult to make the transition from routine soldiering to war: 'A woman said that's what my boys signed up for, that's what they're being paid for, but she's wrong. In this day and age, young laddies join the Army for a career, no' for goin' tae kill someone.'[17] Dealing with children's fears was particularly difficult, not least in the context of television coverage: 'Of course we're frightened, but we can't show it to the children.' 'I try not to watch it when the children are around, but it has a hypnotic effect. It makes us feel closer to them.'[18]

The sense of isolation was strong. A naval officer's wife said, 'I feel as if we wives were waging a war of our own, whereas 90 per cent of the country weren't at war.' In her case, all letters and phone calls stopped for forty-seven days; she didn't know where her husband was until she saw him on television. When this happened, 'she shook; she never knew she could shake like that'. Friends 'were kind and said they understood. But how could they?' She went round in a daze, watching people doing their shopping and knowing that then, because it was a media war, they could switch on their television in the evening and say, 'oh, how's it going today?' Her eleven-year old daughter was brave: 'But one night she came down in floods of tears and asked if her father was going to die.'[19]

For many service personnel, regular telephone calls from the front—a feature of modern war[20]—made their families aware of their feelings. Family support groups were set up—one network in East Anglia was reported to have 400 members[21]—often using phone chains as well as meetings and offices.[22] They were a real feature of the war, giving the minority of society with personal connections to the military a real focus for collective action and self-representation. The support groups, like those formed by miners' wives during the 1984–5 strike, were also the focus of much activity in the wider society, collecting money and material for the troops.

One consequence of the growth in cohesion among military families was that some represented themselves in issues which arose after the war. RAF widows contested media representations of themselves, protesting about a BBC drama in which a Gulf soldier's widow was shown having an affair:

> The over-dramatised and inaccurate portrayal of a widow's behaviour was an insult to our husbands who died during the Gulf conflict and as the result of routine military training.

The son of an officer killed in the Gulf complained at the BBC's 'exploiting such a sensitive subject to produce cheap sensationalist drama ... it was broadcast when wounds are still fresh and so easily reopened.'[23]

More importantly, a group of family members, mainly women, contested the 'cover-up' of the 'friendly fire' incident in which nine soldiers were killed by mistake by American pilots. US forces carried out no formal inquiry and the Ministry of Defence refused to publish the British board of inquiry's report. The Coroner's inquest recorded a verdict of 'unlawful killing' without revealing what really happened, as the key witnesses, the pilots, were not there. The relatives' case was that 'these men must be made accountable for their actions. They cannot just walk away from it.'[24] A solicitor summed up the significance of the new situation: 'No longer are soldiers mere cannon fodder. There is a duty of care.'[25] The press reinforced their case:

> The fog of war argument is a form of higher cynicism. It says it doesn't really matter how someone dies once they are dead. It says the truth is never to be found on a battlefield. It says justice is for lawyers, not for soldiers. Small wonder the women believed they were pitting the logic of their grief against the logic of an officer class which, in ceaselessly repeating that accidents will happen, was saying in effect that their sons were no more than cannon fodder.[26]

Another newspaper concluded that 'the real story is the cover-up by the Prime Minister. John Major could have avoided what is now a diplomatic embarrassment if he had accepted his responsibilities to the families ... at an earlier date.' The families wanted to know 'why their sons died, and for someone to accept responsibility. ... But Major refused to accept or attribute responsibility—even though the government had the information to do so.'[27]

The new activism of the military community contrasted with relative passivity in the wider society. In a crisis widely seen as characterized by a low level of public debate—increasingly the norm for global crises—

relatively few resorted to traditional ways of making feelings felt, such as writing to newspapers or MPs, although Benn, who had a high profile in opposition to war, claimed 8000 correspondents before war broke out.[28] Anti-war groups mobilized smaller numbers than in previous wars— although as we have noted the war was brief, its progress relatively smooth and political support for its objectives overwhelming.

Memberships of support groups and of anti-war campaigns were numbered nationally probably in tens rather than hundreds of thousands, in a population of nearly sixty million. Both sought to engage the support of the wider public, but service support groups were working with the grain of government, media and public opinion, while anti-war groups were very aware of being in a minority. Support groups sought, moreover, social support rather than the political action worked for by anti-war campaigns; they were asking for solidarity with people acting on behalf of the national community, rather than action for an abstract cause. It is not surprising, therefore, that the former achieved wider support and, at least at the minimal level of donations, engaged a significant minority of the population. Many collections were independent of the support groups, and many individual acts of support were made: 250,000 letters and parcels were posted addressed simply to 'a soldier in the Gulf',[29] and blood donations increased from 9000 to 14,000 pints per day.[30]

Nevertheless, it is evident that even in these minimalist terms, support activities for service personnel engaged only a small proportion of the total population. The survey which we conducted shortly after the war in a northern English city (see Appendix) indicated that while about a quarter of respondents claimed to have donated money for British troops, only tiny minorities had been involved in genuinely proactive public work like collecting money, being involved in a support group or, on the other side, in anti-war activism. Almost two-thirds had not even made a donation. Even these figures may overstate the national picture of activism, as they represent a large city in which both support and anti-war groups were active—in smaller places neither may have existed.

Table 10.1 'Active' responses to the Gulf War (%)

Donated money for British forces	25.8
Wrote to a friend or relative in the Gulf	4.9
Wrote to a member of British forces	4.3
Collected money for British forces	2.7
Signed an anti-war petition	2.3
Involved in a support group or helpline	1.0
Took part in an anti-war demonstration	0.4
None of the above	64.1

The other phase of the Iraqi wars in which some people responded actively to distant violence was in the flood of humanitarian aid for Kurdish refugees. This again involved a significant minority, responding to appeals and advertisements by voluntary organizations, or simply to the media campaign, by donations (in money and kind) for the helpless victims. These responses were limited in kind, however, involving little proactive organization or self-representation, but were a financial or material endorsement of the representation of the Kurds made by media and aid agencies.

It is evident, therefore, that studying active responses tells us only a modest amount about people's responses in general. We may assume—but this is arguable—that active responses represented the feelings and opinions of larger numbers of people who did not actually do anything. Even so, the knowledge we have tells us very little about the responses which lay behind donations, whether for British service people or Kurdish refugees.

Independent research on feelings and attitudes

In order to explore the responses of individuals in British society more widely, two kinds of research were undertaken: survey research organized by the author and a colleague and analysis of 'diaries' of individuals' responses kept by panelists of the Mass-Observation Archive at Sussex University. These two forms of research were very different in kind. The survey research replicated the methods of public opinion polls, exploring a wider range of questions designed to highlight aspects of responses neglected by the polls. The diary analysis, on the other hand, took individuals' self-representations in response to a limited prompting by the Archive.

The survey research, technical details of which are described in the Appendix, was undertaken during and immediately after the Gulf War; questions concerned the war, rather than the revolts against the Iraqi regime, which were not known at the time of devising the research. There is therefore a major gap in that no direct evidence is produced of responses to the Kurdish crisis; one of the problems of research into global crises is the difficulty for social scientists of responding to rapidly changing events, given limited resources. Study of the Gulf War could have been planned, on a contingency basis at least, for a month or two in advance (although our actual planning period was less than two weeks, as we found ourselves affected by the uncertainty of the last weeks before war). The form of the war's end and the events which followed it were much less easy to foresee or plan around. Neither governments and military nor media and other civil society institutions planned responses to the Iraqi revolts. Neither did we; but working on a shoestring, we were unable to match the turnaround made by media and aid agencies for whom quick response and flexible budgets are normal.

The survey research was designed first to test the assumption that people in Britain, as in other Western societies, were generally insulated not only from the immediate reality and direct threat of violence (marginal and sporadic terrorist incidents apart) but also, to a very large extent, from information about and images of the ways in which these realities were affecting people in Iraq.

Our assumption was that people's lives were nevertheless linked abstractly to distant violence. As Giddens points out, the transformation of relationships of time and space in modernity means the involvement of people in distant risks and dangers and a well-distributed awareness of these. 'Disembedding mechanisms' in social relations (the dislocation of social relations from given temporal and spatial contexts) have provided large areas of security but 'the new array of risks which have thereby been brought into being are truly formidable'.[31] The circumstances in which we live today have as a result a 'menacing appearance'. We hypothesized that in the Gulf War, many people who were not directly threatened would nevertheless feel themselves to be living with the dangerous situation developing thousands of miles away. Some people in Britain (the relatives of soldiers, for example) were living with this tension in a more personal way than others, but more would be affected.

We were doubtful about the relevance of other perspectives. According to Mann popular militarism now takes a 'spectator sport' form, and members of Western societies consume war as entertainment. Similarly, Luckham argues that we have an 'armament culture', in which images of weaponry are diffused by mass media into popular culture.[32] These theories seemed based on the role of images and ideas of war in peacetime situations, not during actual conflicts, and like many media-based theories, they concentrate more on the production than the consumption of images. When Mann extended his argument to war situations—arguing provocatively that in terms of the presentation of weaponry in the media, 'wars like the Falklands or the Grenada invasion are not qualitatively different from the Olympic Games', this seemed to underestimate people's awareness of violent implications of even the most manipulated media images of war.[33]

Our hypotheses were, first, that despite their 'support' for the war many people would have more complex responses to its 'distant' violence, as well as to the political issues; and second, that these responses would be structured not only by social relations reflected in differences of age, sex, class, party identification and (a novel element of our investigation) prior military/wartime experience but also by their exposure to different media representations. We reasoned that since the media provided not only virtually all the information about the war available to most respondents, but also the only day-by-day interpretations of this information, differential access to media resources would play a significant part in structuring responses. In particular, it seemed important (despite the primacy of television) to investigate the effects of newspaper exposure which offered far fuller and more differentiated interpretative messages.

Our starting point was therefore very close to one expressed in a perceptive newspaper comment:

> Behind the clamour of this media war lies a sombre silence. It's there in the voices of people trying to say what they think, to find what they feel. The war has invaded their lives, cars, homes. They have witnessed many people's experiences and opinions. ... But the war has not touched them. They are only its spectators, thousands of miles away. They may feel pride, dismay, confusion. I think they also feel responsible: responsibility without power.[34]

We wanted to explore the dimensions of this confusion and the sense of responsibility.

Even while they approved of the war, respondents expressed anxiety about it; few confessed either to fascination, or to feeling good about the coalition's successes. One dimension we wished to investigate was how people were personally affected by the war. If the 'spectator sport' and 'armament culture' theories were valid, media coverage would function to 'screen off' the actual violence. Public manifestations of anxiety abounded, however: air travel slumped, there were large increases in calls to the Samaritans at the beginning of the war and students widely panicked about conscription.[35] The *Catholic Herald* reported mass attendance significantly up: almost half of 100 clergy contacted reported growing congregations. 'I think people are feeling very afraid of the war,' one priest said, 'and many feel quite powerless to do anything about it.'[36] Or as a rabbi reported: 'Since the war started, I have slept less than I want to, eaten less than I used to, and prayed with greater intensity than ever before.'[37]

In our survey in the middle of the war, reported anxiety focused partly on individuals in the Gulf to whom people felt close, but it also had wider bases. Thirteen per cent of respondents agreed that they were 'worried about family or friends in the Gulf' (this seems a high proportion but compares with a national MORI finding that 20 per cent of the population had either friends or relatives serving).[38] Of these, 56 per cent claimed that a member of their family (in over half of the cases, a child or teenager) had been 'adversely affected by the violence of the war', compared to 21 per cent in the sample as a whole.

Larger numbers of those without family involvement agreed that they were 'worried about the violence of the war in general' (32 per cent). Only a small proportion 'felt good because of allied or British successes' (12 per cent). On the other hand, 39 per cent claimed not to have been personally affected by the war. Older people and readers of broadsheet newspapers and the *Mirror* were particularly likely to say they were 'worried'; readers of downmarket tabloids were more likely to 'feel good' about British and allied successes in the war. Both these distributions are statistically significant.

Table 10.2 How people reported they were personally affected by the war, by (1) age and sex and (2) newspaper readership

	Worried about family or friends	Feel good	Worried in general	Not affected	N
Men under 45	13	14	27	43	134
Men over 45	11	8	44	36	129
Women under 45	7	16	25	48	122
Women over 45	15	10	41	30	139
All respondents	12	12	34	39	532

Chi squared = 40.1, DoF 25, p = 0.029

Sun and *Star*	16	19	18	44	93
Daily Mirror	14	8	38	39	111
Other tabloids	14	14	25	44	92
Broadsheets	3	10	53	27	62

Chi squared = 36.7, DoF 15, p = 0.0014

The general atmosphere of crisis seems to have given rise to widespread anxiety, which media communicated along with images of high-technology military success. This was so despite the 'screening out' of violence and acceptance of official and widely diffused media explanations of events. Respondents were highly concerned about violence even if they had little concrete evidence of the forms which it was actually taking, although the concern varied between category of victim and social class of respondent. Our survey during the war showed more than 60 per cent of our sample claiming to be 'concerned' or 'very concerned' about loss of life among Iraqi soldiers and more than 85 per cent about Iraqi civilians; over 95 per cent claimed to be concerned about British forces or civilians. Both anxiety and concern will be explored further in discussion of individual responses.

Notes and references

1. For details, see Worcester, 1994; pp. 22–3.

2. *Guardian*, 16 January 1991.

3. *Guardian*, 11 January 1991.

4. *Guardian*, 8 January 1991.

5. *Independent*, 18 January 1991.

6. *Sunday Times*, 20, 27 January, 3 and 10 February 1991; also Rallings, Thrasher and Moon, 1991; unpublished paper based on NOP findings. Approval for military action had risen from 48 per cent in November to 61 per cent just before the war began.

7. *Sunday Times*, 3 February 1991.

8. *Guardian*, 14 February 1991.

9. *Sunday Times*, 27 January 1991.

10. N = 515; don't knows (fifteen cases) excluded.

11. *Observer*, 21 April 1991.

12. Voting intention data is discussed in Part II.

13. *Independent on Sunday*, 20 January 1991.

14. *Guardian*, 4 June 1991.

15. *Independent*, 2 March 1991.

16. *Evening Standard*, 1 March 1991.

17. *Observer*, 20 January 1991.

18. *Independent*, 22 January 1991.

19. *Guardian*, 4 June 1991.

20. See Ender, 1995, for a study of this in Panama. In Britain during the Gulf War, BAe, Nat West and Cable and Wireless launched an appeal for donations to buy phone cards for troops.

21. *Independent*, 25 February 1991.

22. *Independent on Sunday*, 20 January 1991.

23. *Guardian*, 19 May 1992.

24. Mother of victim, Independent Television News, 18 May 1992.

25. *Newsnight*, BBC2, 18 May 1992.

26. *Observer*, 24 May 1991.

27. *New Statesman and Society*, 22 May 1992.

28. *Guardian*, 12 January 1991.

29. *Independent*, 14 February 1991.

30. *Independent*, 19 January 1991.

31. Giddens, 1990.

32. Mann, 1987; Luckham, 1984.

33. See critique in Shaw, 1991; pp. 64–108.

34. Janet Watts, *Observer*, 20 January 1991.

35. I have not come across any published references to the possibility of reintroducing conscription during the Gulf War, which was a strategic nonsense. It was interesting therefore that during discussion of this issue at a conference on War and Memory in Portsmouth (1994), participants insisted remembering seeing such references. The only documentary evidence I know of was the publication by the Militant organization of posters proclaiming 'No Conscription'—a speedy opportunistic response to the fears of young people by a group well informed enough to have known that there was virtually no likelihood of conscription's reintroduction.

36. *Guardian*, 7 February 1991.

37. Rabbi Hugo Gryn, *Independent on Sunday*, 20 January 1991.

38. MORI, 22 January–5 February 1991. Of this 20 per cent, 8 per cent had a relative and 13 per cent a friend.

CHAPTER ELEVEN

Media, perceptions
and representative attitudes

Our surveys focused on issues relating to media coverage because this was how the war had been represented to most members of the population. Only a small minority (approximately the five per cent who reported a member of their immediate family in the Gulf) were likely to have had direct access to individual communications from the Gulf and these may have provided less information than that which was available through mass media.

In exploring the roles of media, we asked three sorts of question: to do with perceptions—to test how far people saw the war in terms consistent with mainstream media coverage; about attitudes to the media themselves; and about attitudes to various aspects of the war—to see how far people's opinions could be related to the media they used. We were able to compare the relationships to people's attitudes of, on the one hand, the newspapers they read, and on the other, factors such as gender, age, tenure status,[1] voting intention and religious affiliation. This enables us to compare the significance for people's attitudes of media consumption and other civil society affiliations.

Perceptions of the war

Respondents to our first questionnaire were asked to choose the one or two most appropriate descriptions of the initial bombing campaign. Most endorsed the dominant views propounded via television and the tabloid press ('precise strikes against strategic targets, with minimum civilian casualties' or 'sorties by brave allied airmen'), with few agreeing that they were 'like video or computer games' or constituted 'intensive bombing with unacceptable civilian casualties', an oppositional view for which coverage gave little warrant. Even those approached for the first time on the second post-war survey gave similar responses.

Almost all respondents recognized that more Iraqi lives had been lost than those of any other nation. However, asked to choose the description of the Amiriya bombing which they found most acceptable, no fewer than 36 per cent agreed that 'Saddam Hussein put civilians in the shelter so as to make propaganda if it was attacked', and 24 per cent agreed 'It was a military communications centre as well as a shelter, and the coalition was right to attack it'. A further 21 per cent agreed 'It was war and there will always be casualties', while only 11 per cent agreed 'It was a civilian shelter and the coalition bombed it by mistake'. On the issue which created most conflict over the role of television, therefore, the majority agreed either with attributing blame for the results of coalition attacks to the enemy (a line promoted by the tabloid press) or with the official military justification. Only a small minority appeared to have clearly received the 'critical' message about a coalition mistake, the danger of which angered right-wing critics of the BBC.

Table 11.1 Perceptions of initial aerial strikes (%)

	Precise strikes/ minimum casualties	Brave sorties	Intensive bombing/ casualties	Like video games	N
1st survey	82	41	8	5	560
2nd survey:					
repeats	86	45	6	4	236
new	80	33	9	8	271

Breakdowns of these findings according to newspaper readership are extremely revealing. Almost half the readers of broadsheets, but fewer than 10 per cent of tabloid readers, saw the bombing as a mistake. Over half of *Sun* and *Star* readers believed the conspiratorial 'Saddam propaganda' line, whereas among other tabloid readers the rational military explanation and the philosophical view that these things happen in war were more frequently chosen. These findings clearly indicate that on a highly propagandized issue, newspaper stances critical of television coverage were very influential.

Table 11.2 Perceptions of the bombing of the Amiriya shelter, by newspaper read (%)

	Military centre	Civilian shelter	Saddam propaganda	Casualties of war	N
Sun and *Star*	21	9	58	12	33
Daily Mirror	30	6	32	32	47
Other tabloid	28	7	39	26	34
Broadsheet	19	45	13	23	19
All respondents	26	14	36	24	168

Chi squared = 39.2, DoF = 9, p = 0.0000

A similar pattern of perceptions applies to the killing of Iraqi troops during their retreat from Kuwait. Sixty-five per cent of respondents saw this as justified in order to destroy the Iraqi military machine in addition to 13 per cent who saw it as necessary to win the war. Only 15 per cent agreed that it was unjustified as the war was already won.

In answer to a question about which countries were most important in the coalition, 87 per cent correctly gauged the USA's leading role, with only 7 per cent seeing the UK in first place; but 76 per cent put the UK second, compared to only 17 per cent for Saudi Arabia. There was, moreover, evidence of the misleading effect of national media coverage in the answers to a question asking what proportion of the sorties flown by the coalition had been flown by British airmen. Although the RAF was responsible for only 2–3 per cent of flights, 42 per cent of respondents opted for the highest proportion offered as a possibility, 'over 30 per cent', and 40 per cent opted for '10–30 per cent'; only 16 per cent opted for '5–10 per cent' with a mere 3 per cent choosing the correct answer, 'under 5 per cent'.

Perceptions reflected more than media coverage, as people interpreted information in accordance with their own views. Asked which leaders had been 'for' and 'against' the war, Labour voters, more likely to oppose the war ($p = 0.000$) than Conservatives, were also more likely to see the Labour leader, Kinnock, as having opposed the war ($p<0.10$). Labour voters were also likely to see other potentially ambiguous figures with nuanced positions, such as the Liberal Democrat leader, Paddy Ashdown, and the Archbishop of Canterbury, Runcie, as having been anti-war (both $p<0.10$).

Table 11.3 Perceptions of political leaders' positions on the war, by voting intention (second survey, new respondents: %)

Voting intention	Disapproving of war	Seeing following as 'opposed to war':			
		Kinnock	Ashdown	Runcie	N
Conservative	2	15	17	49	52
Labour	18	21	33	63	56
Other*	16	30	30	69	60
Chi squared	34.6	5.0	5.7	5.8	
DoF	4	2	2	2	
p	0.000	0.08	0.6	0.6	

* Other includes Liberal Democrat, Green, Don't Know and Wouldn't Vote, as numbers in each category were too small to analyse separately.

Underlying perceptions of issues in the war also appeared to reflect media coverage. The British national 'myth of war', derived from Second

World War experience (according to which dictators should not be appeased but resisted by military force) was widely applied to the Iraqi situation by tabloid newspapers, even more than by Conservative politicians. Our research showed far more tabloid than broadsheet readers believing that Saddam Hussein was like Hitler and/or that he was mad (see Table 11.5 below).

Attitudes to media coverage

Since most people obtained information from mass media, it was also important to gauge how well they thought the media were representing the situation. We asked three sets of questions about television coverage. Overall, 60 per cent of our respondents found it 'informative', while 25 per cent found it 'too informative' and 16 per cent found it 'not informative enough'. However, we divided our sample between 202 who replied early in the conflict, before the Amiriya shelter bombing referred to above (which as we have noted was a landmark in the television coverage), and 307 who replied after this incident.[2] In this 'natural experiment' we found a decline in the proportion agreeing that coverage was too informative which was significant at the conventional 5 per cent level when 'too informative' was compared with the other categories. Fewer respondents may have complained about over-informativeness because the coverage had become less bland or because the level of coverage was itself reduced from the early saturation levels. We also asked about patriotism in television coverage. Overall, 68 per cent found it 'patriotic', with minorities of around 16 per cent each finding it 'too patriotic' and 'not patriotic enough'. There was a small, non-significant increase, from 12 to 18 per cent, in the proportion seeing television news as 'unpatriotic' after the Baghdad bombing.

We also asked whether television news reflected 'a sensible attitude to the war', 'glorified the war too much' or was 'too critical of the war'. Overall, 59 per cent of our sample found that it was 'sensible' (the figure did not change over time). However, the minority seeing television coverage as 'glorifying' the war was as large as 40 per cent before the Baghdad bombing but fell to 29 per cent afterwards; while the minority which saw television as 'too critical' was a miniscule 2 per cent before, but a more significant 13 per cent among later respondents. These figures represent strong evidence of a substantial tendency of viewers to see television as involved in an uncritical glorification of the war and of the effect of the bunker bombing. Only a small minority endorsed the 'too critical' position even after the bunker incident. Even among Conservative voters, more saw television as over-glorifying the war than saw it as too critical, despite Conservative attacks on the BBC. Responses to the same question in our post-war survey confirmed the general pattern. When asked specifically about Amiriya, moreover, 57 per cent agreed that it was right for television to have shown shrouded bodies of the victims, while 35 per cent disagreed.[3]

Asking the same basic questions about national newspaper coverage, we found that, overall, smaller minorities adopted critical positions than was the case for television, although 19 per cent found the newspaper they read 'too patriotic', 30 per cent thought it 'glorified war too much' and 16 per cent were 'dissatisfied'. The differences between the findings for newspapers and television clearly reflect the fact that the former are differentiated products, the latter a relatively uniform product. Although there were some differences between BBC and independent television coverage, and between programmes, these were not sharply defined and it would have made little sense to ask people about programmes or channels when coverage was so uniform.

In choosing their newspaper, people choose a higher or lower level of information, so that informativeness is measured against varying bases. War was liable, however, to raise demands for levels of information different from those normally accepted. In the case of the *Sun* and *Star*, for example, 15 per cent of readers found their paper 'too informative', but equally 16 per cent found it not informative enough. Among readers of the *Daily Mirror*, only 4 per cent found their paper too informative and 20 per cent not informative enough. In contrast, among readers of mid-market tabloids and broadsheets there was much less dissatisfaction on either count. Readers of downmarket tabloids were clearly far less satisfied with their level of information than those of other papers. (This finding was repeated in our second survey.)

A similar pattern can be seen in replies to our question about newspapers' patriotism. Almost a quarter of *Sun* and *Star* readers found their papers too patriotic, as did almost a fifth of *Mirror* readers (although 11 per cent also found it unpatriotic); figures for the mid-market and broadsheet papers were lower. Levels of agreement that newspapers over-glorified the war followed a similar but more pronounced pattern. There is a statistically significant difference in the extent to which respondents assess their own paper as informative and whether or not it glorified the war. Considering that tabloid readers choose their papers knowing of their sensational and generally (with the exception of the *Mirror*) right-wing attitudes, the levels of consumer resistance are significant. A post-Falklands survey also found greater 'dissatisfaction' among tabloid than among broadsheet readers,[4] but our survey, by asking about the tendency of media to 'glorify' war, seems to have shown a larger critical tendency even when readers do not claim to be dissatisfied with their papers' coverage.

Our findings match fairly closely an NOP poll which asked, 'How much do you trust each of the following to tell the truth about what is happening in the Gulf war?' The BBC was trusted a great deal by 69 per cent and ITN, by 67 per cent; briefings by allied military commanders, by 49 per cent, the British government, by 48 per cent and the American government, by 41 per cent. Among newspapers, the *Independent* was trusted by 58 per cent; the *Telegraph*, by 49 per cent; the *Mail*, by 44 per cent; *The Times* and the

Guardian, by 40 per cent; *Today*, by 41 per cent; the *Express* by 29 per cent; the *Mirror*, by 33 per cent; the *Sun* by 29 per cent and the *Star*, by only 24 per cent.[5]

Table 11.4 **Evaluation of national newspapers' coverage of and attitudes to the war, by type of newspaper read (%*)**

	Informative:		Glorifies	Too critical
	Too much	Not enough	too much	
Sun/Star	15	16	41	6
Daily Mirror	7	3	25	5
Other tabloids	4	20	35	9
Broadsheets	5	9	7	4
All papers	8	12	28	6

Chi squared = 26 DoF= 9   Chi squared = 31 DoF = 9
p = <0.002   p = <0.003

* Percentages add up to less than 100, because those finding coverage simply 'informative', or agreeing that it involved a 'sensible attitude to the war', have not been included.

Table 11.5 **Effect of newspaper readership on selected attitudes to the war (raw percentages), and residual effect after controlling for gender, age, tenure status, voting intention and military participation**

	Sun/ Star	Mirror	Mid-market tabloids	Broad- sheets	R2[1]	Sig. of F	Significant 5%	1%
'We have to stand up to dictators' (reason for war)	56	33	35	29	0.038	0.0003	★	★
Saddam 'like Hitler'	48	50	28	16	0.025	0.004	★	★
Saddam 'mad'	42	27	17	8	0.037	0.0004	★	★
'Overthrow Saddam Hussein' (as war aim)	56	51	39	26	0.017	0.02	★	
Use nuclear weapons	16	4	4	3	0.027	0.007	★	
Very concerned about:								
British service personnel	85	86	87	77	0.025	0.03	★	
US service personnel	57	69	57	62	0.029	0.01	★	
Israeli civilians	47	70	51	72	0.007	0.59		
Saudi civilians	48	67	51	73	0.018	0.11		
Saudi service personnel	43	68	45	63	0.029	0.11	★	
Iraqi civilians	28	35	50	64	0.012	0.26		
Iraqi soldier personnel	13	22	31	39	0.012	0.15		
Middle East peace (as war aim)	31	34	28	50	0.008	0.08		

[1] R2 in analysis of the residuals from a regression equation including all controls.

Media and attitudes to the war

We need to distinguish media roles in shaping perceptions of current events (which are clearly critical) and in shaping underlying perceptions and attitudes. It has been widely assumed that television has replaced newspapers both as a primary source of information and as a source of attitudes. Our study suggests, however, that this is too simple a view. We took it for granted that television was the prime source of information on the war for most people, both because of its chronological and visual immediacy and because television news viewing was more universal than newspaper readership. We were much more doubtful about the extension of television's primacy to attitude formation, and this was borne out by the striking correlation of many attitudes to newspaper readership.

There were sharp variations between readers of different papers on a wide range of issues, with a spectrum of attitudes when we divided our sample into four sizeable groups: readers of the *Sun* and the *Star*, of the *Daily Mirror*, of the mid-market tabloids and of broadsheets. Although the pattern of variation itself varied, the spectrum was remarkably consistent, and remained significant in many cases when we controlled for other major variables, as shown in the right hand columns of Table 11.5. These effects also remain after controlling for attitude to television coverage.

These differences in perceptions of and attitudes to the war between readers of newspapers were more extreme and significant than any of the other variations which we measured in our study (see Table 11.6).

The spectrum of attitudes shown in Tables 11.5 and 11.6 cannot be explained mainly by newspapers' party affiliations: attitudes of readers of the Labour-oriented *Mirror* and Conservative-oriented *Sun* and *Star* were often closer to each others' views than either were to readers of Conservative mid-market papers. Nor can this spectrum be explained mainly by class, since the differences between *Sun* and *Star* readers and *Mirror* readers are greater than class-related differences would explain. Although such factors are partial explanations and we could probably construct more complex social profiles of newspaper readerships which would go further in explaining the variations, there is a considerable residuum in many variations which cannot be explained in this manner. If we introduced educational level as a variable,[6] this might explain some newspaper-related variation, since the sorts of papers people read are clearly related to educational experience. It is not clear that this any more than class would explain, say, the differences between *Sun* and *Star* readers and *Mirror* readers.

It seems in any case as implausible to suggest that newspaper identities and ideologies have no (or minimal) significance in shaping readers' attitudes as it would be to suggest that they are the sole (or major) influences. It seems almost perverse to explain political attitudes mainly through 'background' social characteristics and experiences, reflecting social-structural differences. It is far more credible to explain them in terms of people's interactions with mediating ideological forces such as newspapers, which are *directly* involved in providing information and interpretations of events around which attitudes are forming.

Table 11.6 Differences in attitudes according to gender, age, tenure status, voting intention and prior military involvement (chi squared values)

	Gender	Age	Tenure Status	Military Involvement	Voting Intention	Newspaper
'We have to stand up to dictators'	1.7	8.3★★	3.9	0.0	7.0★★	16.8★★★
Saddam Hussein 'like Hitler'	0.2	4.4	4.4	2.4	0.4	27.4★★★
Saddam Hussein 'mad'	4.7★★	5.0★	8.8★★	0.9	1.3	27.9★★★
'Overthrow Saddam Hussein' (as war aim)	8.0★★★	0.6	6.7★★	0.2	3.6	16.8★★
Support use of nuclear weapons	3.1★	0.9	2.3	3.5★	2.6	16.3★★★
Concern for:						
British service personnel	2.0	11.1★★★	4.2	3.2★	6.7★★	3.6
US service personnel	2.5	1.4	0.3	3.5★	2.7	3.7
Israeli civilians	1.1	4.6	1.1	0.6	0.5	14.8★★
Saudi civilians	2.2	1.0	1.1	2.5	0.5	13.4★★★
Saudi service personnel	2.2	3.6	0.3	8.7★★★	0.2	14.8★★★
Iraqi civilians	2.0	3.7	3.6	0.1	0.2	20.5★★★
Iraqi service personnel	4.6★	1.9	1.1	0.0	0.4	13.6★★★
Middle East peace (as war aim)	0.0	1.3	1.6	4.3★	1.5	8.8★★

★★★ significant at 1 per cent
★★ significant at 5 per cent
★   significant at 10 per cent

If educational level did account for much of our 'newspaper' variation, this would not necessarily mean that educational differences rather than newspaper readership 'explained' differences in attitudes. It could rather be interpreted as an expression of an active relationship between educational level and newspaper readership. Newspapers could be seen as means of continuing differentiation of cultural and political identities which, we could speculate, are initially formed to a considerable extent by educational experience.

The findings here suggest that newspapers, although unable to compete with television in terms of instant, visual communication of the war, were nevertheless able to offer much more ideologically complete interpretations of events and stronger advocacy of particular views. Relatively homogeneous television news was legally regulated and politically monitored to produce a relatively neutral product. A differentiated, ideologically and partisan press was able to offer more explicit positions. It is difficult to explain many of the variations in the tables without knowledge of the positions adopted by the newspapers, discussed in Part III. We find, for example, that among *Sun* readers no fewer than 21 per cent favoured using nuclear weapons against Iraq (the figure in Table 11.5 is lowered by combination with *Star* readers). In no other sub-group in our sample, on any dimension, was the percentage supporting this option in double figures. It cannot be accidental that the *Sun*, alone among British newspapers, actually propagandized the use of nuclear weapons. We also find strong, but differentiated, support for the demonization of Saddam Hussein among down-market tabloid readers generally and *Sun* and *Star* readers in particular; this also reflects the personalization of the conflict in these papers.

It is inevitable that the mass media in general and newspapers in particular will have a more immediate role in forming attitudes to current events than any other forces. Most of the other factors which we identified as differentiating attitudes—age, sex, class, politics, religion, military/war experience—represented diffuse elements of social experience and cultural resources for people in British society. While attitudes bound up with these dimensions clearly affected how people felt and responded to the war, they did not provide anything like the immediate, precise and developing interpretations of the press.

Even political and religious positions, which involve ideological interpretations of the world, can have provided people only with general beliefs, which they still had to apply (with the help of the media) to the specific events taking place. Political and religious leaders were not providing their followers with detailed, let alone daily, understandings of and/or positions on the events of the wars. Indeed, some were quite deliberately avoiding such commitments: the leaders of the two opposition parties and the Church of England were the three public figures (out of seven about whom we asked in our second survey) whose position on the war seemed most ambiguous to our respondents.

The media were thus the only institutions continuously interpreting a rapidly developing series of anxiety-producing, threatening and contradictory events to members of society. Although television held the centre stage, newspapers played a special role in this process. They are probably more important as a source of divergent identities in a complex society. In times of crisis, while television assumes primacy as a source of information (and the immediate interpretations which go with it), newspapers play a vital role as a focus of more general interpretations and positions, linked explicitly to the differentiated sets of values which (in buying the product) readers have to some extent chosen for themselves. Where particular events were strongly ideologically represented in the press, as with the Amiriya bombing, newspaper interpretations may overcome television images in forming perceptions and attitudes. Only where television, exceptionally, engages in strong advocacy—as over Kurdistan—does its messages apparently triumph over the press.

Notes and references

1. We used housing tenure status because occupational measures of 'class' proved, as usual, very difficult to construct. By tenure status we meant whether respondents were owner-occupiers, or rented their home from either their local council, a housing association or a private landlord.

2. In fifty-one cases the postmark was illegible.

3. For complementary findings and further discussion, see Morrison, 1992.

4. Morrison and Tumber, 1988.

5. *Independent*, 16 February 1991.

6. Educational questions were unfortunately omitted from our hurriedly drafted questionnaires.

CHAPTER TWELVE

Men and women:
self-representation and memory

Our surveys showed us how people *en masse* responded to standard representations; our categories were often based closely on those represented by media and official discourse. They told us little about how individuals in British society would have represented themselves and how they would utilize standard representations in presenting their own views. In order to investigate this further we needed more qualitative evidence than a survey can provide. I was fortunate to be able to examine the 'diaries' which the Mass-Observation Archive asked their national panel of respondents to keep during the Gulf crisis.[1] Few panelists actually provided diaries, but their self-structured writings represent a rich source of material.

The panel is more female, middle class and middle- or even old-aged than the British population at large. The responses to the Gulf 'directive', of just over half the panel, certainly reflected if they did not exacerbate these biases. The two main analytical themes which emerge—gender differences and how recollections of the Second World War informed the responses of older people to the Gulf conflict—reflect this distribution of the panelists.[2]

Survey data had underlined the importance of both gender and age differences in responses to distant violence. Table 11.6 showed that gender was highly significant on two items: the perception of Saddam Hussein as 'mad' and endorsement of his overthrow as a war aim. Women identified more than men with both of these issues, indicating a pattern of women's 'personalization' of the war around Saddam Hussein. However, our data also indicated that men were more likely than women (36 per cent to 21 per cent) to approve 'strongly' of the war; women were more likely (57 per cent to 36 per cent) to agree that they were 'worried' by the war. Crewe argued, writing about polls on defence in the early 1980s, that gender differences were 'slender': his conclusion that 'fewer than ten percentage points divide men and women in their answers to most questions' is not borne out by these findings.[3]

Our data also indicated age dimensions: older men, like women, did not share the 'excitement' or 'fascination' with the war which some younger men acknowledged. Table 11.6 showed that age was significant in perceptions and attitudes: older people were more likely to perceive Saddam Hussein as like Hitler and to see 'standing up to dictators' as a reason for the war. The major reason for these differences, which the Mass-Observation data help us to explore, is the contrasting experiences of war among older and younger generations. Older people especially tend to interpret new wars in terms of their memories of the Second World War, which was a fundamental life-experience for many people aged in their fifties and upwards in the early 1990s.

Memory, of course, cannot be understood as freestanding. Memories of 1939–45 are products both of the ways individuals appropriated their experiences at the time and of how initial memories have shaped and been shaped by subsequent experience. Memories are also products of national traditions and myths and both sustain and are sustained by these wider forces, shaping collective versions of memory.[4] Traditions and myths, in turn, are constantly renewed in political and ideological contexts, as political leaders seek to turn them to their own advantage and as interpreters, notably in mass media, seek to present new versions for our consumption. This discussion, like other academic studies, can also be understood as just such an attempt, although hopefully less narrowly motivated than many.

I wanted to discover something about how the relationship between old and new experiences worked—for example, the extent to which responses were based on deeply felt memories of the violence and hurt of war or on more ideologically constructed memories of sets of political circumstances. The evidence suggested a great deal, too, about how this relationship was gendered. Some survey respondents had added comments which suggested that fear and anxiety about war came from past experiences. 'I am not a war-monger,' wrote one woman, 'having been blitzed out during the last war. I dread to think of my grandchildren and what they are going to have to live through in the future.' Or from another older woman, 'I have been on the receiving end of bombs from the air, and I would not wish it on anyone.'

It seems plausible to suggest that personal memories like these, although held only by a minority who were affected in this way, are an important source of general anxiety about war in the population. Individual memories no doubt combine with knowledge about the horrors, dangers, hardships and coercion of war, imparted in families as well as by mass media and education, to form a popular perception of war partly at odds with, although doubtless also partly compatible with, more heroic and patriotic myths of past conflicts.[5]

When we look in detail at how people expressed on paper, in their own words, their interest in and approach to the Gulf War, we find striking differences between men and women, especially in the Second World War generation. Women's responses often reflect personal recollections of the horror of war which we have already illustrated. At its strongest, memory is harnessed to a firm rejection of war, as in this comment by a retired secretary in her sixties:

I suppose there are many who did not see the results of the blitz on London and South East England. I saw a mentally and physically handicapped boy left in his wheelchair with his mother dying on the ground beside him, that's war. War in the Gulf—NEVER, NEVER, NEVER.[6]

The same woman, writing a month before the outbreak of war, has a vivid picture of the way in which it will turn out: 'The poor souls who fought in the sand will be left with their legs shot off, maybe half a face missing. War in the Gulf NO, NO, NO'. Another woman, comparing air raid sirens remembered from the Second World War, makes the imaginative leap from her own to the Iraqis' experience: 'It must have been terrible living in Baghdad with air raids every night, something the children will never forget.'[7]

At the other extreme, some older women's fears are for a return of mundane hardships associated with life on the home front. A social worker reports her seventy-one-year-old mother as 'convinced that the Gulf War would bring rationing like they had in World War 2. She advised me to buy up metal items like saucepans.' The daughter, who reports that when she first heard the news of the Iraqi invasion she 'felt very anxious and frightened', also reports her own everyday worries—about petrol shortages, plans to close down local maternity wards to deal with Gulf casualties, and the appeals for blood donors.[8]

Different ways in which concern is expressed reflect the contrasting experiences of women according to their ages during the Second World War. A woman in her fifties, for example, who articulates a common female denial of expertise on the politics of war, gives a child's perspective on war: 'This is not a subject that I am equipped to comment upon but I have lived as a child through World War II and I would not wish that experience on other children.'[9]

It is actually rare to find a woman respondent who does not express concern about the threatening side of war. Doubtless panelists, having volunteered to write about their feelings, are likely to include a higher proportion of more critically minded and literate people (worried readers of broadsheet and mid-market papers) than would be found in the general population. Nevertheless these sentiments are not found in the same way among male panelists, and the patriotic woman whose main point is that 'I object strongly to various councils who are preventing people from displaying the Union flag. I'd like to see it flying from every flagpole. There's a lack of patriotism which I would like to see back again'[10] is actually quite exceptional.

Perhaps the best general impression of contradictory feelings among women who had experienced the Second World War is given in the diary of a retired secretary in her seventies:

(16/11/90) Having lived through two world wars, I cannot believe I could see another.

(16/1/91) It is Dead Line. Memories of World War II are still flooding back.

(17/1/91) Awoke to find war had started. My head felt in a whirl and I started to tremble.

(19/1/91) I met many of my friends of my own age group (late 70s) this afternoon. All were saying how they are reliving the days of World War II.

(3/2/91) The older ones who remember war ... are apprehensive and regretful that we should have arrived at this state of affairs, yet they are fiercely patriotic. [A nurse told her of an eleven-year-old girl who said 'I'm glad we are at war', and when asked why replied, 'I missed the other two!'] 'I wonder how long she will feel like that?'

(27/2/91) I have also observed there is a generation gap, it is the grandparents and their grandchildren who are most apprehensive. The middle generation are confident of victory.

(1/3/91) I still think war is so futile but with dictators such as Saddam Hussein it was necessary. He is a megalomaniac, as Hitler was.[11]

The equation of Saddam with Hitler is volunteered by many of the older women, as by the older men—it is rare that we find exceptions to this view. One was the woman who spotted a different likeness, a physical one of Saddam with Stalin, which she demonstrated with photographs.[12] A less common response was that of the woman who wrote, 'I get sickened by some of the cant and hyperbole too—Saddam Hussein is certainly aggressive, but a "Hitler?"—no!'[13]

Older women are less likely to express the feeling shown by quite a number of younger women, who admit to being confused or even simply uninterested in world events, as in this not untypical comment:

> I've two main responses—one is boredom and the other is worry. I know I should be interested in world affairs, but the Gulf has no direct connection with me, or my family. The news—or is it the speculation—is so unremitting that one gets saturated by the coverage and switches off. ... As yet the crisis is too remote, in place not time.[14]

This complaint is rarer among men, almost all of whom aspire to political or strategic knowledge. Even one unusual man—who confesses, early on in the conflict, that 'I have a mental blockage with this subject—I just shut it out, so that I cannot remember the names of various politicians, generals, etc.'—later finds the common male appetite for this sort of information.[15] Men, younger as well as older, tend to think strategically, politically, logistically and back to the world wars, as in this reflection of a man in his forties, too young to have actually experienced war himself:

> We can deliver a boy with a broken leg or an upset tummy to a UK hospital within, say, 12 hours of him arriving at the Gulf airhead for the flight home— probably comparable with the time from Etaples to Charing Cross in 1914–18! ...

With all that going on, we probably don't think too much about the whys and wherefores: a lot of time is taken up with studying intelligence reports and operational data; little time is devoted to explanation.[16]

However 'what stands out' is that Saddam Hussein is like Hitler, 'if you substitute Kurds for Jews ... , Kuwait for Poland and so on'.

Older men manifest this greater aptitude for things political and military within the context of their own experience of war, often very different from the women's but which is also relived as they write about the Gulf. There is a surprising number of respondents who were actually in the Middle East or North Africa, suggesting that panelists with this background may have been stimulated to write by the Gulf events.

Comments which are thrown up range from these rather desultory and mildly racist remarks: 'My only personal experience of the Middle East was during the war, in Egypt and the Western Desert. ... As far as we were concerned they were all wogs (wily oriental gentlemen) but to be fair I didn't have much to do with them as the army led its own life in vast base camps',[17] to these altogether sharper and more vivid statements (by a retired civil servant in his sixties) which contrast the apparent ease of the Gulf war victory with the horrors of his own war more than four decades previously:

> (8/11/90) My only experience of the Middle East is WWII back and forth across that desert like a yo-yo, hot clammy days and freezing nights.

> (28/2/91) The Gulf War has ended, lost lives, revenge wanted on Hussein, Yanks basking in the glory they could never achieve in Vietnam. ... How could they lose, the odds of 30-to-1 against. Did they face Tobruk, Benghazi, did they hell, 6 weeks was all it took, no Rommel to outwit them. ... But plenty of books telling how it was, what I did, what I saw, then the armchair general giving versions on TV at £75 a throw, we should have done this, we should have done that, Monty was missed.[18]

This point about the difference between the Gulf and the Second World War is reinforced by a teacher, ex-RAF:

> I lived through the phony war in uniform, I can only call this the screwy war. Here we had troops ringing up their Mum from the front—asking for sweets and comics—spilling the beans about all sorts of security matters. ... I wondered at times who was fighting on our side, little boys—and girls. ... We heard of stress—even battle fatigue was mentioned—before a shot was fired. Oh dear! What a do.... I might have written home—I did from Burma—but not for sweets and comics.[19]

Whereas many women relived the fear of being bombed and sympathize with civilians on the receiving end in Iraq, men tended to imagining what it must be like to face the Gulf War as a combatant: 'Imagine,' wrote one, 'as I read in the *Daily Mirror*, of being vapourised by 3,000 degrees Centigrade of a shell passing through a tank and out the other side.'[20]

It is not only those who were in the Middle East whose memories were stimulated. Personal experience and political logic were related in many men's minds, as these comments illustrate:

> Believe me, I am no jingoist. I was born in 1926, and saw the last war, and was in the RN for the last 18 months of it. The nearest thing I had to a hero was Mahatma Gandhi, in my schooldays ... short of letting this monster devour our fellow-men, the military build-up is inevitable. ... Saddam Hussein is another Hitler ... in some ways he is worse.

After the shelter bombing, the same man writes that 'From a personal point of view I'm outraged that civilians might have been placed in harm's way and I blame the Iraqi government and leadership for that.' He agrees with Denis Healey—who has his respect as a 'beachmaster' in 1939–45—quoted as saying, 'If you engage in a very large bombing campaign a lot of civilians are bound to be killed.'[21] Other men make similar points, with a greater implicit acceptance than among women of the inevitability of the horrors of war.[22]

For younger generations, the Second World War is still a pivotal experience which has been passed on in many ways, but it is reinforced by their own memories of wars experienced only via television screens and newspaper columns, as in this comment by a man in his forties:

> I was born during WWII, of now-abused memory, and that war has always been a paradigm to me of the need, when history offers no other way out, to fight and destroy anti-human forces. As a relatively young adult I watched the heroism of the Vietnamese people in their resistance to invasion. No one had the right to ask them to die down under the American onslaught. Pacifism has never made any sense to me, if only because (as Orwell says) it means in practice allowing other people to do the fighting, and dying, on your behalf. But there is no cause in the Gulf comparable to the defeat of fascism or the winning of national liberation.[23]

These comments suggest that, even as individuals' lived memories of 1939–45 die away, records of these memories remain, helping to sustain myths with which, indeed, memories themselves are so powerfully intertwined. Even a post-military society is still a society in which memories of war are both aroused and mobilized in the cultural struggle which has replaced the 'home front' in current conflicts. The success of the tabloids' evocation of Hitler in their presentation of Saddam Hussein is apparent in the Mass-Observation diaries as it is in the survey evidence. It should remind us how potent are the myths of past wars and how propaganda about the past colours perceptions and memories.

Notes and references

1. The request (known in Mass-Observation as a 'directive') was sent out quite early in the crisis, in October 1990, so that responses cover the build-up to war as well as the war itself. The material can be consulted in the Archive which is based at the University of Sussex Library.

2. The Mass-Observation panel for the Gulf directive was made up of 1,100 people, of whom 591 (54 per cent) replied. As the following table shows, the breakdowns by sex of this panel, of the respondents and of a wider group of M-O panelists in the 1980s and 1990s were almost identical.★

3. Crewe, 1985; p. 48.

4. Since memory is, in its most basic meaning, a quality of individual human beings, I am reluctant to use terms such as 'national memory' which imply a common memory among whole populations, when such a common memory does not exist *as memory* (although it may as myth). Hence the term 'collective *versions* of memory' seems appropriate to suggest the active construction of memories *for* people which tends to be involved.

5. That a widespread awareness of the horror of war is brought by television viewers to their viewing of newsreels is also suggested by Morrison's (1992, p. 33) report of responses to uncut footage of the Amiriya shelter bombing compared to that actually broadcast.

6. M-O A: DR 666.

7. M-O A: DR 1424.

8. M-O A: DR 826.

9. M-O A: DR 68.

10. M-O A: DR 1559.

11. M-O A: DR 36.

12. M-O A: DR 2053.

13. M-O A: DR 2258.

14. M-O A: DR 1673.

15. M-O A: DR 828.

16. M-O A: DR 1810.

17. M-O A: DR 2134.

18. M-O A: DR 2185.

19. M-O A: DR 2506.

20. M-O A: DR 38.

21. M-O A: DR 276.

22. This acceptance of the inevitability of the horrors of war does not, however, imply that men make light of them, as Major appears to have found to his cost when his proposed 1994 'celebration' (rather than commemoration) of the 50th anniversary of D-Day aroused outrage among veterans, many of whom remembered the large numbers of their comrades who had fallen in the Normandy landings.

23. M-O A: DR 1671.

★	Total participants in M-O panels		Gulf directive: panel		Gulf directive: respondents	
men	700	30.5 per cent	341	31 per cent	181	30.6 per cent
women	1,596	69.5 per cent	759	69 per cent	410	69.4 per cent
totals	2,296		1,100		591	

I read and analysed the files of 149 respondents (92 women, 57 men), i.e. just over 25 per cent of the total.

— Part V —

Comparisons and
Perspectives

CHAPTER THIRTEEN

From Kurdistan to Bosnia and Rwanda

The Kurdish crisis is the only clear-cut case, of all the conflicts in the early 1990s, in which media coverage compelled intervention by the Western powers. Although this crisis marked an important shift in the principles of global politics, in which national sovereignty and non-intervention were subordinated to human rights and international intervention, the precedent was limited. This was because what the media did was to make explicit a nexus of responsibility already established by the actions of the Western-led coalition in the Gulf War and their appeals for the overthrow of the Iraqi regime. We can therefore ask: was the Kurdish case the exception rather than a new rule? The answer, however, is not simple: while this case involved a simple equation of Western responsibility, media coverage and international intervention which has not been replicated elsewhere, the elements of the equation are present in variable degrees in other situations. In this chapter I develop a comparative discussion to suggest how these relationships work out in the broad range of cases as a preliminary to a more general conclusion in the final chapter of this book. Discussion in this chapter is based not on primary research but on secondary information: it indicates hypotheses for further research.

Media and the making of 'global crises'

I have argued that in the post-Cold War era, global crises may be constituted even where the interests of major powers are not involved in a direct or obvious way, if there is a world-wide *perception* of large-scale violations of life and globally legitimate principles. I also argued that the existence of a global crisis can be confirmed by the occurrence of, or significant pressure for, internationally legitimate *intervention* (humanitarian, political or military) to resolve the crisis. I indicated that media coverage had much to do with the constitution of global crises in these senses.

The Iraqi wars illustrate some of the range of possibilities. The invasion of Kuwait was a global crisis brought about by old-fashioned reasons of state—Western powers and others saw their interests as well as international law violated—rather than because of media coverage of the effects of invasion. Indeed, there was no direct coverage which was partly why the plight of Kuwaitis (let alone Palestinians and South Asians in Kuwait) was never the main issue in the Gulf War. It was rather the principles of defeating aggression and returning Kuwait to independent statehood around which the war was fought.

In the aftermath, the first and (probably, in terms of people involved and lives lost) largest revolt against Saddam Hussein's regime was that of the largely Shia people of southern Iraq, centred on Basra. This revolt, its brutal suppression and the flood of refugees which followed, never constituted a global crisis. There was no serious pressure for intervention, although US troops occupied a sizeable part of southern Iraq and were within easy striking distance of Basra and other centres of the revolt. The refugee crisis resulting from the later Kurdish revolt and its suppression, on the other hand, did become a global crisis, resulting in huge media and public pressure for intervention, to which Western leaders succumbed.

Both revolts resulted from the defeat of the Iraqi regime in the Gulf War, and Western responsibility for this defeat and for inciting revolt was identical in each case. We must clearly look for other reasons why one revolt became a global crisis and the other did not. We might examine the importance of timing: the southern revolt erupted when Bush had just halted military action, when coalition governments and peoples were celebrating the liberation of Kuwait, the end of the war and the prospective return of their troops. It was unfortunate for the rebels that their calls for assistance cut across popular feelings of relief—reflected in the media— that the war was over and politicians' calculations that this was the time to cash in on success. In contrast, by the time the Kurds' situation became desperate, the initial relief over the war's ending had faded and media and people were more open to consider their need for help.

However, the southern revolt and its dire consequences continued until well after the Kurdish crisis attracted world attention and yet never became global issues. Whatever the importance of timing, it was not as important as access for Western reporters and above all cameras and the portable satellite dishes by which film is transmitted to television studios. It is difficult to avoid the conclusion that the unfilmability of Basra and other southern cities was the central difference in Western responses compared to Kurdistan. The majority of Shia refugees fled to Iran, which media organizations regarded largely as a no-go area. Within the Kurdish crisis, too, nearly all attention was focused on refugees on the border with Turkey to the neglect of those in or near Iran.

Another factor at work here was the media's (and Western governments') difficulty in focusing on more than one crisis at a time: the south could never be more than an adjunct to the Kurdish story. This factor also affected the wider significance of the Iraqi wars. During the nine months from August 1990–April 1991 inclusive, Iraqi stories dominated international news in Western media. But 1991 was also a fateful year for emerging post-Cold War realities in which two other major crises came to a head. In July the wars of Slovenian and Croatian independence began, opening a period of wars and genocide unprecedented in the European continent since 1945. A month later the failed coup against the Gorbachev regime occurred, signalling the break-up of the Soviet Union.

Therefore for three-quarters of the year preceding these two world-shaking events, the world's governments and media alike were pre-occupied with Iraq. There was some awareness, of course, that momentous events were happening in the USSR. When Soviet military attacked a Lithuanian radio station in January 1991 (just before the attack on Iraq), killing twelve people, there was briefly some attention and media com-mentary criticizing the muted responses of Western governments (explained by their need to keep the USSR onside against Iraq). But generally throughout this nine-month period the Soviet and Yugoslav crises received very limited Western attention, from both governments and media. Viewing television news and reading newspapers from early 1991, I was struck by how the Soviet and Yugoslav stories occasionally surfaced, only to disappear almost without trace for days and weeks, except from inside the broadsheets, in contrast to the intensive coverage of the revolutions of 1989. The main reason was minimal governmental attention to these same crises: if Western governments had been actively concerned, media attention would have followed.

The importance of this case is that it concerns developments which even by traditional statist standards were of major importance to the West: the Soviet events from a world point of view, those in Yugoslavia from at least a European standpoint. Western governments and media were to pay them enough attention in due course. But the year from mid-1990 to mid-1991 was crucial to the development of both crises, and attention was diverted elsewhere.

If this could happen with crises which were manifestly of geopolitical importance, it is not difficult to understand how crises of less clear-cut significance never became global crises. None of the wars within and between the former Soviet republics received more than passing attention from Western governments, media and the UN. These included the long-running inter-state war between Armenia and Azerbaijan; the major civil war in Tzadjikistan, with international dimensions involving Afghanistan and Iran; various civil wars in Georgia; and the war in Moldova between Romanian- and Russian-speaking parties. Only the war between the Russian army and separatists in Chechnya, in 1994–5, attracted major world attention because it involved Russia directly and brought into question the evolution of the Russian state, although for the same reasons any serious intervention was out of the question.

One reason for the neglect of post-Soviet crises was probably the tacit assumption of Western media as well as governments that, despite the collapse of the USSR, successor states—mostly members of the loose Russian-dominated Confederation of Independent States—were within the Russian sphere of influence. The only likely exceptions to the acceptance of Russian hegemony over its 'near abroad' were the Baltic states—because of their European orientation and Western acceptance that their original independence had been illegitimately usurped by Stalin—and Ukraine—because of its size and geopolitical significance. A major conflict between Russia and Ukraine would have had global repercussions, although in the early 1990s they just about succeeded in managing their differences.

Respect for the geopolitical interests of major non-Western powers cannot be invoked as an explanation for the lack of serious Western or UN attention to other wars. In parts of Asia, Latin America and Africa, civil wars have been endemic in recent decades. During the Cold War, these conflicts were interpreted in terms of global conflict between the Western and Soviet blocs. Some wars, like those in the 1980s in Angola, Mozambique, Ethiopia, Afghanistan, Nicaragua and Cambodia, were seen as surrogate conflicts of the blocs and their ideologies. Others, like the Iran–Iraq war, the Palestinian–Israeli conflict and the anti-apartheid struggle in South Africa, while not seen directly as East–West issues, were interpreted in terms of their significance for the global struggle of the blocs.

With the end of the Cold War, most of these conflicts have ended or changed form. In general, Western involvement with and attention to them has declined. In Ethiopia, the fall of the Soviet-backed regime and the success of the Eritrean separatists has taken the country out of the world's politics and headlines. In Cambodia, the UN mounted its most elaborate political intervention to date, organizing elections which replaced the Vietnamese-backed regime with a monarchist-led coalition, excluding the genocidist Khmer Rouge (formerly receiving Chinese and tacit Anglo–American support) from power; governments and media lost interest after the elections. In Mozambique, a similar operation to reconcile the Frelimo regime and the Renamo guerrillas, deprived of their respective Soviet and South African backers, received virtually no media coverage. Once a more amenable right-wing government was installed in Nicaragua, in a historic compromise with the former Sandanista regime, US and world attention virtually disappeared.

These declines of governmental and media attention could be seen as inevitable given shifts from war and extreme crisis to reconciliation and reconstruction. What is more striking, therefore, is that where major civil wars continued after 1989, Western governments and media also showed minimal interest. In Cambodia, the continuing war between the new coalition and the Khmer Rouge was virtually ignored except when Westerners were taken hostage. In Afghanistan, when the Soviet-backed regime fell after Gorbachev withdrew military support, a new civil war among victorious Islamic factions was of minimal interest to the world, although the USA had previously supplied them.

Perhaps the most striking case is Angola, where after the USA and South Africa had withdrawn their support from UNITA, and the USSR and Cuba theirs from the MPLA government, UNITA refused to accept the results of UN-sponsored elections and launched a new phase of civil war. Although hundreds of thousands may have died in the ensuing bloodbath, Western governments and media alike largely turned a blind eye. Events quite as horrific as those in Iraq, Bosnia or Rwanda made only the most occasional headlines. The UN and voluntary agencies had a modest presence, but otherwise there was little response.

In contrast to these desperate wars which failed to become global crises, several conflicts which did not become all-out wars received massive Western attention. Foremost among these were the Palestinian–Israeli and South African conflicts. Both involved violent struggle, the *intifada* and revolt and repression in the townships as well as guerrilla actions, but culminated in political accommodations—albeit on very different terms— between regimes and their main political opponents. Why did these conflicts receive great diplomatic and media attention, while Angola and Afghanistan were left to take their much more violent courses?

Gowing describes media conflict coverage as like

> supermarket war video—editorially, we can pick and choose—just like walking down the shelves of breakfast cereal. One day Nagorno Karabakh. The next day Tajikistan. Perhaps Georgia, or Afghanistan. Then a bit of Angola, Liberia or Yemen and perhaps Algeria if we are lucky.[1]

But the real question is why television rarely chooses these exotic brands, preferring to stick to old favourites.

The explanation for this pattern of responses by Western governments, media and civil societies centres around two concepts: strategic interests and histories of linkage. What distinguished Palestine–Israel and South Africa were that they remained strategically important to Western states even after the Cold War and that there were important histories of linkage with Western societies. Palestine–Israel lay at the heart of the many-sided regional conflicts in the Middle East, the world's major oil-supplying and most heavily armed region. The Israeli settler population was closely linked to the powerful Jewish lobby in the USA, and the USA and other Western states had been involved with negotiations over the problem over decades. Similarly, South Africa is the most powerful industrial state in Africa, the single-most important key to the sub-Saharan continent. Even more than Israel, South Africa was in many ways as much a part of the West as, say, Australia and New Zealand. There were deep historic links with Britain and other European states, and for decades the West had set itself against apartheid. These conflicts and attempts at settlement could not but be matters of concern to Western states, societies and media.

These reasons set Palestine–Israel and South Africa, like Iraq, apart from a general rule of state and media indifference. Just as in the case of Iraq, in these instances strategic interests were powerful; and just as in the Kurdish case there was linkage with previous Western intervention, so in these cases there were (much longer and stronger) histories of involvement. In Palestine–Israel and South Africa, however, Western intervention was primarily diplomatic and economic rather than military and humanitarian: there was no full-scale war, no massive destruction and less instantaneous misery.

The question therefore remains: were the Iraqi wars exceptions to the general Western responses to war and suffering? The first part of the answer is fairly obvious: the Gulf is the only crisis of the post-Cold War years to date in which the West has seen its strategic interests engaged sufficiently to go to war. The second is less so: some of the elements of that series of events have been present in a number of other crises since 1991. I shall now turn from the general run of wars which have remained local in significance to other wars which have become global political crises. First I deal in some detail with the post-Yugoslav wars, which have received by far the most extensive political, military, humanitarian and media attention of all post-Iraqi wars. Then I deal more briefly with other instances of crises which have achieved global significance.

Media, intervention and non-intervention in the post-Yugoslav wars

The break-up of Yugoslavia was a major European if not world event. Yugoslavia had a unique role in Cold War history. It was the main independent Communist state, outside Soviet and Chinese spheres of influence; in between Eastern and Western Europe; a forerunner of 'market socialism'; a bastion of workers' co-operatives idealized by the new left; and leader of the world nonaligned movement. It was also a multinational state, a patchwork of republics and ethnic groups. For West Europeans its Mediterranean coast was a common holiday destination like Greece or Spain, within hours of Britain by air and Germany by car.

The eruption of the wars of Yugoslav succession (I shall call them the 'post-Yugoslav wars'), the first in continental Europe since the 1940s, could only be of profound significance for European states, societies and media.[2] Unlike Third World wars which had continued apace since 1945 and conflicts in the Caucasian and Central Asian regions of the former USSR, the ex-Yugoslav wars were demonstrably within Europe, on the borders of the European Community and in a state which had seemed a likely candidate for membership. The EC saw the ex-Yugoslav crisis as its responsibility, and its foreign ministers attempted forlornly to negotiate a peaceful solution.

The wars of Slovenian (1991), Croatian (1991–2) and Bosnian (1992–5) independence were therefore major European crises.[3] Since Europe is still a pivotal region and Western Europe a component of the Western bloc, they were also global crises. They were, however, crises in which EC states, after their initial failures in mediation, wished to limit intervention to diplomatic and humanitarian actions, and which the USA regarded as European affairs. Only after the failure of EC diplomacy and monitoring to influence the course of events were UN troops introduced, initially to police cease-fire lines in Croatia and then to protect humanitarian convoys in Bosnia-Herzegovina.[4]

Western and UN interventions in ex-Yugoslavia were undertaken for almost completely opposite reasons to those in Iraq. Whereas in Iraq the objective was to reverse the occupation of Kuwait, in ex-Yugoslavia there was no aim of undoing Serbian occupations of large parts of Croatia and Bosnia (or Croatian occupation of Bosnia). On the contrary, UN forces had strictly limited mandates; the United Nations Protection Force (UNPROFOR) in Bosnia was established to protect UN personnel, not the civilian population (although to a limited degree it did this in some situations) let alone to reverse aggression.[5] EC and UN negotiators and the 'Contact Group' of major powers produced successive 'peace plans' which largely legitimated Serbian and Croatian gains in Bosnia.

Western media were operating, therefore, on different terrain from that in Iraq. On the one hand, since UN forces were not fighting a war and their intervention was partial, incremental and multilateral (not dominated by a single power like the USA in Iraq), there was no overall plan for media management. While local media in ex-Yugoslavia were, with a few honourable and courageous exceptions, utterly controlled and propagandistic, Western media were not compelled to toe either a UN or a national line (although some were voluntarily nationalistic about 'their' troops among UN forces).

On the other hand, when journalists reported on horrific events in ex-Yugoslavia, the nexus of Western responsibility was weak. The EC's recognition strategy towards Croatia and Bosnia had naïvely encouraged the view that it was possible to achieve independence from Yugoslavia without confronting Serbian-controlled military power; but there had been no prior war against Serbia and the EC; the USA and the UN had incited no one to fight. When journalists argued that the West should save victims in Bosnia, they were appealing to a general sense of the responsibility which went with power rather than a specific sense connected to prior Western actions. In Iraq they cut with the grain of Western policy; in ex-Yugoslavia they cut across it.

Western policy—in the sense of an underlying agreement not to intervene militarily to prevent or reverse Serbian and Croatian aggression—was largely implicit. Concretely a lack of policy, or shifting, confused and contradictory policies, were often more evident. There was never the unity of the West and the UN which the USA mobilized in the Gulf. The EC appeared to lead but it was divided and, once war broke out, in disarray. Germany's lead in the early diplomatic phase gave way to British and French leadership: they committed the largest number of UN troops but were also the most cautious of all Western states.

The stances of national governments often seemed confused and changeable. The USA, especially under Clinton—who as a presidential candidate in 1992 had promised more vigorous action to support Bosnia but who as president vacillated hopelessly—wanted to influence events but not to put forces on the ground. Russia sought to block many of the limited anti-Serbian measures which the West could agree, gaining more influence as Western weakness and divisions became apparent. The UN bureaucracy in New York was notably reluctant to initiate action; Secretary-General

Boutros-Ghali not only bowed to major powers but seemed to believe that Bosnia should not be prioritized over other crises. On the ground there were differences of direction between UNPROFOR and the United Nations High Commission for Refugees (UNHCR) and voluntary agencies who were actually helping civilian victims.

In contrast to the Gulf War, there was no clear governmental position from which Western and global media might take their cue. Television channels and newspapers varied in general and at particular moments in their endorsement, if at all, of the West's underlying reluctance to get involved. In general, the contrast between the West's strength of purpose in the Gulf and its weakness in ex-Yugoslavia meant that media found it difficult wholeheartedly to endorse governments' inaction. Reporters who witnessed or filmed the aftermath of appalling atrocities often found themselves, as in Kurdistan, urging implicitly or explicitly that 'something must be done'. Non-intervention might seem good *realpolitik* to political leaders, but it hardly made a principled stand for the leader columns. While some rationalized the West's position, others constantly nudged the powers further and a few took a strongly critical stance—urging for example the lifting of the arms embargo which mainly hit the Bosnian government.

The media often signified the realities which the politicians wished to convey. While American media like their government tended to be verbally supportive of the Bosnian state, British media often reflected their government's studied neutrality towards aggressors and victims. British newspapers, especially tabloids, wrote simply about 'Muslims', 'Croats' and 'Serbs', thus presenting the wars as conflicts between ethnic groups. British television too picked up the language of 'warring groups' or 'factions' which put all on a par. For much of the Bosnian war, the BBC subtly endorsed an ethnic account by always referring to the legitimate and pluralist Bosnian government, which prided itself on its own and its forces' multi-ethnic composition, as 'the mainly Muslim Bosnian government'. (In 1995 they reverted to 'the Bosnian government'.)

Virtually no one in British media departed from usage which referred to the Serbian nationalist regime of Radovan Karadzic, responsible for the largest genocide, as the 'Bosnian Serbs'—although over 200,000 people of Serb origin remained in government territory as late as 1995, some of them active opponents of or even fighters against Karadzic's regime in Pale. Likewise, the leaders of the Croatian mini-state, responsible for genocide against Muslims in Mostar and central Bosnia, were the 'Bosnian Croats'— although more Croats lived in government areas than the Croatian statelet and many opposed Croatian nationalism. After several years of war, these designations were employed even by British opponents of the Serbians and Croatians; ethnic nationalism had triumphed in the language of British media.

Despite these implicit accommodations to the official line, media in Britain and elsewhere often played critical roles, implicitly generating pressure for intervention, Kurdish-style. Certainly this is how media were perceived by government and politicians, who complained that the 'something must be done' brigade in the media were forcing their hand. This question would repay detailed study of the kind we have given to the Gulf and Kurdistan. Some evidence has been presented by media analysts, but no one has yet presented a close analysis of the kind offered on the Iraqi case. As a guide to such work rather than a substitute for it, the remainder of this section offers a schematic outline of the main issues in understanding media coverage of the ex-Yugoslav wars in the light of this book's analysis.

The outbreak of each of the wars, in Slovenia and Croatia in 1991 and Bosnia in 1992, was thoroughly covered in Western media. The focus was on the major urban bombardments, with horrifying footage of the levelling of Croatian cities such as Osijek and Vukovar, the shelling of historic Dubrovnik and the beginnings of the siege of Sarajevo. The question which needs to be investigated is how far Western media really conveyed the nature of the genocide—the systematic village-by-village and town-by-town clearing of millions from their homes, the brutal house-by-house killing of tens of thousands. Another issue is the adoption of the term 'ethnic cleansing', which originated with its Serbian practitioners: another disturbing indication of how the nationalist agenda was accepted.

The problem with this genocide is that much occurred not in well-publicized contests for towns and cities but in areas which Serbian and Croatian forces already controlled when fighting began. Genocide occurred chiefly behind rather than on the front lines; it was easily shielded from the direct gaze of the world's press. While the world was aware of the suffering of Sarajevo, Muslim and Croat communities throughout Serbian-controlled Croatia and Bosnia, and Muslim and Serb communities in Croatian-controlled Bosnia were expelled and often slaughtered. Just as in southern Iraq, killing on a massive scale failed to make headlines largely because it could not be filmed. Although, as in Iraq, there were eye-witness accounts by victims, what appeared in the media chiefly depended on where journalists and their cameras could go. This tied coverage disproportionately to Sarajevo and later to the movements of Western UN troops whom journalists tended to accompany.

Visual images were so important. There were reports of Serbian concentration camps—ignored by Western governments and the UN—from the start of the Bosnian war, but it was not until ITN, with the *Guardian*'s Ed Vulliamy, actually managed to visit and film emaciated inmates at one camp, in August 1992, that the story became big news. This was the most important case in which journalists actually 'discovered' a major atrocity and were able to make it a political issue.[6] Because of the emotive label, 'concentration camp', Serbian camps were quickly identified with Nazi extermination camps. Although the camps were not devoted to extermination in the same way, the pattern of killing and abuse in them made the link entirely plausible. The international public outcry fuelled demands for Western intervention, took Western governments off-guard and caused Serbian leaders to make a major public climbdown and disown the camps.

Although huge media coverage attended this exposé, it was not sustained once the story returned to the 'routine' of ethnic cleansing: burning of villages, killings, rapes, etc. Instead, most ongoing attention was still devoted to Sarajevo and, especially, the shuffling to and fro of Western peace envoys, the various plans (the compromises of which grew ever more sordid but were little criticized), the heroic efforts of peace convoys and the movements of increasing numbers of UN troops. As in winter 1992 and spring 1993 the Serbians mopped up their gains in eastern Bosnia and the Croatians in western Bosnia and Herzegovina, Western media made little of the spread of genocide. Towns and villages fell in the most appalling circumstances with only isolated reports, if any. People fleeing the Serbian capture of Cespa, for example, reported that children were so hungry that they were eating grass in the besieged town before its capture, but there were no Western reporters in Cespa so the story never took off.

In the Serbian siege of Srebrenica in spring 1993, Western media finally witnessed the desperate plight of a besieged small town overflowing with refugees of previous 'cleansing', starving and under daily bombardment. Coverage was so damning that, as with the concentration camps, the UN was moved to act—this time on the initiative of non-aligned members of the Security Council—and declared Srebrenica to be a 'safe area'.[7] After Serbians had terrorized its people for weeks and reduced the enclave to a minimal area, they finally allowed UN troops to enter, so permitting its survival as an isolated ghetto, dependent on Serbian permission for convoy access and UN troop movements.

Once the Srebrenica crisis had been resolved, media coverage again subsided largely to low-level reporting of the daily bombardment of the Bosnian capital. The next media panic was a perfect illustration both of the ability of reporters to highlight a problem and of the superficial nature of media panics and governments' responses. A BBC reporter discovered a little girl in a Sarajevo hospital, Irma Hadzimuratovic, who would die without treatment outside Bosnia. Once he had exposed her case, media quickly found other children in the same plight and generated a daily campaign for action. This resulted in John Major's announcement of a special airlift, 'Operation Irma', for two dozen children. Media had certainly helped a small number of needy children; they had spotlighted the routine misery of people in Sarajevo, but they had narrowed that distress down to the suffering of a few children. The point was underlined as Major excluded adult victims, especially injured combatants, from his airlift; hundreds of thousands remained trapped after a handful had been saved. Major's rescue was also put into perspective by an airlift of four hundred ill and wounded of all ages to Italy. Irma Hadzimuratovic remained at Great Ormond Street children's hospital in London until she died on 1 April 1995.

The arbitrary nature of the media spotlight was further underlined by the selective treatment of the Croatian offensive against Muslims in late 1993. Croatian forces burnt out and killed Muslim villagers throughout central Bosnia, but this only made headlines on British television because reporters accompanied their national forces. There were graphic scenes of horror in the village of Ahmici, as well as of British troops helping survivors to flee (but not of preventing killings or pursuing killers). However as Gowing points out, the exposure of Croatian atrocities suited NATO governments because it 'diluted the public consensus against the Serbs'.[8]

In contrast, the centrepiece of the Croatian offensive, their attempt to 'cleanse' Mostar—Bosnia's second city and mainly Muslim before the war—in order to make it the capital of an ethnically pure Croat state, received only intermittent coverage on British television and little in the press. In the siege of east Mostar, remaining Muslims were bombarded night and day, near-starving and crowded in the cellars of a ruined city in some of the most miserable scenes anywhere in ex-Yugoslavia. Yet because access for outsiders was very difficult, mostly the siege went unfilmed and unreported at the time, and Mostar, unlike Sarajevo or even Srebrenica, never became a media *cause célèbre*. As Gowing puts it, the lack of a battlefield satellite dish was crucial; one isolated BBC report had a big impact, he claims, on nearby UNPROFOR staff, but failed to shake policy. He quotes a UN official who claimed that television coverage of the city 'would have changed the whole balance on Mostar. It would have given us [the UN] strong leverage.'[9]

In contrast to this ignoring of mass slaughter—and Mostar's neglect can stand for the majority of Bosnian towns and villages—one atrocity in Sarajevo, out of all the thousands in the first two years of the war, again showed the power of media to ignite world political reactions. The killing of seventy people in a market in Sarajevo in February 1994 prompted the most potent of all media panics. Beamed around the world, the outrage at the massacre was followed by NATO's most decisive air intervention to date, and before long the UN had imposed an exclusion zone for heavy weaponry around the city and partially lifted the siege. And yet, within weeks, in a sorry re-run of Srebrenica twelve months earlier, the neighbouring 'safe area' of Gorazde was threatened with Serbian capture. Once more media showed the world how the UN allowed the attackers to keep their target, full of refugees, under constant bombardment and to overrun most of the enclave. Once again it was at the eleventh hour that the UN responded to the world outcry and made enough noises to convince the Serbians to pull back—as they may well have intended to do in any case.

For almost a year after Gorazde, coverage declined to its lowest level since the start of the post-Yugoslav wars. There were probably a number of reasons for this. The diplomatic 'peace process' was largely stalled. The military situation was largely stalemated, leading to a four-month ceasefire in early 1995. Neither the easing of the situation in Sarajevo nor its deterioration from late 1994 was as big news as the market massacre. The modest gains of the Bosnian army from late 1994 were not really news either; like the Kurds, the Bosnians were more photogenic as helpless victims than as combatants in their own cause. Even the Serbian attack on another safe area, at Bihac in early 1995, was not as big news as earlier sieges, although (or because) it followed a similar pattern.

The biggest Bosnian story of mid-1995 was the Serbian capture of hundreds of UN troops. This action, in response to a single NATO air strike and widely seen in the context of increasing isolation and division of the Bosnian–Serbian leadership, excited media as little else because Western troops were involved. Although little harm befell them—British soldiers were released unharmed except for several injured in a car crash—the situation received saturation coverage. Certainly this exposed the weakness of the UN's position in relation to the Serbians and helped force the Western powers to deploy more troops to protect their existing forces. It was notable, however, that the more brutal side of the Serbian response to the NATO strike—a massacre by shellfire of seventy people, mainly youths sitting in cafes in the centre of Tuzla—received minimal attention compared to the massacre in Sarajevo a year earlier. Film of the dead and funerals was overshadowed by clips of cheery British soldiers tucking into food provided by their Serbian captors.

Shortly afterwards, some of the most shocking events of the entire Bosnian war put the media's 'success' in stimulating the UN's 'safe havens' policy in the starkest possible relief. Two enclaves, Srebrenica, scene of the 1993 bombardment which stimulated the development of the policy, and Zepa, were overrun by Serbian forces despite the presence of UN garrisons. The Western powers decided not to reinforce the UN, which offered no resistance, and the US and British governments even appeared willing to allow Gorazde, the largest eastern Bosnian safe haven, to fall as well. Television showed streams of refugees, women and children bussed out of the towns and some men who had found their way on foot through Serbian lines, arriving in Bosnian-held Tuzla. While reporters raised some questions about the fate of most of the Bosnian Muslim men from the two enclaves, they were unable to film their killing at the hands of Ratko Mladic's Serbian troops. The most that can be said is that the media contributed, together with US satellite information, to providing evidence for the International War Crimes Tribunal's indictment of Mladic and Karadzic over these incidents.

The turnaround of the post-Yugoslav wars in late 1995 is attributable almost entirely to military and diplomatic initiatives in which media coverage played only the most indirect roles, and which can be traced to developments in US policy as well as the actions of the combatants. On the one hand, Croatian and Bosnian forces, with the backing of the USA, made major military gains, capturing the Serbian 'Krajina' inside Croatia and large parts of north-western Bosnia. On the other, the Clinton administration seems to have decided that further escalation of the war might produce upheavals that would threaten the prospect of accommodation with Serbia proper, and thus the chance of a successful outcome to American policy in the Balkans. Seeking—as in the Middle East, Northern Ireland and elsewhere—foreign policy successes to bolster his flagging campaign for re-election, Clinton moved to put unprecedented pressure on Serbia, Croatia and Bosnia to agree a settlement (adopted in Dayton, Ohio in November 1995 as this book was going to press).

Western media's roles in these developments were limited. They reported the Croatian offensive in the Krajina in a largely positive way, following Western policy, and made relatively little of the gross human rights abuses involved. They gave less attention to the Croatian and Bosnian gains in Bosnia, or to any of their excesses. The 'peace settlement' appears fragile, but it is to be backed by 60,000 NATO troops, including 20,000 Americans—forces which, at an earlier stage of the conflict, might have deterred the Serbians and prevented genocide. Western media have largely welcomed the settlement, and while many have pointed out its practical difficulties, few have commented sharply on its acceptance of the results of ethnic cleansing in both Croatia and Bosnia and its legitimization of apartheid in the division of Bosnia. One positive outcome was the prospect of restoring a unified Sarajevo, but the likely terms of reunification hardly held great hopes for a genuine pluralism and multiculturalism—Mostar had been 'reunited' under EU administration for over a year, with continuing ethnic divisions between the Bosnian and Croatian sectors. Gorazde's people were however saved from the fate of Srebrenica and Zepa.

After almost five years of the post-Yugoslav wars, the balance of forces was turning against the more extreme genocidists, but no large-scale reversal of genocide or return of refugees to their homes was in prospect. It is worth asking what role Western media played in this outcome. On the one hand, nothing the media had done caused the Western powers or the UN to prevent or reverse genocide on a large scale and, as we have emphasized, they incorporated many of their governments' assumptions even into the language in which they reported the conflicts. With the exceptions of a few commentators in the broadsheets and occasional contributions on television, media had hardly challenged the overall policy of the West or the UN towards ex-Yugoslavia.

On the other hand, the fairly constant coverage of Sarajevo may have created implicit pressure on the West not to allow the capital to be overrun by Serbian forces or to starve. The high level of overall coverage, in contrast to many other wars, had fed the 'something must be done' attitude in Western countries, at least in the earlier phases of the war. This in turn provided much of the impetus towards UNHCR and voluntary agencies' relief operations, and hence to UN military protection for these operations. The peaks of moral concern generated by coverage of issues like the concentration camps, the first Srebrenica crisis and the market massacre helped push the West and the UN into particular measures which have provided minimal protection for some, but not most, victims, for some periods. Even UNPROFOR, despite its often cravenly submissive attitude to Serbian forces, provided a buffer—however inadequate—for some vulnerable Bosnian communities and the Bosnian government, enabling them to survive and even to fight back. And finally, Clinton's fear of negative coverage of a continuing Bosnian war, and repeated Serbian humiliations of the West, may have contributed to his seeking the 1995 'settlement'.

Other global crises of the early 1990s

Of course, as Gowing points out from his conversations with policy-makers, 'the overall inability to control TV crews in Bosnia has become a pivotal fact in convincing governments NOT to become involved in future conflicts—unless, that is, the military/UN operational objective can be achieved within a matter of days, before public support begins to wane.'[10]

No other global crisis has had the sustained coverage, over years, as the ex-Yugoslav wars. Few, as we have noted, received intensive coverage at all: most have been occasional and transitory stories in Western media, leading to no serious pressure for, let alone actual, intervention by the UN or Western governments. Most crises have not been 'global' in the new sense which we have defined in this book, even though in some the local effects were as large scale and drastic as in Iraq and Bosnia.

Four other crises can be identified as having received large-scale media coverage. Two directly involved former superpowers intervening in their spheres of influence and were major news stories mainly because of their interventions. In Haiti, the USA intervened in 1994—under UN auspices—to conclude the three-year crisis arising from the overthrow of the democratically elected president, Bertrand Aristide. The USA has had a long history of intervening in Caribbean and Central American states—often to help overthrow elected governments rather than restore them—and so the Haiti intervention was within the general pattern.

Media coverage certainly had a major role in embarrassing the Clinton administration for failing to solve Haiti's human rights' crisis. Film of atrocities committed under the military rulers created pressure for action to make the situation on the ground conform to Clinton's rhetoric. Nevertheless, this was clearly a situation in which US policy—Clinton's apparently genuine support for democratic reform in the Americas—defined the situation, and media acted to goad the administration to live up to its word. In the end it was very much the administration's calculation of the benefits and timing of intervention. The media were mobilized to cover the invasion and helped deliver a substantial boost to Clinton's poll ratings.

The Russian intervention in Chechnya in 1994–5 was actually within the Russian Federation, in an autonomous republic whose government had proclaimed independence over two years earlier. Although the Yeltsin government had long been urged to end the secession, by Russian nationalists in parliament and the media, and media had covered the local civil war in Chechnya in 1994, it is not clear that coverage played a major part in propelling the invasion. Rather it appears to have been a desperate gamble by Yeltsin himself or elements within the government and army to gain some new credibility. Russian media coverage of the resulting war largely rebounded on the government, as television viewers saw extensive film of Russian soldiers destroying the city of Grozny and causing widespread death and misery among its citizens, many of them Russians. International coverage was considerable precisely because Russia itself was involved, but, as we have already noted, serious Western or UN intervention was ruled out for the same reason, although Western governments were obliged to make protestations of concern.

Leaving aside Iraq, ex-Yugoslavia and these two great power crises, only two other crises of the 1990s have received large-scale media coverage and have become global in the sense we have used: Somalia and Rwanda. Given the large number of wars which have not been transformed in this way, why did Somalia and Rwanda become global crises? What made them different from all the others?

The answers seem to be strikingly different in the two cases. Relationships between media coverage and governments' policies were very different, and the outcomes were quite opposed. In Somalia, the dictatorship of Siad Barre had been overthrown in 1990, and it quickly became clear that central government had collapsed. A many-sided civil war had developed; much of economic life disintegrated and mass starvation occurred. International agencies withdrew from the country because they deemed it unsafe for their workers. Western television and press coverage of the crisis was, relative to many, considerable. The reasons were that the condition of much of the population became critical and—an important connection—there were echoes of the 1984–5 famine in neighbouring Ethiopia, which had become a global television *cause célèbre*.[11] However coverage was intermittent and did not succeed in building up a sustained campaign, like the Kurdish campaign which we have described. Coverage throughout much of 1992 made it clear that the situation was desperate; there was a groundswell of opinion for intervention, but no sign that governments were ready to act. In May, the Bosnian war had broken out, and the West was trying to avoid being embroiled there.

Intervention in Somalia came not in response to a fever pitch of media coverage but when it seemed that constant exposure of Somalis' miseries had failed to secure action. Intervention (in December 1992) was at first a unilateral action of the USA, although UN legitimation was sought. It seems to have been very much the personal decision of President Bush, who had lost his bid for re-election the previous month and was caretaker president pending the inauguration of Clinton in January 1993. There was speculation that Bush wished to leave a difficult situation for his successor, but a desire to leave on a note of international boldness recalling his success in the Gulf seems a more obvious explanation. Strategically, Somalia was seen as a relatively easy operation, the potential enemies being local warlords and the terrain relatively easy to operate in. In these respects it contrasted sharply with Bosnia, where the Serbians had a powerful armed force and the terrain was notoriously difficult. One motive may have been to distract from the clamour for intervention in Bosnia, particularly since the exposure of the concentration camps there.

Despite these apparent advantages, the Somali operation became a textbook case of how not to intervene. The USA was successful in bringing a certain amount of aid to people in need, especially in the early stages of the operation, although much was diverted to the armed bands.[12] The US did not understand Somali society, with its complicated clan structure, or its politics.[13] Despite good intentions, it was unable to work effectively with Somali groups to foster local political structures. US and UN forces were not prepared for dealing with local warlords, and after twenty-three Pakistani UN troops were killed, the USA embarked on an ill-fated campaign against one leader, General Aideed. This ended in the public humiliation of US troops, with the filming of the body of an American soldier being dragged on a rope in the dust behind his killers' vehicle. Such images played a large part in reinforcing American opposition to 'humanitarian' interventions, although President Clinton did subsequently succeed in his intervention in Haiti.

In Somalia, although media coverage of famine played a part in creating pressure for intervention, and coverage of US and UN failures played a part in eventual withdrawal, neither intervention nor failure and withdrawal could be said to be *largely* the result of media coverage. US intervention, as in the Gulf and Haiti, was clearly an autonomous military–political decision rather than a bowing to media pressure as in Kurdistan. While media magnified the weaknesses of the intervention, they did not generate overwhelming pressure for withdrawal.

In contrast, the situation in Rwanda appears to be closest of all to a 'pure' media-defined crisis, as in Kurdistan. The death in a plane crash of the ruthlessly anti-democratic president, Juvenal Habyaramina, was the signal for a planned campaign of mass killings across the central African state by the *interahamwe* militia and civilians mobilized by the ruling party. The genocide targeted both opposition politicians and members of the minority Tutsi tribe. The orgy of murder was vast and rapid: within little more than a month, in April–May 1994, it is widely agreed that at least half a million and possibly up to a million men, women and children, most of them Tutsis, had been killed—many simply with machetes. The speed of the killings meant that any international response, to be effective, would have had to have been rapid. Four hundred Belgian UN troops were stationed in Rwanda, but these were used only to rescue European civilians; they then withdrew leaving the local population to its fate. The few members of Western voluntary organizations in Rwanda were unable to do much to help, and most of them were evacuated.

In this situation the role of Western media organizations was critical. A few locally based reporters were able to provide Western television with graphic accounts of the early phases of genocide, while as the evidence grew of the enormity of the events, mainstream journalists went in, providing film of the aftermath of the killings, interviews with survivors and eye-witnesses and the surge of refugees who spontaneously formed huge but totally unsupported camps, mainly across the border in Tanzania. The coverage of the refugees was highly reminiscent of the plight of the Kurds. (Newspapers provided much less effective coverage than television, even less than in Kurdistan.)

As in Kurdistan, television commentary was often of the 'something must be done' kind, an implicit call for action by the West. The character and scale of the horror, as portrayed by television, generated pressure on the UN to intervene, and indeed the Security Council did resolve to send a force; but due to the unwillingness of states to commit troops, no significant UN force arrived until after the genocide was over. Voluntary aid organizations built on the television pictures in large-scale appeals for funds and rapid efforts to bring food, clean water, medicines and shelter to the refugees.

The Rwandan situation was resolved not by media-driven UN action, but by the military success of the opposition Rwandan Patriotic Front, which quickly conquered most of the country. The only significant Western intervention was unilateral action by France, more than two months after the worst television pictures of slaughter, ostensibly for humanitarian purposes, but also it seemed to block a total RPF victory. The French occupied south-western Rwanda (the RPF had invaded from the north-east) and created an enclave to which many Hutus (the majority tribe from which the killers had been drawn) fled from the RPF. French troops therefore defended many of those deemed responsible for the genocide.

Even more than in Kurdistan or Bosnia, the media found the politics of the situation difficult to deal with. Although it was clear that some Hutu had been among the victims of the genocide, and the RPF contained Hutu as well as Tutsi, the media could generally only describe the conflict in ethnic terms. The media found it easier to represent the Tutsi (like the Muslims in Bosnia) as victims than it did to acknowledge the political–military struggle of the RPF (which like the Bosnian government tended to be treated as just another ethnic faction).[14]

As the RPF consolidated its hold, a second wave of refugees developed, this time Hutu fleeing the feared revenge of the RPF and Tutsis. Over a million eventually fled to new camps, this time chiefly across Rwanda's western border in Zaïre. Once again, living conditions were appalling, and in late 1994 there was massive coverage of this new Rwandan crisis and huge new aid efforts by the UN and voluntary agencies. Since the genocide had been carried out by militia and youth drawn extensively from the Hutu population, it was inevitable that the new camps included many of those responsible for mass murder.

Some coverage highlighted the agencies' problems in dealing with members of the genocidist militia and attempts to reconstruct them in the camps. However most coverage of the second refugee crisis presented the problem as it had presented the first, in purely humanitarian terms. The failure to explicate the political situation clearly and the tendency to resort to simple ethnic categories meant that media ended by conflating the two as human tragedies. The first, mainly Tutsi, refugees had fled from the worst genocide of recent times which greatly exceeded in size and speed even the Serbian 'ethnic cleansing' in Bosnia. The second, mainly Hutu refugees, who included many murderers, fled from a new government which had not actually perpetrated extensive violence on the Hutu population and had sought national reconciliation.

Clearly refugees of the second wave, like the first, were in desperate situations in *ad hoc* camps and deserved large-scale coverage and humanitarian assistance.[15] Clearly, too, Hutu fears were not completely unrealistic, although they were exaggerated by the former ruling party and militia. The RPF might have failed to live up to its message, although Western reporters found little evidence of abuses until an incident in April 1995 when RPF troops killed up to three thousand Hutu refugees in a camp inside Rwanda which the new government wanted cleared in order to disperse people to their home towns and villages. (The UN, having turned its back on the earlier genocide, now took a strong line with the RPF.)

None of these facts warranted the equation of the two situations, reducing them both to simple humanitarian disasters. While media did some contextualizing, this reductionist tendency was clear. Western and African governments and the UN had their own reasons for wishing to avoid intervention in Rwanda—although given the lightly armed character of the genocidists, a relatively modest but swift military intervention might have had easier success than elsewhere in halting and preventing killings. The limitations of media coverage were hardly the reason for the UN's failure to intervene effectively to save hundreds of thousands of lives. On the contrary, despite its limitations, the media coverage constituted, as in Kurdistan, the chief pressure for intervention. The fact that intervention did not follow reflects the fact that in Rwanda, as in all the other cases we have examined, there were no strongly perceived Western strategic interests and no connection of responsibility which the Kurds were able, it now appears almost uniquely, to exploit.

Notes and references

1. Gowing, 1994 (see also fuller version, Shorenstein Barone Center on the Press, Politics and Public Policy, Harvard University, 1994).

2. Since the federation of Serbia and Montenegro continues to call itself Yugoslavia, I shall refer to 'ex-Yugoslavia' to describe the whole of Yugoslavia as it existed from 1945–91.

3. These wars need also to be seen in the context of the other Yugoslav crises, notably the suppression of the Albanian majority in 'Kosova'—as they call it, although the minority Serbs know it as Kosovo—and the

destabilization of Macedonia by Serbia's ally, Greece.

4. For simplicity's sake, Bosnia-Herzegovina will be referred to as Bosnia in the remainder of this discussion.

5. For a graphic account of the role of the UN, and especially UNPROFOR, see Rieff, 1995.

6. For accounts, see Gowing, 1994, pp. 16–28; Vulliamy, 1994, pp. 98–117; Guttman, 1993, pp. 28–40.

7. Details of this episode are provided by Gowing, 1994; pp. 19–23.

8. Gowing, 1994; p. 24.

9. Gowing, 1994; pp. 8, 30–1. Mostar was saved later by the wider strategic interest in which Croatia and Bosnia, at US urging, formed an alliance against the Serbians. Under EC administration, the ruins of east Mostar were patched up, but Muslims were still ghettoized, with little access to prosperous, still Croatian-controlled west Mostar, let alone the outside world.

10. Gowing, 1994; p. 4.

11. See Philo, 1993.

12. Alex de Waal disputes even the widely credited initial success of the operation in alleviating famine (de Waal, 1994; pp. 19–20).

13. See Lewis, 1994.

14. de Waal, 1994, pp. 25–30, makes similar criticisms of Oxfam, which called for UN military intervention rather than support for the RPF.

15. Many in humanitarian agencies felt, however, that the UN failed to confront the genocidists in the camps who misappropriated aid; the French branch of Médicins sans Frontières withdrew from the Zaïre camps (Anne-Marie Huby, letter, *Guardian*, 24 December 1994). MSF later called for trials for crimes against humanity, criticizing the 'aid only' approach (*Guardian*, 25 January 1995).

CHAPTER FOURTEEN

Civil society, media and public opinion in the new global crises

The discussion of responses in Western societies to the ex-Yugoslav and other wars has focused almost entirely on media—in contrast to the discussion of the Iraqi wars which analysed how various civil society institutions were involved. In reality the contrast is between the Gulf War, which was understood *as a war* by most people and institutions in Western societies, and all other crises including Kurdistan which were not understood in this way. Our study of British civil institutions revealed that apart from media and humanitarian agencies, there was little evidence of effective responses to the Kurdish crisis. There is little to suggest anything different in any other crisis (although a detailed study would be necessary to confirm that).

Individuals responded, certainly, primarily through donations to disaster relief and in some European countries by direct help to Bosnian refugees, but hardly in other ways (not, for example, in political action). Public opinion mattered, in that governments calculated in the Kurdish case, at various points during the war in Bosnia but to a much lesser extent elsewhere, that the clamour of the media and support for agencies represented public opinion and sometimes acted accordingly.

National and ideological limits of civil society

What this shows is that most national institutions are conditioned to dealing with wars in which national armed forces—'our' troops—are involved. Traditional institutions like political parties and churches have histories of response to such wars, and their ideologies contain elaborated moral and political concepts which enable them to respond. Divisions develop and debates take place, often along predictable lines. Patriotism is a concept which informs much debate, an overarching concept justifying actions which in other circumstances would not be acceptable. Political and religious leaders, especially, articulate ideologies which have been developed over a number of wars, mostly in support of the national government and its allies (the concept of alliance is well developed from two world wars and other conflicts).

Most dissent to war within these institutions is dissent from war in general, not from the reasons for the particular war. This was particularly evident in the Gulf, since almost all opponents of the war agreed with the need to condemn the Iraqi government and its invasion of Kuwait. Most agreed on the need for some sort of sanctions against Iraq short of war. The argument was almost entirely about means.

This was also true of social-movement mobilization, although as we saw this was limited in scope. The dominant anti-war strand was pacifist in orientation, and although Marxist opposition was also represented, this too was a sort of general opposition to war. Marxist opponents of the Gulf War would have been opposed to any war undertaken by the 'capitalist' and 'imperialist' governments of Britain and the West and saw this war as a strong instance—because of oil—of this general case. Because few British soldiers were killed and no real hardships attended the British population, the anti-war movement had few concrete focal points for its general concerns (only the plight of the Iraqi and Palestinian detainees, the threats to Muslims in some areas and the few military dissenters functioned in this way, but they were of limited significance to most of the population).

What is striking is that both the traditional institutions of civil society and 'new' social-movement opposition failed to develop effective responses to the other Iraqi wars and the consequent refugee crises. The lack of responses during the Kurdish crisis might be put down to the swiftness of developments and institutional inertia. This is, however, a surprising weakness for social movements which have often been defined by rapid, spontaneous reactions. It cannot be explained simply by this factor, as a similar pattern seems to have obtained in the Bosnian war, which has lasted several years. We need to ask why major national institutions *and* social movements both seem barely capable of representing either the victims of war in distant places or (still less) those who are struggling in these conflicts for justice, democracy and other Western ideals.

The explanation which seems to work best is that the ideologies—the thought patterns with which people within institutions approach global conflicts—are linked to support or opposition to the nation-state in the context of inter-state war. We are either for 'our' state in its contests with other states—and each institution, whether church or political party or intellectual position, has its own way of explaining that—or we are against—and again there are different sorts of justifications. Some institutions, such as the British Conservative party or anti-war movements, are entirely on one side of the divide, while others, like the Labour party, the churches, the schools and the Muslim community straddle the divide in different ways.

What most civil society institutions had in common was their difficulty in shifting mindsets from pro- and anti-state attitudes to the Gulf War to the very different problem of representing the people and issues involved in the Kurdish crisis. It follows that we cannot expect these institutions to find it easy to deal with crises like Bosnia and Rwanda, except in echoing minimalist humanitarian concerns. Even these weak responses arise from agenda developed by other institutions like television news, newspapers and aid agencies.

Who and *what* civil society institutions are representing is also important. I found that they are still very much geared to the national society. This is particularly clear in the case of the traditional representative institutions, the political parties and churches. However internationalist a social-democratic party or a Christian church is in theory, their practices are so closely tied to the national context that they can primarily only represent the nation-state, 'our' soldiers and wider Western interests with which these are interwoven. This is where, in the end, the balance of the carefully judged phrases of a Kinnock or a Runcie is likely to lie.

What is interesting about the oppositional sectors of national civil society is how much, in the end, they are geared to a similar model of representation, even if they represent particular groups within a national context rather than the nation-state and the presumed common interest of national society. In contesting the dominant view, they appeal to abstract universals: peace and reconciliation in the pacifist view; the international working class in the Marxist view; world Islam or pan-Arabism in some Muslim views. In reality, however, they are attempting to represent particular constituencies in the national society—the radical middle class, the oppositional working class, British Muslims facing discrimination.

What is most notable about oppositional sectors is their weak ability to represent groups of people threatened in other parts of world society. So to a large extent the Labour left and the peace movement were unable to switch to representing the Kurds. The Marxist left could call for 'Arab solutions to Arab problems', so rejecting Western 'imperialism', but found it less easy to represent specific groups of Arabs repressed by an Arab regime. British Muslims found it easier to identify with a self-styled champion of world Islam against Western values than to reject that champion's genocidal policies and to champion themselves the much more oppressed people of Iraq. It is striking, given the previous history of peace movements against wars and weapons systems, that no significant mass movement of solidarity with Bosnia has arisen over more than three years of war.[1] Under what conditions would it be possible to develop movements of that kind?

The problems are therefore twofold. First, parties, churches, anti-war movements and Muslim institutions are themselves directly representative institutions geared to the national society. Second, their ideologies of the world are largely geared to old, statist contexts of international relations rather than the new realities of globalization. Intellectuals and schools, on the other hand, may be more flexible, since their *raison d'être* is not to represent groups within the national society (although they may do that) or even the national society and state (although most do represent them to some degree) but to encourage discussion, extend debate and express plurality (although not all achieve all these in practice). It it notable, however, that in the Iraqi wars only some media and aid organizations could be said to represent strongly the combatants and victims of distant violence. Civil society as a whole represented the Iraqi wars primarily as an inter-state conflict and represented British national or sectional interests within that. Media and humanitarian organizations represented them, partly, as contexts in which people fought, suffered and needed our voices and practical support.

Media and global representation

Media represented people involved in distant violence, in the senses of showing their situations *and* of advocacy, better than other national institutions. Media shared, of course, in the function of national representation. There was enormous variation in the ways in which media balanced the two roles of national and global representation. Many, especially tabloid newspapers, were involved in national to the detriment of global representation. There was a striking contrast in most media between the managed product of the Gulf War and the active representation of distant victims in Kurdistan. Even those media which took up the task of representing victims of violence did so, as we saw, in limited and partial ways. Gowing's general survey endorses our judgement that film access is crucial: 'the main principle is: no pictures, then no serious coverage of a conflict'.[2]

The crucial question is under what circumstances this active representation of victims may become effective and influence state policy. The variation discussed in this book, within the Iraqi wars between the Gulf, Kurdistan and the Shi'ite revolt, and between and within other wars, is widely acknowledged. Cornelio Sammarunga of the International Committee of the Red Cross, complaining of the neglect of many crises, argued that the aid policies of Western governments were set by the sensationalist priorities of television: 'Television is driven by images which is an inappropriate way for others to make policy.'[3] According to Lawrence Martin, in 1992, 'The very fact that there are soon to be British troops in Bosnia is testimony to media influence.'[4]

Academic analyses do not see media as so instrumental in determining government and military policies. Patrick O'Heffernan argues that media and military are involved in 'mutual exploitation', with both dependency and tension. He argues that foreign policy 'is the end point of a long chain of events, people and institutions that collect and shape information, options and political leverages, and it very specifically includes a self-interested media'. For him,

> Mass-media influence on foreign policy is issue-specific, with certain categories of issues more likely to successfully utilise the media to develop policy elite support. Environmental issues, *those involving human rights or human suffering,*

and issues that touch Americans ... are far more likely to move forward on the foreign policy agenda as a result of media exposure than more abstract or complex 'high politics' issues such as arms control or trade terms.[5]

Clearly, although he does not say so, this is because these issues are far more likely to mobilize public opinion.

Mobilizing opinion and influencing policy are, however, different things. Gowing, a news practitioner turned researcher, quotes the British Foreign Secretary, Douglas Hurd, as saying of the horror in Rwanda, 'I can hardly bring myself to watch.' Gowing comments that

> Emotions across Whitehall have been identical through the wars in Slovenia. Then Croatia and Bosnia. And in Somalia. The pictures have cried out that 'something must be done.' But they never forced a fundamental change of political will that stopped the conflicts.[6]

Gowing also quotes a British official as saying that on Bosnia, 'TV almost derailed policy on several occasions, but the spine held. It had to. The secret was to respond to limit the damage, and be seen to react without undermining the specific [policy] focus.' Official statements expressed horror and outrage, 'usually misread in TV and newspaper reporting as signals of a hardening of policy', but they were what one official described as 'pseudo-decisions for pseudo-action'.

Gowing's conclusions are that Bosnia and Somalia were 'diplomatic watersheds', in which Western powers turned their backs on intervention prompted by television coverage of killing or disaster:

> In future, real-time television coverage of the proliferation of regional conflicts will create emotions, but ultimately make no difference to the fundamental calculations in foreign policy making. No journalist should delude himself otherwise, however ghastly the horrors he witnesses and reports on. It is likely something will be done but only with symbolic expressions of concern or token humanitarian gestures.[7]

Gowing concludes, therefore, that television is likely to be limited to tactical and localized rather than strategic policy impacts. Short-term exposés do not necessarily have major effects on public opinion (although clearly a major campaign, like Kurdistan, does). Most of the time television's impact is on 'the small elite of newspaper editors, leader writers, op-ed columnists and motivated politicians who do monitor real-time television'. This is where the impact of television is feared: 'Without exception, ministers and officials who played down the impact of real-time television on themselves pointed to this numerically tiny but politically powerful elite as the group which does influence foreign policy-making based on what it sees on television.'[8] Gowing's interviews with policy-makers thus support this book's argument that newspapers have a distinctive role in media impact; their coverage and editorializing complements television's instant impact and often helps to convert it into political leverage.

Gowing argues that even the tactical impacts which do occur are the result of unexpected events and situations where policy is underdeveloped. He quotes Kofi Annan, UN Under Secretary-General for Peacekeeping: 'When there is a problem, and the policy has not been thought through, there is a knee-jerk reaction. They have to do something or face a public relations disaster.' Such moments are ones of 'policy panic', when 'governments get into a policy mess. They end up committing themselves further than they ever wanted to.'[9] These are what Freedman has called 'symbolic security politics', 'whereby military operations known to be ineffectual are mounted largely for public show'.[10]

The important issue is whether Gowing is right to limit the influence of television and press to the tactical and the cosmetic. The Kurdish intervention is a clear exception, a major diversion from planned policy forced overwhelmingly by television through its effects both on élite and popular opinion, albeit working on strategic and political commitments already made. Certainly, the changes of policy elsewhere which can be attributed to television have been much more minimal. The UN's 'humanitarian' intervention in Bosnia can be considered a gigantic diversion from the larger issue of halting genocide and aggression. But the intervention has had some achievements, it has clearly become a sizeable commitment for some European powers, and it is not certain that it would have been undertaken at all without media coverage of the war. Likewise, although I have argued that US intervention in Somalia was not a simple result of media pressure, it is difficult to believe it would have been on the agenda at all without prior media coverage. Similarly, although there was no effective intervention to halt the Rwandan genocide, the issue would not have been on the UN's and governments' agendas at all without television coverage.

Media coverage affects the form of military intervention, as well as whether intervention takes place. There is a 'CNN curve' of 'public demand for military intervention, followed by public protest when casualties are suffered'.[11] Badsey calls this a 'double bind' fear of the media and fear of casualties. To be more precise, it is fear of two types of coverage which work in opposite directions: that of atrocities against civilians which supports intervention, and coverage of military casualties which works to limit it. The latter has been influential

in the strong American preference for military intervention by air rather than ground forces. ... From the perspective of a government seeking to limit media involvement, air power—and increasingly missile power—represents by far the best instrument for military intervention in another country, especially in a single raid, since the media's ability to check and verify the story is severely limited. Media coverage of the air campaign in the Gulf war confirmed that the use of bomb- or missile-camera videotape released after the operation may allow the military to dictate the story to the media, virtually depriving them of their 'gatekeeper' function in deciding which news is to be passed to the public, and how it is to be presented. For the same reasons, however, the media can be profoundly suspicious of what they are offered, while countries which have been subject to air attacks have grown more politically sophisticated in their ability to provide the media with another dimension to the story.[12]

In these senses the public relations aspect is not just an add-on to states' policies but an integral part of policy formation. States have to balance continuously their strategic objectives in relation to other states and military–political formations with their relationships with audiences, electorates and groups within the national society. Media coverage of conflict constantly disturbs any hope of a simple, controlled balance between these two aspects of states' activities. Disturbance can come even where states 'know' what they are doing, as in Iraq, and even more where they are less clear about objectives, as in Bosnia.

It may be that the loss of certainty over strategy in the aftermath of the Cold War opened up a particular window for media influence which, as Gowing suggests, Western states now wish to close down after their experiences in Bosnia and Somalia. It is certain, however, that the possibility of uncertainty and indecision has not been removed. Therefore the situation which allows media to influence public perceptions and policy has hardly been abolished.

Representing distant violence, developing global civil society

This study has emphasized the importance of media in the representation—in the sense of advocacy as well as portrayal—of distant violence in Western and global society. It has emphasized the importance of media and humanitarian organizations in contrast not only to traditional civil society institutions—such as parties and churches, intellectual groupings and schools—but also to social movements and the emerging institutions of ethnic minority communities. In contrast to much theorizing which has highlighted the role of civil society, it has emphasized how civil society is still nationally based and how limited is its capacity to represent those fighting and suffering in far-off wars. In contrast to theories which emphasize the roles of social movements, it has highlighted a lack of social movements to respond to the situation of people in the distant conflicts of the post-Cold War world.

This study has also shown, however, many important limitations of media in the representation of distant violence. Media attention is often brief, sporadic, narrowly victim-oriented and far too dependent on the availability of visual images and hence portable satellite dishes. News media generally take their cue from national governments and international organizations and follow their strategic directions. Only rarely do they contest or modify them. Despite global reach, the main media are still primarily Western and national organizations. Television rarely provides any but the simplest, usually implicit, editorial line as an alternative to government policies. Newspapers editorialize but frequently in terms of a shrill patriotism. Tabloids are the narrowest representatives of purely national civil society. Even liberal broadsheets are erratic in their advocacy of sustained policies to assist people in zones of conflict.

While this study argues against the eulogization of civil society or social movements and the demonization of the media, its conclusion is not that the representation of distant violence can be left safely in media hands. On the contrary, media's achievements stand out only because of the failure of most other sectors of civil society. Western civil societies in general, and there is no reason to believe that the story we have found in Britain would not be substantially replicated elsewhere, are hardly well adapted to the challenges of global society. While economics and culture are rapidly integrating world society, civil society remains largely trapped in national forms which prevent it from responding fully to new global challenges, particularly to the plight of vulnerable groups in zones of conflict.

This study shows that this situation exists partly because of the national framework of civil institutions. It is also, however, because of the ideological frameworks developed by nation-states and adapted to the global confrontation of the Cold War era. Consequently new conflicts and challenges are interpreted in terms of concepts of nation and international order inherited from the past. Even dissident views are largely trapped within these old ideologies.

The challenge which this book highlights is how to develop a global civil society in which the globally vulnerable will be well represented. One criticism I have made repeatedly is that media—and humanitarian organizations—are much better at representing people in conflict as victims than as protagonists. What is missing above all is the ability of people in conflict situations to represent themselves. Western-dominated global media rarely take seriously the self-representation of individuals, communities and organizations in zones of conflict.

Within Western society, the issue is how to articulate new visions of a responsible global community. Clearly further development of critical media—of newspapers which criticize governments and define alternatives in addition to television broadcasts which show what is happening—is vital. It is not, however, enough. The development of *globalist* campaigning organizations—of which humanitarian and human rights organizations are the best but not perfect current models—is also essential. It is necessary to transform institutions in national civil societies with globalist thinking, to awaken and strengthen feelings and concepts of global responsibility.

In order to extend global civil society it is also crucial to nurture new ideas: developing global society as a community as well as a market; overcoming the distancing which affects our responses to people in other situations; actively asserting responsibility. Developing these concepts will challenge many ideas and ideologies, of left as well as right, inherited from the past.

Notes and references

1. It is indicative that the CND, which campaigned—as I have outlined—against the Gulf War (and before that the Falklands) has had nothing to say about Bosnia. Its campaigning magazine, *CND Today*, has literally ignored the issue throughout three years of conflict. On the other hand, former European Nuclear Disarmament (now European Dialogue) activists have been in the forefront of advocating 'civil society' links between Western Europe and Bosnian towns and cities. Another prominent 'social movement' campaign involving Bosnia was the women's movement campaign against the Serbian use of rape to humiliate Muslim women. This campaign was limited, however, in failing to set rape in the context of women's experiences of genocide in general: their expulsions from their homes, the murder of many women, the murder of husbands, children and other family members, etc.

2. Gowing, 1994; p. 3.

3. Cornelio Sammarunga, *Guardian*, 14 October 1994.

4. Lawrence Martin, *Times Higher Educational Supplement*, 20 November 1992.

5. O'Heffernan, 1994; p. 240.

6. Gowing, 1994; pp. 7, 11, 12.

7. Gowing, 1994; p. 15.

8. Gowing, 1994; pp. 17–18.

9. Gowing, 1994; p. 19.

10. Lawrence Freedman, *Independent*, 19 May 1993.

11. *International Herald Tribune*, 26 October 1992, quoted in Badsey, 1994; p. 3.

12. Badsey, 1994; p. 14.

The survey research

In early January 1991, we planned two surveys, the first during the aerial attack phase of the Gulf War and the second after the commencement of the land war. In the event, the first was carried out during the second half of the war, and the second in its immediate aftermath. Substantive questions in the first questionnaire, framed in mid-January at the very beginning of the war, were asked in a general way. In the second questionnaire we were able to ask more specific questions about events which occurred in the conflict, but the questionnaire was designed before the revolts and refugee crises became apparent.

The surveys were based on random samples of the local population in Hull (an industrial, working-class, Labour-voting city in Northern England) and Beverley (its adjacent middle-class, Conservative-voting suburban area). The area chosen is not typical in all ways of the UK population, and there are some recognizable biases in our sample (e.g. a small overrepresentation of Labour voters compared to the national situation and a virtual absence of ethnic minorities). There was, however, no overriding reason why the Hull/Beverley population should have had substantially different attitudes to the war from those of the population nationally. Indeed asking a question about basic approval/disapproval of the war which had been asked by a national poll, we too obtained 80 per cent approval from our sample, so that we can claim some correspondence between ours and national polls. Our interest, moreover, was in establishing relationships between different aspects of attitudes to the war, and between these attitudes and a range of social variables, rather than to engage in precise, predictive opinion polling.

Our selection of a random sample from the electoral register avoided the recognized dangers of quota samples, on which all national UK opinion polls are based. For our first survey, questionnaires were sent by post to 1,300 people between 7 and 11 February, and replies were coded by the date of the postmark. By 22 February, when a ceasefire was imminent, we had received approximately 500 replies, giving a response rate of nearly 40 per cent. Since the register we used had been compiled in October 1989, and so included many who had moved or died, this was a good response which compares well with other postal questionnaires in similar situations.

For our second survey, questionnaires were sent to approximately 400 of the original respondents, who had agreed to receive a second questionnaire, together with almost 1,000 additional people drawn at random from the same electoral register. Questionnaires were sent out at the end of March, one month after the end of the war, and replies came in during April and the beginning of May—effectively the period when the media focused on the Kurdish crisis, although our questions, framed in advance, did not mention this. Despite the urgency of the war itself having disappeared, our overall response rate remained none the less only just under 40 per cent (although lower among the new element of our sample).

First questionnaire: attitudes to the Gulf War

For some of the following questions you should tick only one box; for others, when you might agree, at least in part, with several of the proffered alternatives, we are asking you to tick no more than two.

1   What is your attitude to the involvement of British forces in the Gulf War?

strongly approve	approve	disapprove	strongly disapprove
☐	☐	☐	☐

2   Do you think that sanctions should have been given longer to work, before military force was used?

yes	no	don't know
☐	☐	☐

3   Why do you think Britain went to war? (tick the one or two you most agree with)

☐ to get Iraq out of Kuwait
☐ because we support the United Nations
☐ to protect oil supplies
☐ because we have to stand up to dictators
☐ because we support America
☐ none of these
☐ don't know

4   What should the allies' war aims be? (tick the one or two you most agree with)

☐ to get Iraq out of Kuwait
☐ to destroy Iraq's military machine
☐ to overthrow Saddam Hussein
☐ to occupy Iraq
☐ to achieve a Middle East peace settlement, including the Palestine question
☐ shouldn't be fighting
☐ don't know

5   What do you think of Saddam Hussein? (tick the one or two you most agree with)

☐ he is a dangerous man

☐ he is like Hitler

☐ he is standing up for the Arabs

☐ he is mad

☐ none of these

☐ don't know

6   What should happen to Saddam Hussein if or when the allies defeat Iraq? (tick one only)

☐ should be left in power if Iraq withdraws from Kuwait

☐ should be left to Iraqi people to deal with

☐ should be killed

☐ should be brought to trial for war crimes

☐ none of these

☐ don't know

7   Which of these statements comes closest to expressing your view of the role of violence in this war? (tick one only)

☐ I believe that nuclear weapons should be used against Iraq to win the war

☐ I believe that the minimum violence necessary to win should be used against Iraq

☐ I do not believe that the violence of the war against Iraq can be justified

☐ none of these

☐ don't know

8   Which of these statements do you think best describes the allied air attacks on Iraq in the opening phase of the war? (tick the one or two you most agree with)

☐ sorties by brave allied airmen

☐ precise strikes against strategic targets, with minimum civilian casualties

☐ like video or computer games

☐ intensive bombing with unacceptable civilian casualties

☐ none of these

☐ don't know

9 How concerned are you about the loss of life among the following groups of people? (tick one box in each row)

	very concerned	not concerned	concerned
British service personnel	☐	☐	☐
Israeli civilians	☐	☐	☐
American service personnel	☐	☐	☐
Saudi civilians	☐	☐	☐
Saudi service personnel	☐	☐	☐
Iraqi civilians	☐	☐	☐
Iraqi service personnel	☐	☐	☐

10 Do you watch television news of the war regularly?

yes ☐   no ☐

11 If you watch TV news of the war regularly (at least once most days), which of these reasons would you give for doing so? (tick one or two which most apply to you)

☐ I want to be informed about the war

☐ I feel worried by the war

☐ I feel frightened by the war

☐ I find the war fascinating

☐ I find the war exciting

☐ none of these

☐ don't know

12 If you don't watch TV news of the war regularly, which of these reasons would you give for not doing so? (tick one or two which most apply to you)

☐ I haven't got access to a TV

☐ I'm not interested or too busy to watch TV news of the war

☐ I find TV coverage of the war boring or repetitive

☐ I find better coverage of the war in the press or radio

☐ I find TV coverage of the war worrying

☐ I find TV coverage of the war frightening

☐ none of these

☐ don't know

13 Which of these statements would you say applies generally to TV's coverage of the Gulf War? (tick only one in each of (a), (b) and (c))

(a) informative too informative not informative enough

☐ ☐ ☐

(b) patriotic too patriotic not patriotic enough

☐ ☐ ☐

(c) glorifies war too much sensible attitude towards war too critical of war

☐ ☐ ☐

14 Do you read one of the following national daily newspapers regularly? Please tick the one you read most often.

☐ Sun ☐ Star ☐ Mirror

☐ Today ☐ Telegraph ☐ Independent

☐ Times ☐ Guardian ☐ Yorkshire Post

☐ other ☐ none

15 How satisfied are you with its war coverage?

very satisfied satisfied dissatisfied very dissatisfied don't know

☐ ☐ ☐ ☐ ☐

16 Which of these statements would you say applies to your paper's coverage of the Gulf War? (tick only one in each of (a), (b) and (c))

(a) informative too informative not informative enough

☐ ☐ ☐

(b)   patriotic   too patriotic   not patriotic
                                                enough
        ☐   ☐   ☐

(c)   glorifies war   sensible attitude   too critical of war
        too much   towards war
        ☐   ☐   ☐

17 Do you read the Hull Daily Mail regularly?

yes   no
☐   ☐

If yes, how satisfied are you with its war coverage?

very satisfied   satisfied   dissatisfied   very dissatisfied   don't know
☐   ☐   ☐   ☐   ☐

18 Which of these statements would you say applies to the Hull Daily
    Mail's coverage of the Gulf War? (tick only one in each of (a), (b) and
    (c))

(a)   informative   too informative   not informative
                                                enough
        ☐   ☐   ☐

(b)   patriotic   too patriotic   not patriotic
                                                enough
        ☐   ☐   ☐

(c)   glorifies war   sensible attitude   too critical of war
        too much   towards war
        ☐   ☐   ☐

19 Have you been affected personally by the war in any of the following
    ways? (tick one)

    ☐ I feel worried about family members or friends in the Gulf
    ☐ I feel good because of British and allied successes
    ☐ I feel worried by the violence of the war in general
    ☐ I haven't been affected personally by the war
    ☐ don't know

20 Would you say that any other member of your family has been adversely affected by the violence of the war?

yes ☐ no ☐ don't know ☐

If yes, tick any of the following whom you would say have been affected:

☐ child (14 and under) ☐ teenagers and young people (15–24)
☐ adult (25–64) ☐ older person (65+)

If you have ticked any of these, are the people in question:

☐ male ☐ female ☐ both

If yes, could you describe how they have been affected?

21 Would you give us the following details of yourself and your family? (This is to enable us to compare the views of men/women, different age groups, supporters of various parties, etc.) Please tick the descriptions which apply to you.

Sex: ☐ male ☐ female

Age: ☐ 15–24 ☐ 25–34 ☐ 35–44 ☐ 45–54
     ☐ 55–64 ☐ over 65

Religion: ☐ Church of England ☐ Roman Catholic
          ☐ other Christian ☐ Muslim ☐ Jewish
          ☐ other ☐ none

22 Is where you live:

☐ owned by you ☐ rented from the council
☐ rented from a housing association ☐ rented privately
☐ other

23 Are you currently employed?

yes ☐ no ☐

If yes, please state job title:
If no, are you:

registered unemployed housewife student retired
☐ ☐ ☐ ☐

24 How would you vote if there was a General Election tomorrow?

Conservative   Labour   Liberal Democrat   Green
☐   ☐   ☐   ☐

other (please specify)   wouldn't vote   don't know
☐   ☐   ☐

25 Have you served in the armed forces?

yes   no
☐   ☐

If yes, in which of the following? (tick all that apply)

Second World War   National Service   Falklands War
☐   ☐   ☐

Regular forces in peacetime   Reserves   Territorials
☐   ☐   ☐

26 At the present time, are you, or any other member of your immediate family:

	yes	no
(a) serving in the armed forces	☐	☐
(b) employed by a firm which makes any defence equipment	☐	☐

27 Is any member of your immediate family serving in the Gulf?
yes   no
☐   ☐

28 Is any member of your immediate family a civilian in the Gulf?
yes   no
☐   ☐

29 Is there any other comment you would like to make about the Gulf War?

We are also interested in finding out whether people's views change as the war continues through different stages. If you have no objection to answering a second questionnaire of this kind, please tick.   ☐

Second questionnaire: attitudes after the Gulf War

1–4 Repeated questions 1, 2, 8 and 9 from first questionnaire.

How you saw the war

5   Over 100,000 sorties were flown by coalition air forces during the Gulf
    War. What percentage of these do you think were flown by British air-
    men?

Under 5%	5–10%	10–20%	20–30%	30–50%	over 50%
☐	☐	☐	☐	☐	☐

6   Which countries played the largest part in the coalition against Iraq
    during the Gulf War? Please rank the following countries in terms of
    their importance in the war (write 1 against the country you think
    played the most important part, 2 against the second most important,
    up to a maximum of 5).

Egypt	France	Italy	Kuwait	Morocco	Syria
☐	☐	☐	☐	☐	☐

Saudi Arabia	United Kingdom	United States
☐	☐	☐

7   Which countries suffered the largest losses of life in the Gulf War?
    Please rank the following countries in terms of their numbers of casu-
    alties (write 1 against the country you think suffered the most casual-
    ties, etc.)

Iraq	Israel	Saudi Arabia	United Kingdom	United States
☐	☐	☐	☐	☐

8   Who do you think should take moral responsibility for the killing of
    large numbers of Iraqi soldiers and civilians in coalition air attacks?

    ☐ Saddam Hussein and the Iraqi leadership

    ☐ George Bush, John Major and other coalition leaders

    ☐ Both Iraqi and coalition leaders

    ☐ None of these/don't know

9   Coalition forces ended the war in occupation of part of southern Iraq.
    Which of the following statements comes closest to expressing your
    view of what the coalition should have done in this situation?

    ☐ I was opposed to the war in any case or I thought the war should
      have ended earlier

☐ They should have withdrawn from Iraq altogether

☐ They were right to end the war where and when they did

☐ They should have gone on to capture Baghdad and overthrow Saddam Hussein

☐ They should have helped the people in Basra who were trying to overthrow Saddam Hussein

☐ None of these/don't know

Media coverage

10–13   Repeated questions 13, 14, 16 and 17 from first questionnaire.

14   On 13 February coalition planes bombed a shelter in Baghdad, causing hundreds of civilians to be killed. Which of the following statements is closest to your view of this incident?

☐ It was a military communications centre as well as a shelter, and the coalition was right to attack it

☐ It was a civilian shelter and the coalition bombed it by mistake

☐ Saddam Hussein put civilians in the shelter so as to make propaganda if it was attacked

☐ It was war and there will always be casualties

☐ None of these/don't know

15   British television journalists reported on this incident from inside the bombed shelter and television news showed pictures of shrouded bodies. Do you think they were right to do so?

yes   no   don't know
☐   ☐   ☐

16   Large numbers of Iraqi soldiers were killed by coalition air attacks during their retreat from Kuwait. Which of these comes closest to your view of these killings?

☐ They were justified in order to win the war

☐ They were justified, in order to destroy the Iraqi war machine as well as win the war

☐ They were unjustified, as the Iraqis were withdrawing from Kuwait and the war was already won

☐ Don't know

17 Some television news bulletins and newspapers showed film or printed pictures of the bodies of Iraqis killed by coalition attacks during their retreat from Kuwait. Do you recall seeing any film or pictures of this kind? Tick any of the following media in which you saw them:

on television news   in a national newspaper   in the *Hull Daily Mail*

☐   ☐   ☐

18 Do you think that those news programmes and papers which showed such film were right to do so?

yes   no   don't know

☐   ☐   ☐

The aftermath

19–23   Questions on post-Gulf War issues: arms sales, defence spending, post-war Kuwait and Palestine (not discussed in this book).

Impact on domestic politics

24 Repeated question 24 (voting intention) from first questionnaire.

25 Please rank these issues in terms of their importance in deciding how you will vote in the next General Election (write 1 next to the issue you think most important, 2 next to the second, etc.).

Defence policy   Education   Gulf victory   Health service

☐   ☐   ☐   ☐

Inflation   Interest rates   Pensions   Poll tax   Unemployment
             /mortgages

☐   ☐   ☐   ☐   ☐

26 Has the outcome of the Gulf War made you more or less likely to vote for the following parties?

	more likely	less likely	neither more or less likely
Conservative	☐	☐	☐
Labour	☐	☐	☐
Liberal Democrat	☐	☐	☐
Green	☐	☐	☐

27 Which of the following public figures do you think were in favour, and which opposed to the war?

	for war	against war	don't know
John Major	☐	☐	☐
Neil Kinnock	☐	☐	☐
Paddy Ashdown	☐	☐	☐
Edward Heath	☐	☐	☐
Tony Benn	☐	☐	☐
The Pope	☐	☐	☐
Archbishop of Canterbury (Runcie)	☐	☐	☐

28 How would you rate the performance of the following during the Gulf War?

	very good	good	not very good	bad
George Bush	☐	☐	☐	☐
John Major	☐	☐	☐	☐
Neil Kinnock	☐	☐	☐	☐
Paddy Ashdown	☐	☐	☐	☐

29 Do you agree with the government's decision to hold a commemoration (victory) parade in London?

yes	no	don't know
☐	☐	☐

30 Which of these statements best expresses your view of those publicly opposed to the war while it was being fought?

☐ I agree with opposition to the war

☐ I disagree with opposition to the war, but support the rights of those opposed to the war to express their views

☐ I disagree with opposition to the war, and believe it should be banned

☐ none of these/don't know

Your involvement

31 Please tick any of the following which you did during the Gulf War:

☐ donated money or goods for the British forces

☐ collected money or goods for the British forces

☐ wrote a letter to a friend or relative in the Gulf

☐ wrote a letter to a member of the British forces (not a friend or relative)

☐ was involved in a support group or helpline for people with relatives in the Gulf

☐ signed an anti-war petition or statement

☐ took part in an anti-war demonstration

☐ took part in a pro-war demonstration

☐ none of the above

32–33 Repeated questions 19 and 20 from first questionnaire.

Personal details

34–42 Repeated questions 21–29 from first questionnaire.

43 Is there any other comment you would like to make about this survey?

Education questionnaire: children, teachers and schools in the Gulf War

The war in your school

How would you describe the responses of the children you teach to the news of the first coalition air attacks on Iraq, in January?

How many pupils in the classes you teach expressed anxiety about family members in the Gulf?

none	1 or 2	3 or more
☐	☐	☐

What forms did this anxiety take, and how did you respond to it?

How many pupils expressed anxiety about the war in general?

none	a few	most
☐	☐	☐

Were they mainly

boys	girls	both
☐	☐	☐

What forms did this anxiety take, and how did you respond to it?

Did you observe any sort of behaviour disturbance which seemed to be related to the war? (If yes, please describe.)

Did the war affect pupils' play and games in any way? (If yes, please describe.)

How many pupils expressed clear views in favour of the war?

none	a few	most
☐	☐	☐

Were they mainly

boys	girls	both
☐	☐	☐

How many pupils expressed clear views against the war?

none	a few	most
☐	☐	☐

Were they mainly

boys   girls   both
☐   ☐   ☐

Did the war polarise pupils' views along ethnic lines? (If yes, please give details.)

Did you personally deal with the war in a teaching situation?

not at all   once or twice   frequently
☐   ☐   ☐

If yes, what sorts of issues did you raise, and how?

Did you discuss the issue of moral responsibility for violence in war with your pupils? If yes, please describe how and with what results.

Was the war dealt with in assemblies (whole school, year groups, etc.)?

not at all   once or twice   frequently
☐   ☐   ☐

Did your school have any policy on the problems raised for children by the war? (If yes, please describe.)

Please rank the following issues, as far as possible, according to the importance which you think they had (a) in pupils' questions and discussions about the war, (b) in your own approach, and (c) in school policy. (Write 1 for most important issue, 2 for next most important, etc.)

	pupils	self	school
concern for pupils' family members	☐	☐	☐
environmental issues in war	☐	☐	☐
moral issue of killing in war	☐	☐	☐
personality of Saddam Hussein	☐	☐	☐
political aspects in general	☐	☐	☐
racial/religious/ethnic aspects	☐	☐	☐
support for British troops	☐	☐	☐

Did your pupils write letters to, or collect goods for, British service personnel in the Gulf?

If yes, did the initiative for this come from

the pupils   yourself   the school

☐   ☐   ☐

Please describe the response of the pupils to these activities.

Did your pupils produce written work, drawings, etc. on any aspect of the war? (If yes, please describe.)

Did the war result in any conflict among teachers, or between teachers, governors and the LEA, over the policy to be adopted? (If yes, please describe.)

Did your union or professional association produce any guidelines on issues arising for teachers from the war? If so, how much assistance do you feel that they gave you?

Have you any comment on how television coverage of the war affected your pupils?

Have you any comment on how national press coverage of the war affected your pupils?

Were the activities (connected to the war) of children in your school publicised in the local press, radio or TV? (If yes, please describe, and send copies of press cuttings if possible.)

Would you like to make any other comments on the effects or implications of the Gulf War on the children you teach, on your school, and on yourself as a teacher?

Your school: ☐ primary   ☐ secondary comprehensive

                 ☐ grammar   ☐ 6th form college

                 ☐ FE college

Composition: ☐ co-educational   ☐ boys   ☐ girls

                 ☐ LEA   ☐ RC   ☐ C of E

                 ☐ self-governing   ☐ independent

Catchment area: ☐ inner-city   ☐ council estates

                 ☐ suburban   ☐ small/medium town

                 ☐ rural

Proportion of pupils belonging to all ethnic minorities:

Proportion of Muslim pupils:

Yourself: under 25   25–34   35–44   45–54   55+
☐   ☐   ☐   ☐   ☐

Sex: ☐ M   ☐ F   Union/association:

Grade of post: Main subject(s):

Age group(s) taught: 4–7   7–9   9–11   11–13   13–16   16–19
☐   ☐   ☐   ☐   ☐   ☐

What was your attitude to the involvement of British forces in the Gulf?

strongly   approved   disapproved   strongly
approved   disapproved

☐   ☐   ☐   ☐

Do you read any of the following daily papers regularly? Please tick the one you read most often.

☐ Express   ☐ Guardian   ☐ Independent

☐ Mail   ☐ Mirror   ☐ Star

☐ Sun   ☐ Telegraph   ☐ Times

☐ Today   ☐ other   ☐ none
                (specify)

During the Gulf crisis, was any member of your immediate family in the Gulf, as a civilian or a member of the armed forces?

How would you vote if there was a General Election tomorrow?

Conservative   Labour   Liberal Democrat   Green
☐   ☐   ☐   ☐

other   wouldn't vote   don't know
☐   ☐   ☐

Would you be willing to answer further questions from us, if we contacted you again?

Bibliography

Article 19 (1994) *Forging War: The Media in Serbia, Croatia and Bosnia-Hercegovina*. London: Article 19.

Badsey, Stephen (1994) *Modern Military Operations and the Media*. Camberley, Surrey: Strategic and Combat Studies Institute.

Baudrillard, Jean (1991) 'La Guerre de Golfe n'a pas eu lieu', *Libération*. 29 March.

Bell, Steve (1991) *The Presentation of Dissent in the British Media during the Gulf War*. MA dissertation, University of Leeds.

Brown, Ben and Shukman, David (1991) *All Necessary Means*. London: BBC.

Brittain, Victoria (ed.) (1991) *The Gulf Between Us*. London: Virago.

Crewe, Ivor (1985) 'Two and a half cheers for the Atlantic Alliance' in Gregory Flynn and Hans Rattinger, *Public Opinion and Atlantic Defence*. London: Croom Helm.

de Waal, Alex (1994) 'African encounters', *Index on Censorship*. **23** 6.

Ender, Morten G. (1995) 'GI phone home: the use of telecommunications by soldiers of Operation Just Cause', *Armed Forces and Society*. **21** 3, pp. 435–54.

Freedman, Lawrence and Karsh, Efraim (1993) *The Gulf Conflict 1990-91*. London: Faber.

George, Bruce (1991) *The British Labour Party and Defense*. London: Praeger.

Giddens, Anthony (1990) *The Consequences of Modernity*. Cambridge: Polity.

Glasgow University Media Group (1985) *War and Peace News*. Milton Keynes: Open University Press.

Glenny, Misha (1992) *The Fall of Yugoslavia: The Third Balkan War*. London: Penguin.

Gowing, Nik (1994) Real-Time TV Coverage from War: Does it Make or Break Government Policy?, 'Turbulent Europe' conference paper, British Film Institute.

Gramsci, Antonio (1971) *Selections from the Prison Notebooks*. London: Lawrence and Wishart

Guttman, Roy (1993) *A Witness to Genocide*. Shaftesbury: Element.

Halliday, Fred (1990) 'The crisis of the arab world: the false answers of Saddam Hussein', *New Left Review*. **184**. Nov–Dec, pp. 69–75.

Hallin, Daniel (1986) *The Uncensored War*. New York: Oxford University Press.

Harris, Robert (1992) *Gotcha! Government, Media and the Falklands War*. London: Faber.

Hiro, Dilip (1992) *Desert Shield to Desert Storm: The Second Gulf War*. London: HarperCollins.

Hobsbawm, Eric and Ranger, Terence (1983) *The Invention of Tradition*. Cambridge: Cambridge University Press.

Husband, Charles (1994) 'The Political Context of Muslim Communities' Participation in British Society' in Bernard Lewis and Dominique Schnapper (eds) *Muslims in Europe*. London: Pinter.

Kuper, Adam (1981) *Genocide*. Harmondsworth: Penguin.

Lewis, Ioan (1994) *Making History in Somalia: Humanitarian Intervention in a Stateless Society*. London: LSE Centre for the Study of Global Governance.

Luckham, Robin (1984) 'Of arms and culture', *Current Research on Peace and Violence*. VII 1, pp. 1–64.

Magas, Branka (1993) *The Destruction of Yugoslavia: Tracking the Break-Up 1980-92*. London: Verso.

Mandelbaum, Michael (1982) 'Vietnam: the television war', *Daedalus*. **III** pp. 157–169.

Mann, Michael (1987) 'Roots and contradictions of modern militarism', *New Left Review*. **162**, pp. 35–50.

Mannheim, Karl (1936) *Ideology and Utopia*. London: Kegan Paul.

Marx, Karl and Engels, Friedrich (1965) *The German Ideology*. London: Lawrence and Wishart.

Morrison, David (1992) *Television and the Gulf War*. London: Libbey.

Morrison, David and Tumber, Howard (1988) *Journalists at War*. London: Sage.

Mowlana, Hamid, Gerbner, George and Schiller, Herbert L. (eds) (1992) *Triumph of the Image: The Media's War in the Persian Gulf - A Global Perspective*. Oxford: Westview.

Norris, Christopher (1992) *Uncritical Theory: Post-modernism, Intellectuals and the Gulf War*. London: Lawrence and Wishart.

O'Heffernan, Patrick (1994) 'A Mutual Exploitation Model of Media Influence in US Foreign Policy' in Bennett, W. Lance and Paletz, David L. (eds) *Taken by Storm*. London: University of Chicago Press.

Parsons, Anthony (1995) *From Cold War to Hot Peace: UN Interventions 1947-1994*. London: Michael Joseph.

Philo, Greg (1993) 'From Buerk to Band Aid: the Media and the 1984 Ethiopian Famine' in John Eldridge (ed.) *Getting the Message: News, Truth and Power*. London: Routledge.

Philo, Greg and McLaughlin, Greg (1993) *The British Media and the Gulf War*. Glasgow: Glasgow University Media Group.

Pinter, Harold (1992) 'Blowing up the media', *Index on Censorship*. **21** 5, pp. 2–3.

Rallings, Colin, Thrasher, Michael and Moon, Nick (1991) 'British Public Opinion During the Gulf War'. Unpublished paper.

Rieff, David (1995) *Slaughterhouse: Bosnia and the Failure of the West*. London: Vintage.

Runcie, Robert (1991) "A Just War" in Brian MacArthur (ed.) *Dispatches from the Gulf War*. London: Bloomsbury.

Said, Edward (1993) *Representations of the Intellectual: The 1993 Reith Lectures*. London: Vintage.

Searle, Chris (1992) 'The gulf between: a school and a war', *Race and Class*. **33** 4, pp. 1–14.

Sharp, Jane M. O. (1993) *Bankrupt in the Balkans: British Policy in Bosnia*. London: Institute for Public Policy Research.

Shaw, Martin (1991) *Post-Military Society: Militarism, Demilitarization and War at the end of the Twentieth Century*. Cambridge: Polity.

(1994) *Global Society and International Relations*. Cambridge: Polity.

(1994) 'Civil society and global politics: beyond a social movements approach', *Millennium: Journal of International Studies*. **23** 3, pp. 647–68.

Shaw, Martin and Carr-Hill, Roy (1991) *Public Opinion, Media and Violence*. Hull: Hull University Department of Sociology & Social Anthropology.

(1994) 'Churches and War: Surveys of Attitudes during the Gulf Conflict' in Peter G. Forster (ed.) *Contemporary Mainstream Religion*. Aldershot: Gower.

Sheridan, Dorothy (1993) 'Writing to the archive: Mass-observation as autobiography', *Sociology*. **27** 1, pp. 27–40.

Taylor, Philip M. (1992) *War and the Media: Propaganda and Persuasion in the Gulf War*. Manchester: Manchester University Press.

Vulliamy, Ed (1994) *Seasons in Hell*. London: Simon & Schuster.

Wellman, Derek (1991) 'How they fought the war in Parliament', *Just Defence Newsletter*. Spring, p. 4.

Werbner, Pnina (1994) 'Islamic Radicalism and the Gulf War: Lay Preachers and Political Dissent among British Pakistanis' in Bernard Lewis and Dominique Schnapper (eds) *Muslims in Europe*. London: Pinter.

Wilcken, Patrick (1995) 'The intellectuals, the media and the Gulf War', *Critique of Anthropology*. **15** 1, pp. 37–8.

(1995) *The Intellectuals, the Media and the Gulf War*. London: Prickly Pear Press.

Worcester, Robert (1991) *British Public Opinion*. Oxford: Blackwell.

(1994) 'The Middle East crisis and British public opinion', *The Public Perspective*, November–December.

Index